Counterfactuals

Counterfactuals

DAVID LEWIS

Blackwell Publishing

© 1973 by David Lewis

BLACKWELL PUBLISHING
350 Main Street, Malden, MA 02148-5020, USA
108 Cowley Road, Oxford OX4 1JF, UK
550 Swanston Street, Carlton, Victoria 3053, Australia

The right of David Lewis to be identified as the Author of this Work has been asserted in accordance with the UK Copyright, Designs, and Patents Act 1988.

First published by Basil Blackwell Ltd 1973
First publishing in the USA by Harvard University Press 1973
Reissued by Blackwell Publishers 2001
Reprinted 2003, 2005

Library of Congress Cataloging-in-Publication Data

Lewis, David K., 1941-
    Counterfactuals / David Lewis.
        p. cm.
    First published: 1973.
    Includes bibliographical references and index.
    ISBN 0–631–22495–5 (hardback.: alk. paper) — ISBN 0–631–22425–4 (pbk. : alk. paper)
    1. Counterfactuals (Logic)   I. Title.

BC199.C66 L48 2000
160—dc21

00-059899

A catalogue record for this title is available from the British Library.

The publisher's policy is to use permanent paper from mills that operate a sustainable forestry policy, and which has been manufactured from pulp processed using acid-free and elementary chlorine-free practices. Furthermore, the publisher ensures that the text paper and cover board used have met acceptable environmental accreditation standards.

For further information on
Blackwell Publishing, visit our website:
www.blackwellpublishing.com

IN MEMORY OF RICHARD MONTAGUE

Contents

Preface

The principal changes in this revised printing are in Section 6.1, where I have corrected two major errors in my discussion of completeness results for the V-logics. Both of them were spotted by Erik C. W. Krabbe in 1976. I am most grateful to him for finding the trouble, and also for very helpful correspondence about alternative methods of repair. One error was in my construction of the canonical basis on pages 127–130: I falsely claimed that the set of co-spheres of cuts around a given index would be closed under unions.* In order to ensure such closure, it is necessary to construct the canonical basis differently. The other was in the axiom system for **VC** given on page 132. I left out the rule of Interchange of Logical Equivalents; however I tacitly appealed to this rule in proving completeness, so my proof did not apply to the axiom system I had given.

In addition I have corrected minor errors on pages 35, 55 and 129, also spotted by Krabbe; removed misprints; and brought some references up to date.

I have had more to say about counterfactuals and related matters. These further thoughts might appropriately have been added to this book; but since they are to be found elsewhere, I have been content to add an appendix giving citations and abstracts.

David Lewis
1986

---

* Erik C. W. Krabbe, 'Note on a Completeness Theorem in the Theory of Counterfactuals', *Journal of Philosophical Logic* **7** (1978): 91–93.

Acknowledgements

I am grateful to Kit Fine, Hans Kamp, David Kaplan, Richard Montague, J. Howard Sobel, Robert Stalnaker, Richmond Thomason, and many other friends and colleagues for encouragement and for valuable discussions about counterfactuals over the last five years.

I am grateful also to the American Council of Learned Societies for financial assistance, and to Saint Catherine's College, Oxford, for hospitality, during the year when most of this book was written.

David Lewis
Princeton, June 1972

1. An Analysis of Counterfactuals

1.1 Introduction

'*If kangaroos had no tails, they would topple over*' seems to me to mean something like this: in any possible state of affairs in which kangaroos have no tails, and which resembles our actual state of affairs as much as kangaroos having no tails permits it to, the kangaroos topple over. I shall give a general analysis of counterfactual conditionals along these lines.

My methods are those of much recent work in possible-world semantics for intensional logic.* I shall introduce a pair of counter-factual conditional operators intended to correspond to the various counterfactual conditional constructions of ordinary language; and I shall interpret these operators by saying how the truth value at a given possible world of a counterfactual conditional is to depend on the truth values at various possible worlds of its antecedent and consequent.

Counterfactuals are notoriously vague. That does not mean that we cannot give a clear account of their truth conditions. It does mean that such an account must either be stated in vague terms—which does *not* mean ill-understood terms—or be made relative to some parameter that is fixed only within rough limits on any given occasion of language use. It is to be hoped that this imperfectly fixed parameter is a familiar one that we would be stuck with whether or not we used it in the analysis of counterfactuals; and so it will be. It will be a relation of comparative similarity.

Let us employ a language containing these two counterfactual conditional operators:

$$\square\!\!\rightarrow$$

* See, for instance, Saul Kripke, 'Semantical Considerations on Modal Logic', *Acta Philosophica Fennica* 16 (1963): 83–94; Richard Montague, 'Pragmatics', in R. Klibansky, *Contemporary Philosophy* (La Nuova Italie Editrice: Firenze, 1968): 102–122, reprinted in Montague, *Formal Philosophy* (Yale University Press: New Haven, 1974); Dana Scott, 'Advice on Modal Logic', in K. Lambert, *Philosophical Problems in Logic* (D. Reidel: Dordrecht, 1970); and David Lewis, 'General Semantics', *Synthese* 22 (1970): 18–67.

read as '*If it were the case that _____, then it would be the case that . . .*',
and

read as '*If it were the case that _____, then it might be the case that . . .*'.
For instance, the two sentences below would be symbolized as shown.

If Otto behaved himself, he would be ignored.
Otto behaves himself □→ *Otto is ignored*

If Otto were ignored, he might behave himself.
Otto is ignored ◇→ *Otto behaves himself*

There is to be no prohibition against embedding counterfactual conditionals within other counterfactual conditionals. A sentence of such a
form as this.

$$((\psi \;\Box\!\!\rightarrow ((\chi \;\Box\!\!\rightarrow \psi) \;\diamondsuit\!\!\rightarrow \phi)) \;\diamondsuit\!\!\rightarrow \chi)$$
$$\Box\!\!\rightarrow (\phi \;\Box\!\!\rightarrow (\psi \;\diamondsuit\!\!\rightarrow ((\chi \;\Box\!\!\rightarrow \phi) \;\diamondsuit\!\!\rightarrow (\phi \;\Box\!\!\rightarrow \psi))))$$

will be perfectly well formed and will be assigned truth conditions,
although doubtless it would be such a confusing sentence that we
never would have occasion to utter it.

The two counterfactual operators are to be interdefinable as follows.

$$\phi \diamondsuit\!\!\rightarrow \psi =^{df} \sim(\phi \;\Box\!\!\rightarrow \sim\psi),$$
$$\phi \;\Box\!\!\rightarrow \psi =^{df} \sim(\phi \diamondsuit\!\!\rightarrow \sim\psi).$$

Thus we can take either one as primitive. Its interpretation determines
the interpretation of the other. I shall take the 'would' counterfactual
□→ as primitive.

Other operators can be introduced into our language by definition
in terms of the counterfactual operators, and it will prove useful to do
so. Certain modal operators will be thus introduced in Sections 1.5 and
1.7; modified versions of the counterfactual in Section 1.6; and 'comparative possibility' operators in Section 2.5.

My official English readings of my counterfactual operators must
be taken with a good deal of caution. First, I do not intend that they
should interfere, as the counterfactual constructions of English sometimes do, with the tenses of the antecedent and consequent. My official
reading of the sentence

We were finished packing Monday night □→ *we departed Tuesday
    morning*

comes out as a sentence obscure in meaning and of doubtful grammaticality:

> *If it were the case that we were finished packing Monday night, then it would be the case that we departed Tuesday morning.*

In the correct reading, the subjunctive 'were' of the counterfactual construction and the temporal 'were' of the antecedent are transformationally combined into a past subjunctive:

> *If we had been finished packing Monday night, then we would have departed Tuesday morning.*

Second, the 'If it were the case that ____ ' of my official reading of □→ is not meant to imply that it is not the case that ____ . Counterfactuals with true antecedents—counterfactuals that are not counterfactual— are not automatically false, nor do they lack truth value. This stipulation does not seem to me at all artificial. Granted, the counterfactual constructions of English do carry some sort of presupposition that the antecedent is false. It is some sort of mistake to use them unless the speaker does take the antecedent to be false, and some sort of mishap to use them when the speaker wrongly takes the antecedent to be false. But there is no reason to suppose that every sort of presupposition failure must produce automatic falsity or a truth-value gap. Some or all sorts of presupposition, and in particular the presupposition that the antecedent of a counterfactual is false, may be mere matters of conversational implicature, without any effect on truth conditions. Though it is difficult to find out the truth conditions of counterfactuals with true antecedents, since they would be asserted only by mistake, we will see later (in Section 1.7) how this may be done.

You may justly complain, therefore, that my title 'Counterfactuals' is too narrow for my subject. I agree, but I know no better. I cannot claim to be giving a theory of conditionals in general. As Ernest Adams has observed,* the first conditional below is probably true, but the second may very well be false. (Change the example if you are not a Warrenite.)

> *If Oswald did not kill Kennedy, then someone else did.*
> *If Oswald had not killed Kennedy, then someone else would have.*

Therefore there really are two different sorts of conditional; not a single conditional that can appear as indicative or as counterfactual depending on the speaker's opinion about the truth of the antecedent.

---

* 'Subjunctive and Indicative Conditionals', *Foundations of Language* **6** (1970): 89–94.

The title 'Subjunctive Conditionals' would not have delineated my subject properly. For one thing, there are shortened counterfactual conditionals like '*No Hitler, no A-bomb*' that have no subjunctives except in their—still all-too-hypothetical—deep structure. More important, there are subjunctive conditionals pertaining to the future, like '*If our ground troops entered Laos next year, there would be trouble*' that appear to have the truth conditions of indicative conditionals, rather than of the counterfactual conditionals I shall be considering.*

1.2 Strict Conditionals

We shall see that the counterfactual cannot be any strict conditional. Since it turns out to be something not too different, however, let us set the stage by reviewing the interpretation of strict conditionals in the usual possible-world semantics for modality. Generally speaking, a strict conditional is a material conditional preceded by some sort of necessity operator:

$$\Box(\phi \supset \psi).$$

With every necessity operator $\Box$ there is paired its dual possibility operator $\Diamond$. The two are interdefinable:

$$\Diamond\phi =^{\mathrm{df}} \sim\Box \sim \phi, \quad \text{or} \quad \Box\phi =^{\mathrm{df}} \sim\Diamond \sim \phi.$$

If we like, we can rewrite the strict conditional using the possibility operator:

$$\sim\Diamond(\phi \mathbin{\&} \sim\psi).$$

Or we could introduce a primitive strict conditional arrow or hook, and define the necessity and possibility operators from that.‡

A necessity operator, in general, is an operator that acts like a restricted universal quantifier over possible worlds. Necessity of a certain sort is truth at all possible worlds that satisfy a certain restriction. We

---

* Notation: sentences of our language are mentioned by means of lower-case Greek letters ϕ, ψ, χ *et al.*; sets of sentences by means of Greek capitals. Logical symbols and the like are used autonymously, and juxtaposition of names of expressions signifies concatenation of the expressions named. Possible worlds are mentioned by means of the lower-case letters h, i, j, k; sets of worlds by means of capital letters; and sets of sets of worlds by means of script capitals.

‡ In this section only, I use the unmarked box and diamond to stand for *any* arbitrary paired necessity operator and possibility operator. When next they appear, in Section 1.5, they will be reserved thenceforth for a specific use: they will be the 'outer' necessity and possibility operators definable in a certain way from the counterfactual (or they will be analogously related to operators analogous to the counterfactual). The dotted box and diamond, $\boxdot$ and $\Diamond$, will be likewise reserved when they appear in Section 1.7.

call these worlds *accessible*, meaning thereby simply that they satisfy the restriction associated with the sort of necessity under consideration. Necessity is truth at all accessible worlds, and different sorts of necessity correspond to different accessibility restrictions. A *possibility operator*, likewise, is an operator that acts like a restricted existential quantifier over worlds. Possibility is truth at some accessible world, and the accessibility restriction imposed depends on the sort of possibility under consideration. If a necessity operator and a possibility operator correspond to the same accessibility restriction on the worlds quantified over, then they will be a dual, interdefinable pair.

In the case of *physical necessity*, for instance, we have this restriction: the accessible worlds are those where the actual laws of nature hold true. Physical necessity is truth at all worlds where those laws hold true; physical possibility is truth at some worlds where those laws hold true.

In the case of physical necessity, which possible worlds are admitted as accessible depends on what the actual laws of nature happen to be. The restriction will be different from the standpoint of worlds with different laws of nature. Let i and j be worlds with different laws of nature, and let k be a world where the laws of i hold true but the different laws of j are violated. From the standpoint of i, k is an accessible world; from the standpoint of j it is not. Accessibility is in this case—and most cases—a relative matter. It is the custom, therefore, to think of accessibility as a relation between worlds: we say that k is *accessible from* i, but k is not accessible from j. We say also that i stands to k, but j does not stand to k, in the *accessibility relation* for physical necessity and possibility.

In general: to a necessity operator $\Box$ or a possibility operator $\Diamond$ there corresponds an accessibility relation. The appropriate accessibility relation serves to restrict quantification over worlds in giving the truth conditions for $\Box$ or $\Diamond$. For any possible world i and sentence ϕ, the sentence $\Box\phi$ is true at the world i if and only if, for every world j such that j is accessible from i, ϕ is true at j. Likewise $\Diamond\phi$ is true at i if and only if, for some world j such that j is accessible from i, ϕ is true at j. More concisely: $\Box\phi$ is true at i if and only if ϕ is true at every world accessible from i; $\Diamond\phi$ is true at i if and only if ϕ is true at some world accessible from i. It follows that the strict conditional $\Box(\phi \supset \psi)$ is true at i if and only if, for every world j such that j is accessible from i, the material conditional $\phi \supset \psi$ is true at j; that is, if and only if, for every world j such that j is accessible from i and ϕ is true at j, ψ is true at j. More concisely: $\Box(\phi \supset \psi)$ is true at i if and only if ψ is true at every accessible ϕ-world. ('ϕ-world', of course, abbreviates 'world at which ϕ is true', and likewise for parallel formations.)

(A) NECESSITY

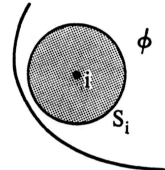

$\Box\phi$

(B) POSSIBILITY

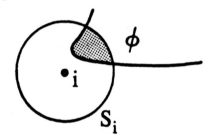

$\Diamond\phi$

(C) STRICT CONDITIONAL

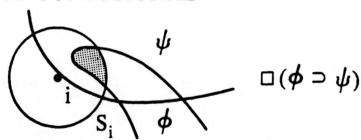

$\Box(\phi \supset \psi)$

FIGURE 1

It suits my purposes better not to use the customary accessibility relations, but instead to adopt a slightly different—but obviously equivalent—formulation. Corresponding to a necessity operator $\square$, or a possibility operator $\diamondsuit$, or a kind of strict conditional, let us have an assignment to each world i of a set S_i of worlds, called the *sphere of accessibility* around i and regarded as the set of worlds accessible from i.* The assignment of spheres to worlds may be called the *accessibility assignment* corresponding to the modal operator. It is used to give the truth conditions for modal sentences as follows.

A sentence $\square\phi$ is true at a world i if and only if ϕ is true throughout the sphere of accessibility S_i around i (as shown in Figure 1(A)).

A sentence $\diamondsuit\phi$ is true at a world i if and only if ϕ is true somewhere in the sphere S_i (as shown in Figure 1(B)).

A strict conditional sentence $\square(\phi \supset \psi)$ is true at i if and only if $\phi \supset \psi$ is true throughout the sphere S_i; that is, if and only if ψ is true at every ϕ-world in S_i (as shown in Figure 1(C)).

Let us consider various examples of accessibility assignments for various sorts of necessity, with particular attention to the corresponding strict conditionals.

Corresponding to *logical necessity*, and the logical strict conditional, we assign to each world i as its sphere of accessibility S_i the set of *all* possible worlds. Thus the logical strict conditional $\square(\phi \supset \psi)$ is true at i if and only if ψ is true at all ϕ-worlds whatever; there are no inaccessible ϕ-worlds to be left out of consideration.

Corresponding to *physical necessity*, and the physical strict conditional, we assign to each world i as its sphere of accessibility S_i the set of all worlds where the laws of nature prevailing at i hold; so the physical strict conditional $\square(\phi \supset \psi)$ is true at i if and only if ψ is true at all those ϕ-worlds where the laws prevailing at i hold.

Corresponding to a kind of time-dependent necessity we may call *inevitability at time t*, and its strict conditional, we assign to each world i as its sphere of accessibility the set of all worlds that are exactly like i at all times up to time t, so $\square(\phi \supset \psi)$ is true at i if and only if ψ is true at all ϕ-worlds that are exactly like i up to t.

Corresponding to what we might call *necessity in respect of facts of so-and-so kind*, and its strict conditional, we assign to each world i as its sphere of accessibility the set of all worlds that are exactly like i in respect of all facts of so-and-so kind, so $\square(\phi \supset \psi)$ is true at i if and only if ψ is true at all ϕ-worlds that are exactly like i in respect of all facts of so-and-so kind.

* Warning: in some mathematicians' usage, a sphere is a hollow surface. Think of my spheres rather as solid regions, like spheres of influence. In mathematicians' usage, solid 'spheres' are called *balls*.

A degenerate case: corresponding to what we may call *necessity in respect of all facts*, or *fatalistic necessity*, we assign to each world i as its sphere of accessibility the set of all worlds that are exactly like i in all respects whatever. Since 'all respects whatever' includes likeness in respect of identity or nonidentity to i, i alone is like i in all respects whatever; thus each world i has as its sphere of accessibility the set $\{i\}$ having i as its sole member. Then $\square\phi$ is true at i if and only if ϕ is true at i; and the fatalistic strict conditional $\square(\phi \supset \psi)$ is true at i if and only if the material conditional $\phi \supset \psi$ is true at i.

Sometimes we do not insist that each world i must belong to its own sphere of accessibility S_i. Corresponding to *deontic* (or *moral*) *necessity*, we assign to each world i as its sphere of accessibility the set of all morally perfect worlds. Then $\square\phi$ is true at i if and only if ϕ is true at every morally perfect world. A morally imperfect world like ours does not belong to its own sphere of accessibility.

We have another degenerate case: corresponding to what I may call *vacuous necessity*, we assign to each world i as its sphere of accessibility the empty set, making $\square\phi$ true at i for any sentence ϕ and world i whatever.

We may compare the strictness of different strict conditionals. The more inclusive are the spheres of accessibility, the stricter is the conditional. Suppose we have necessity operators $\square_1$ and $\square_2$, corresponding to the assignment to each world i of spheres of accessibility S_i^1 and S_i^2 respectively. Then the strict conditional $\square_2(\phi \supset \psi)$ is *stricter at* world i than $\square_1(\phi \supset \psi)$ if and only if S_i^2 properly includes S_i^1. One strict conditional is *stricter* than another if and only if the first is stricter at every world. Note that any strict conditional is implied by any stricter conditional with the same antecedent and consequent.

Thus the logical strict conditional is stricter than any other; the material conditional is the least strict of all the conditionals that obey the constraint that every world is self-accessible; and the physical strict conditional, for instance, falls in between. The vacuous conditional is the least strict conditional of all.

It may happen, of course, that two strict conditionals are incomparable. It may be that they are incomparable at some world because neither sphere includes the other. Or they may be comparable at every world, but one may be stricter at some worlds and the other at other worlds.

Counterfactuals are related to a kind of strict conditional based on comparative similarity of possible worlds. A counterfactual $\phi \,\square\!\!\rightarrow\, \psi$ is true at a world i if and only if ψ holds at certain ϕ-worlds; but certainly not all ϕ-worlds matter. '*If kangaroos had no tails, they would topple over*' is true (or false, as the case may be) at our world, quite without regard to those possible worlds where kangaroos walk around on crutches, and stay upright that way. Those worlds are too far away from ours. What is meant by the counterfactual is that, things being pretty much as they are—the scarcity of crutches for kangaroos being pretty much as it actually is, the kangaroos' inability to use crutches being pretty much as it actually is, and so on—if kangaroos had no tails they would topple over.

We might think it best to confine our attention to worlds where kangaroos have no tails and *everything* else is as it actually is; but there are no such worlds. Are we to suppose that kangaroos have no tails but that their tracks in the sand are as they actually are? Then we shall have to suppose that these tracks are produced in a way quite different from the actual way. Are we to suppose that kangaroos have no tails but that their genetic makeup is as it actually is? Then we shall have to suppose that genes control growth in a way quite different from the actual way (or else that there is something, unlike anything there actually is, that removes the tails). And so it goes; respects of similarity and difference trade off. If we try too hard for exact similarity to the actual world in one respect, we will get excessive differences in some other respect.

There is a simpler argument that there is no world where kangaroos have no tails and everything else is as it actually is. Consider all the material conditionals of the form

$\phi \supset$ *kangaroos have tails*

such that ϕ is true at the actual world. If kangaroos had no tails and everything else were as it actually is, then these conditionals would be true as they actually are, for these conditionals are part of the 'everything else'. Also, in most cases, the antecedents would be true as they actually are, for (at least when the antecedent is irrelevant to whether kangaroos have tails) the antecedents also are part of the 'everything else'. But then, unless the world is one where *modus ponens* goes haywire (so that logic itself is not as it actually is!), kangaroos do have tails there after all. I know of nothing wrong with this argument, but I admit that it looks like an unconvincing trick; so I prefer to rely on the considerations of the previous paragraph.

It therefore seems as if counterfactuals are strict conditionals corresponding to an accessibility assignment determined by similarity of worlds—overall similarity, with respects of difference balanced off somehow against respects cf similarity. Let S_i, for each world i, be the set of all worlds that are similar to at least a certain fixed degree to the world i. Then the corresponding strict conditional is true at i if and only if the material conditional of its antecedent and consequent is true

throughout S_i; that is, if and only if the consequent holds at all antecedent-worlds similar to at least that degree to i.

If we take any one counterfactual, this will do nicely. But trouble may
come if we consider several counterfactuals together. (1) '*If I (or you,
or anyone else) walked on the lawn, no harm at all would come of it; but if
everyone did that, the lawn would be ruined.*' (2) '*If the USA threw its
weapons into the sea tomorrow, there would be war; but if the USA and
the other nuclear powers all threw their weapons into the sea tomorrow
there would be peace; but if they did so without sufficient precautions
against polluting the world's fisheries there would be war; but if, after
doing so, they immediately offered generous reparations for the pollution
there would be peace; . . . .*'* (3) '*If Otto had come, it would have been a
lively party; but if both Otto and Anna had come it would have been a
dreary party; but if Waldo had come as well, it would have been lively;
but. . . .*'

These sequences have the following general form. I include with
each asserted counterfactual also the negated opposite, for in the cases I
imagine these negated opposites also are held true.

$$\phi_1 \mathrel{\Box\!\!\rightarrow} \psi \qquad\qquad \text{and} \quad \sim(\phi_1 \mathrel{\Box\!\!\rightarrow} \sim\psi),$$
$$\phi_1 \,\&\, \phi_2 \mathrel{\Box\!\!\rightarrow} \sim\psi \qquad \text{and} \quad \sim(\phi_1 \,\&\, \phi_2 \mathrel{\Box\!\!\rightarrow} \psi),$$
$$\phi_1 \,\&\, \phi_2 \,\&\, \phi_3 \mathrel{\Box\!\!\rightarrow} \psi \quad \text{and} \quad \sim(\phi_1 \,\&\, \phi_2 \,\&\, \phi_3 \mathrel{\Box\!\!\rightarrow} \sim\psi),$$
$$\vdots$$

With a little ingenuity, it seems possible to prolong such a sequence
indefinitely. No one stage in the sequence refutes the theory that the
counterfactual is a strict conditional based on similarity, but any two
adjacent stages do. The counterfactual on the left at any stage contradicts the negated counterfactual on the right at the next stage. Take the
first and second stages: no matter how the spheres of accessibility may
be assigned, if ψ is true at every accessible ϕ_1-world, then ψ is true at
every accessible ($\phi_1 \,\&\, \phi_2$)-world. So if the counterfactual is any strict
conditional whatever, then $\phi_1 \mathrel{\Box\!\!\rightarrow} \psi$ implies $\phi_1 \,\&\, \phi_2 \mathrel{\Box\!\!\rightarrow} \psi$ and
contradicts $\sim(\phi_1 \,\&\, \phi_2 \mathrel{\Box\!\!\rightarrow} \psi)$. Likewise $\phi_1 \,\&\, \phi_2 \mathrel{\Box\!\!\rightarrow} \sim\psi$ implies
$\phi_1 \,\&\, \phi_2 \,\&\, \phi_3 \mathrel{\Box\!\!\rightarrow} \sim\psi$ and contradicts $\sim(\phi_1 \,\&\, \phi_2 \,\&\, \phi_3 \mathrel{\Box\!\!\rightarrow} \sim\psi)$, and
so on down the sequence.

The left-hand counterfactuals make trouble for the theory that the
counterfactual is a strict conditional, even without their negated

---

* J. Howard Sobel first brought such combinations of counterfactuals to my
attention, pointing out that they are characteristic of the situations in which act-
and rule-utilitarianism seem to prescribe different courses of action. Sobel has
applied my theory of counterfactuals in examining the claim that act- and rule-
utilitarianism are extensionally equivalent; see his 'Utilitarianisms: Simple and
General', *Inquiry* **13** (1970): 394–449.

opposites. If those at two adjacent stages both are true, then according to the theory the second is true vacuously. So are all those beyond it. Beginning at the beginning: if ψ is true at every accessible ϕ_1-world but $\sim\psi$ is true at every accessible $(\phi_1 \& \phi_2)$-world, then there must not be any accessible $(\phi_1 \& \phi_2)$-worlds—nor any accessible $(\phi_1 \& \phi_2 \& \phi_3)$-worlds, nor. ... Then if the lower counterfactuals are true, it is no thanks to their consequents: if a strict conditional is vacuously true, then so is any other with the same antecedent. From the premises that if Otto had come it would have been lively and that if Otto and Anna had come it would have been dreary, it follows that if Otto and Anna had come then the cow would have jumped over the moon. Since that does *not* follow, the counterfactual is not a strict conditional.

If we treat the counterfactual as a strict conditional based on similarity, then the best we can do for our troublesome sequences is to keep changing our minds about which such strict conditional it is. We may be able to make the two sentences at any one stage true by an appropriate choice of a sphere of accessibility based on similarity, but we must choose anew for each stage. If so, we have the situation shown

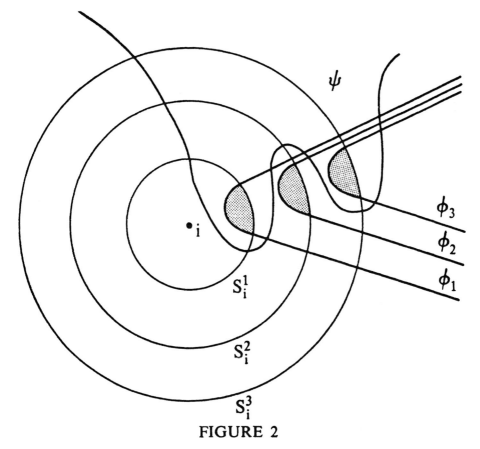

FIGURE 2

in Figure 2. Suppose we have a sphere S_i^1 around i that is right for the first stage: ψ is true at every ϕ_1-world in S_i^1, and—since there are ϕ_1-worlds in S_i^1—it is not the case that $\sim\psi$ also is true at every ϕ_1-world in S_i^1. Then S_i^1 is wrong for the second stage. So is any sphere smaller than S_i^1. But by changing our minds about the degree of similarity to i that we require, perhaps we can find a sphere S_i^2 that is right for the second stage. S_i^2 corresponds to less stringent standards of similarity than S_i^1, and to a stricter conditional. (The stringency of the standards of similarity goes inversely with the strictness of the conditional. *Less* stringent standards of similarity bring *more* worlds into accessibility, making it *more* difficult for anything to hold at all those worlds.) S_i^2 is wrong for the first stage; in order to handle the second stage we had to expand the sphere of accessibility to reach some $(\phi_1 \ \& \ \phi_2 \ \& \ \sim\psi)$-worlds, and these falsify the first-stage counterfactual. S_i^2 is wrong also for the third stage. So is any sphere smaller than S_i^2. But by changing our minds once again, perhaps we can find a still larger sphere S_i^3—a still less stringent standard of similarity, a still stricter conditional—that is right for the third stage. It is wrong for the second and first, however; and for the fourth, if the sequence continues. In short: it may be that for every stage of the sequence, there is a choice of strictness that is right for that stage. But as we go down the sequence, we need stricter and stricter conditionals. The choice that works at any one stage makes false all the counterfactuals at previous stages, and all the negated opposites at subsequent stages. If counterfactuals are strict conditionals we have no hope of deciding, once and for all, how strict they are.

It will not help to plead vagueness. If counterfactuals were strict conditionals based on similarity, indeed they would presumably be vague ones. The assignment of spheres of accessibility for them would be fixed only within rough limits. This might happen both because our ways of trading off respects of similarity and difference against each other are not well fixed and because the degree of overall similarity to a world i that is set as a condition of membership in the sphere of accessibility around i is not well fixed. Both sources of vagueness would tend to make some counterfactuals indefinite in truth value, since the truth value will come out differently under different equally acceptable resolutions of the vagueness. But the counterfactuals and their negated opposites in our troublesome sequence are *not* necessarily especially indefinite in their truth value. I think it is clear from my examples that such a sequence could consist of counterfactuals and their negated opposites all of which are as definitely true as counterfactuals ever are (except for those paragon counterfactuals in which the antecedent logically implies the consequent).

Neither will it help to plead dependence on context. If counterfactuals were vague strict conditionals, no doubt context would resolve some of the vagueness, and different contexts would sometimes resolve it differently. But our problem is not a conflict between counterfactuals in different contexts, but rather between counterfactuals in a single context. It is for this reason that I put my examples in the form of a single run-on sentence, with the counterfactuals of different stages conjoined by semicolons and 'but'. While one context may favor a delineation of baldness on which Dudley is bald, and another may favor a delineation on which he is not, no context can favor a delineation on which he both is and is not. There is no such delineation. While one context might favor a level of strictness on which the first-stage pair in our sequence are both true, and another may favor a greater strictness on which the second-stage pair are both true, and still another may favor a still greater strictness on which the third-stage pair are both true, and so on, none can favor a strictness on which the four sentences from the pairs at two adjacent stages are all true. There is no such strictness.

It is still open to say that counterfactuals are vague strict conditionals based on similarity, and that the vagueness is resolved—the strictness is fixed—by very local context: the antecedent itself. That is not altogether wrong, but it is defeatist. It consigns to the wastebasket of contextually resolved vagueness something much more amenable to systematic analysis than most of the rest of the mess in that wastebasket.

1.3 Variably Strict Conditionals

Counterfactuals are like strict conditionals based on similarity of worlds, but there is no saying how strict they are. They come in as many different strictnesses as there can be stages in my sequence of counterfactuals and their negated opposites. I suggest, therefore, that the counterfactual is not any one strict conditional, but is rather what I shall call a *variably strict conditional*. Any particular counterfactual is as strict, within limits, as it must be to escape vacuity, and no stricter.

Corresponding to any (constantly) strict conditional, as we have seen, there is an assignment to each world i of a single sphere of accessibility S_i around i. Corresponding to a variably strict conditional, on the other hand, there must be an assignment to each world i of a *set* $\$_i$ of spheres of accessibility around i, some larger and some smaller. Such an assignment is required to meet certain formal constraints, laid down in the following definition. We shall see later how, and to what extent, these constraints are justified.

Let $\$$ be an assignment to each possible world i of a set $\$_i$ of sets of possible worlds. Then $ is called a (*centered**) *system of spheres*, and the members of each $_i$ are called *spheres* around i, if and only if, for each world i, the following conditions hold.

(C) $_i$ is *centered on i*; that is, the set $\{i\}$ having i as its only member belongs to $_i$.

(1) $_i$ is *nested*; that is, whenever S and T belong to $_i$, either S is included in T or T is included in S.

(2) $_i$ is *closed under unions*; that is, whenever $\mathcal{S}$ is a subset of $_i$ and $\bigcup\mathcal{S}$ is the set of all worlds j such that j belongs to some member of $\mathcal{S}$, $\bigcup\mathcal{S}$ belongs to $_i$.

(3) $_i$ is *closed under* (*nonempty*) *intersections*; that is, whenever $\mathcal{S}$ is a nonempty subset of $_i$ and $\bigcap\mathcal{S}$ is the set of all worlds j such that j belongs to every member of $\mathcal{S}$, $\bigcap\mathcal{S}$ belongs to $_i$.

The system of spheres used in interpreting counterfactuals is meant to carry information about the comparative overall similarity of worlds. Any particular sphere around a world i is to contain just those worlds that resemble i to at least a certain degree. This degree is different for different spheres around i. The smaller the sphere, the more similar to i must a world be to fall within it. To say the same thing in purely comparative terms: whenever one world lies within some sphere around i and another world lies outside that sphere, the first world is more closely similar to i than the second. Conversely, if S is any set of worlds such that every member of S is more similar to i than any non-member of S, then S should be one of the spheres around i. (An exception: we may or may not count the set of *all* worlds as one of the spheres around i, although it vacuously meets the condition just given.)‡

Our four formal constraints in the definition of a centered system of spheres are justified because, if they were not met, the spheres could not very well be regarded as carrying information about comparative similarity of worlds.

(C) Surely each world i is as similar to itself as any other world is to it;

---

* We may omit the qualifying adjective 'centered' for the most part, restoring it only when we have need to discuss systems of spheres that are perhaps not centered: that is, assignments $ that satisfy conditions (1), (2), and (3) but perhaps not (C).

‡ Whether or not a quantitative concept of similarity 'distance' between worlds makes sense, I need only the non-quantitative, comparative concept given by means of a system of spheres. In topology also we find a non-quantitative concept of distance, given sometimes by means of a system of 'neighborhoods'. Neighborhoods are something like my spheres, but there is one important difference: because topological neighborhoods around a point are not in general nested, they yield a purely qualitative concept of distance—not quantitative, but not even comparative. We can say whether one point or point-set is at all separated from another; but if A and B both are separated from C we cannot say whether one separation exceeds the other.

therefore i should belong to every (nonempty) sphere around i. Almost as surely, no other world is quite as similar to a world i as i itself is; even if there were a world j qualitatively indiscernible from i (imagining for the moment that possible worlds are not the sort of things that obey a non-trivial law of identity of indiscernibles) we might still argue that i does, and j does not, resemble i in respect of being identical to i. Therefore some sphere around i should contain i and exclude all other worlds; that is, $\{i\}$ should be a sphere around i.

(1) If some $\$_i$ were not nested, we would have two spheres S and T in $\$_i$, and two worlds j and k, such that j lies within S but outside T, and k lies within T but outside S. If S and T both carried information about comparative similarity to i, then j would be more similar than k to i (because j does and k does not lie within the sphere S) but also k would be more similar than j to i (because k does and j does not lie within T). We cannot have it both ways.

(2) Suppose j does, and k does not, lie within the union $\bigcup S$ of a set $\$$ of spheres around i. It follows that j does, and k does not, lie within some sphere S in $\$$, and hence that j is more similar than k to i. Therefore $\bigcup S$ is a set such that any world within it is more similar to i than any world outside it, and such a set should be a sphere around i.

(3) Similarly, suppose j does, and k does not, lie within the intersection $\bigcap S$ of a nonempty set $\$$ of spheres; then j does, and k does not, lie within some sphere S in $\$$; so j is more similar than k to i. $\bigcap S$ is a set such that any world within it is more similar to i than any world outside it, and hence should be a sphere around i.

Note that conditions (2) and (3) of closure under union and intersection are automatically satisfied when there are only finitely many spheres around i, or in the case of a finite subset $\$$ of an infinite $\$_i$. If there is a biggest sphere in $\$$ (one that includes all the others) it is $\bigcup S$. If there is a smallest sphere in $\$$ (one that is included in all the others) it is $\bigcap S$. By nesting, every finite set of spheres around a world has a biggest and a smallest. But not so an infinite set: it may have bigger and bigger spheres without end, or smaller and smaller spheres without end. It would simplify things considerably if we could rule out this annoying possibility by fiat; but we shall see that such a fiat would be unjustifiable.

Condition (2) of closure under unions implies that the empty set is a sphere around each i; for in (2) I did not require $\$$ to be nonempty, and by definition the union of empty $\$$ is empty. To include the empty sphere is technically convenient, but unintuitive; however, it can easily be verified that the presence of the empty sphere has no effect at all on the truth conditions to be given with reference to the system of spheres.

More important, I have left it open whether or not the set of all possible worlds is to be one of the spheres around each world i; or in other words, whether or not the union $\bigcup \$_i$ of all spheres around i is to exhaust the set of worlds; or, in still other words, whether or not every possible world is to lie within some or other sphere around i. If $\bigcup \$_i$ is the set of all worlds, for each i, I will call $\$$ *universal*. If not, then I regard the worlds that the spheres around i do not reach—those that lie outside $\bigcup \$_i$—as being all equally similar to i, and less similar to i than any world that the spheres do reach. We will see that any such world will be left out of consideration in determining whether a counterfactual is true at i. It is as if, from the point of view of i, these remotest worlds were not possible worlds at all.

Now that we have set up this Ptolemaic astronomy, we are ready to use it to give truth conditions for counterfactual conditionals, as follows.

$\phi \,\Box\!\!\rightarrow\, \psi$ is true at a world i (according to a system of spheres $\$$) if and only if either

(1) no ϕ-world belongs to any sphere S in $\$_i$, or

(2) some sphere S in $\$_i$ does contain at least one ϕ-world, and $\phi \supset \psi$ holds at every world in S.

Alternative (1) gives the vacuous case: either ϕ is true at no world, or it is true only at worlds outside $\bigcup \$_i$. Then our counterfactual is vacuously true at i. We shall say in this case that ϕ is not *entertainable*, at i, as a counterfactual supposition. Alternative (2) gives the principal case: ϕ is an entertainable supposition at i, and within some sphere around i that is big enough to reach at least one ϕ-world—call such a sphere ϕ-*permitting*—ψ is true at all ϕ-worlds. In brief: a counterfactual is vacuously true if there is no antecedent-permitting sphere, non-vacuously true if there is some antecedent-permitting sphere in which the consequent holds at every antecedent-world, and false otherwise.

Figure 3 depicts the four cases that might arise for a counterfactual $\phi \,\Box\!\!\rightarrow\, \psi$—two ways for it to be true at a world i, and two ways for it to be false.

In case (A), there is no ϕ-permitting sphere. Even the outermost sphere around i does not reach the ϕ-worlds, if indeed there are any. Then every counterfactual with antecedent ϕ is vacuously true at i; for instance, both $\phi \,\Box\!\!\rightarrow\, \psi$ and its opposite $\phi \,\Box\!\!\rightarrow\, \sim\!\psi$. It does not matter (and so is not shown) where the ψ-worlds are, or even whether there are any.

In case (B), there is a ϕ-permitting sphere around i within which ψ holds at all ϕ-worlds—namely, the next-to-outermost sphere. $\phi \supset \psi$ holds throughout this sphere. Therefore $\phi \,\Box\!\!\rightarrow\, \psi$ is non-vacuously true. One such sphere is enough to make it true; it does no harm that there also is a larger ϕ-permitting sphere—the outermost—that reaches

(A) VACUOUS TRUTH

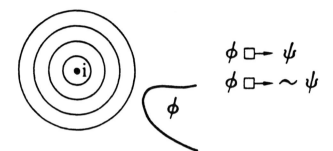

$$\phi \,\Box\!\!\rightarrow \psi$$
$$\phi \,\Box\!\!\rightarrow \sim\! \psi$$

(B) NON-VACUOUS TRUTH

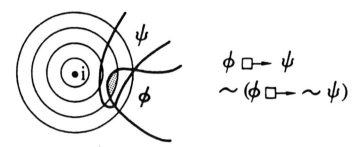

$$\phi \,\Box\!\!\rightarrow \psi$$
$$\sim (\phi \,\Box\!\!\rightarrow \sim\! \psi)$$

(C) FALSITY- - OPPOSITE TRUE

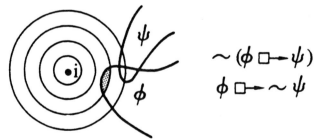

$$\sim (\phi \,\Box\!\!\rightarrow \psi)$$
$$\phi \,\Box\!\!\rightarrow \sim\! \psi$$

(D) FALSITY - - OPPOSITE FALSE

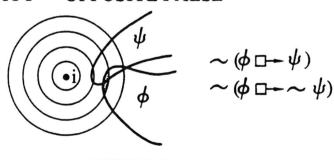

$$\sim (\phi \,\Box\!\!\rightarrow \psi)$$
$$\sim (\phi \,\Box\!\!\rightarrow \sim\! \psi)$$

FIGURE 3

ϕ-worlds where ψ is false. The opposite counterfactual $\phi \;\square\!\!\rightarrow\; \sim\psi$ is false: there are ϕ-permitting spheres, and both of them contain ϕ-worlds where the new consequent $\sim\psi$ is false.

Case (C) is the other way around. There are ϕ-permitting spheres, but none in which ψ holds at every ϕ-world, so none throughout which $\phi \supset \psi$ holds. Therefore $\phi \;\square\!\!\rightarrow\; \psi$ is false. In the inner one of the two ϕ-permitting spheres, $\sim\psi$ holds at every ϕ-world; so the opposite counterfactual $\phi \;\square\!\!\rightarrow\; \sim\psi$ is true.

In case (D), finally, there are ϕ-permitting spheres, and both of them contain a mixture of ϕ-worlds where ψ holds and ϕ-worlds where $\sim\psi$ holds. Therefore $\phi \;\square\!\!\rightarrow\; \psi$ and its opposite $\phi \;\square\!\!\rightarrow\; \sim\psi$ both are false.

Let us reconsider the sequences of true counterfactuals and their true negated opposites that drove us to give up the theory that the counterfactual is a constantly strict conditional based on similarity:

$$\phi_1 \;\square\!\!\rightarrow\; \psi \qquad \text{and} \quad \sim(\phi_1 \;\square\!\!\rightarrow\; \sim\psi),$$
$$\phi_1 \;\&\; \phi_2 \;\square\!\!\rightarrow\; \sim\psi \qquad \text{and} \quad \sim(\phi_1 \;\&\; \phi_2 \;\square\!\!\rightarrow\; \psi),$$
$$\phi_1 \;\&\; \phi_2 \;\&\; \phi_3 \;\square\!\!\rightarrow\; \psi \quad \text{and} \quad \sim(\phi_1 \;\&\; \phi_2 \;\&\; \phi_3 \;\square\!\!\rightarrow\; \sim\psi),$$

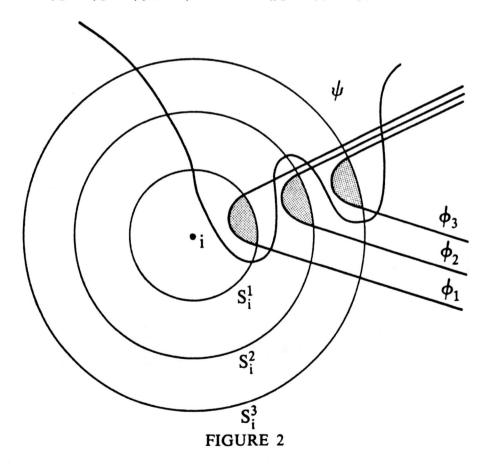

FIGURE 2

and so on. Figure 2 portrayed our difficulty: taking the counterfactual as a constantly strict conditional, we had to choose one of the spheres $S_i^1, S_i^2, S_i^3, \ldots$ to be *the* sphere of accessibility around i, but no choice was right. S_i^1 was right for the first stage of the sequence but not the second, S_i^2 was right for the second stage but not the first or third, and so on. Now Figure 2 portrays the solution: taking the counterfactual as a variably strict conditional, we do not need to choose. The several spheres are all present in $\$_i$ together. S_i^1 is there to make the first-stage counterfactual non-vacuously true, S_i^2 is there to make the second-stage counterfactual non-vacuously true, and so on. The stages can coexist in peace.

1.4 The Limit Assumption

If there are only finitely many spheres around some world i, then any nonempty set of these spheres has a smallest member: a sphere in the set that is included in every other sphere in the set. In particular, for any entertainable antecedent, the set of antecedent-permitting spheres has a smallest member. This smallest antecedent-permitting sphere is the intersection of the set of all antecedent-permitting spheres around i. It contains the antecedent-worlds closest to i: all and only those of the antecedent-worlds than which no other antecedent world is closer to i.

The same may be true even if there are infinitely many spheres around i, provided we have no infinite descending sequence of smaller and smaller spheres without end. (That is: if the ordering of the spheres by inclusion is a well-ordering.) For instance, if we could number the spheres in such a way that sphere 0 is the smallest (the empty set), sphere 1 is the next smallest (the sphere $\{i\}$), sphere 2 is the next smallest, and so on, then there would be a smallest member of every set of spheres, and in particular there would be a smallest antecedent-permitting sphere for every entertainable antecedent.

If there are sequences of smaller and smaller spheres without end, then there are sets of spheres with no smallest member: take the set of all spheres in any such sequence. Yet it might still happen that for every entertainable antecedent in our language, there is a smallest antecedent-permitting sphere. For our language may be limited in expressive power so that not just any set of worlds is the set of ϕ-worlds for some sentence ϕ; and, in that case, it may never happen that the set of ϕ-permitting spheres is one of the sets that lacks a smallest member, for any antecedent ϕ.

The assumption that, for every world i and antecedent ϕ that is entertainable at i, there is a smallest ϕ-permitting sphere, I call the

Limit Assumption. It is the assumption that as we take smaller and smaller antecedent-permitting spheres, containing antecedent-worlds closer and closer to *i*, we eventually reach a limit: the *smallest* antecedent-permitting sphere, and in it the *closest* antecedent-worlds.

If the consequent of a counterfactual holds at all antecedent-worlds within some antecedent-permitting sphere around *i*, then also the consequent holds at all antecedent-worlds in any smaller antecedent-permitting sphere. In particular, the consequent holds at all antecedent-worlds in the smallest antecedent-permitting sphere, if such there be. Conversely, if the consequent holds at all antecedent-worlds in the smallest antecedent-permitting sphere, then the consequent holds at all antecedent worlds in some antecedent-permitting sphere. Under the Limit Assumption, therefore, we could make the truth conditions for counterfactuals simpler: a counterfactual is true at *i* if and only if either (1) there is no antecedent-permitting sphere around *i*, or (2) the consequent holds at every antecedent-world in the smallest antecedent-permitting sphere around *i*. Simpler still: a counterfactual is true at *i* if and only if the consequent holds at every antecedent-world closest to *i* (where we do not call an antecedent-world outside $\bigcup \$_i$ 'closest', even if it is an antecedent-world than which there is none closer).

Unfortunately, we have no right to assume that there always are a smallest antecedent-permitting sphere and, within it, a set of closest antecedent-worlds. Suppose we entertain the counterfactual supposition that at this point

—————————

there appears a line more than an inch long. (Actually it is just under an inch.) There are worlds with a line 2″ long; worlds presumably closer to ours with a line $1\frac{1}{2}$″ long; worlds presumably still closer to ours with a line $1\frac{1}{4}$″ long; worlds presumably still closer .... But how long is the line in the *closest* worlds with a line more than an inch long? If it is $1 + x$″ for any *x* however small, why are there not other worlds still closer to ours in which it is $1 + \frac{1}{2}x$″, a length still closer to its actual length? The shorter we make the line (above 1″), the closer we come to the actual length; so the closer we come, presumably, to our actual world.* Just as there is no shortest possible length above 1″, so there is no closest world to ours among the worlds with lines more than an

* 'Presumably', here and elsewhere, because it depends on the technique of printing. Suppose the actual line was printed by a digital process of some sort, and the shortest length above 1″ that is possible using this process is $1\frac{1}{8}$″. Then perhaps some world at which this process is used to give a $1\frac{1}{8}$″ line is closest, being closer to ours than any world at which a process unlike the actual process is used to give a slightly shorter line. Thus this and other examples are not quite decisive; but they should suffice at least to deter us from rashly assuming that there *must* be a smallest antecedent-permitting sphere.

inch long, and no smallest sphere permitting the supposition that there is a line more than an inch long.

When there is no smallest antecedent-permitting sphere, our truth conditions amount to this: if there are antecedent-permitting spheres, then as we take smaller and smaller ones without end, eventually we come to ones in which the consequent holds at every antecedent-world.

1.5 'Might' Counterfactuals and Outer Modalities

My interpretation of the 'would' counterfactual as a variably strict conditional, together with my definition

$$\phi \diamondsuit\!\!\rightarrow \psi =^{df} \sim(\phi \,\square\!\!\rightarrow \sim\psi)$$

of the 'might' counterfactual in terms of the 'would' counterfactual, yield derived truth conditions for the 'might' counterfactual as follows.

$\phi \diamondsuit\!\!\rightarrow \psi$ is true at a world i (according to a system of spheres \$) if and only if both

(1) some ϕ-world belongs to some sphere S in $\$_i$, and
(2) every sphere S in $\$_i$ that contains at least one ϕ-world contains at least one world where $\phi \,\&\, \psi$ holds.

Under the Limit Assumption, we could restate the derived truth conditions for 'might' counterfactuals thus: $\phi \diamondsuit\!\!\rightarrow \psi$ is true at i if and only if ψ holds at some ϕ-world in the smallest ϕ-permitting sphere around i. More simply: a 'might' counterfactual is true at i if and only if the consequent holds at some antecedent-world closest to i. (Again, an antecedent-world outside $\bigcup\$_i$ must never count as a closest antecedent-world to i, not even if there are none closer.) But if the Limit Assumption does not hold, then these simplified restatements will not do; the 'might' counterfactual is then true if and only if, as we take smaller and smaller antecedent-permitting spheres around i without end, and thereby confine our attention to antecedent-worlds closer and closer to i, we never leave behind all the antecedent-worlds where the consequent holds.

If the 'would' counterfactual $\phi \,\square\!\!\rightarrow \psi$ is non-vacuously true, then the 'might' counterfactual $\phi \diamondsuit\!\!\rightarrow \psi$ also is true. If $\phi \,\square\!\!\rightarrow \psi$ and its opposite $\phi \,\square\!\!\rightarrow \sim\psi$ are both false, then $\phi \diamondsuit\!\!\rightarrow \psi$ and its opposite $\phi \diamondsuit\!\!\rightarrow \sim\psi$ are both true; for this is the case in which ψ is true at some of the closest ϕ-worlds and $\sim\psi$ is true at others of them. But when $\phi \,\square\!\!\rightarrow \psi$ is false and its opposite $\phi \,\square\!\!\rightarrow \sim\psi$ is true, ψ holds at none of the closest ϕ-worlds and $\phi \diamondsuit\!\!\rightarrow \psi$ is therefore false. Finally, when ϕ is not entertainable and $\phi \;\square\!\!\rightarrow\; \psi$ is therefore vacuously true, $\phi \;\diamondsuit\!\!\rightarrow\; \psi$ is again false.

Let T be a sentential constant true at every world; let $\perp$ be a sentential constant false at every world. (Or, if you prefer, let T abbreviate some arbitrarily chosen truth-functional tautology and let $\perp$ abbreviate its contradictory negation.) Then the 'would' counterfactual $\phi \;\square\!\!\rightarrow\; \perp$ cannot be true otherwise than vacuously, when ϕ is not entertainable. Therefore the 'might' counterfactual $\phi \;\diamondsuit\!\!\rightarrow\; \mathsf{T}$, definitionally equivalent to $\sim(\phi \;\square\!\!\rightarrow\; \sim\mathsf{T})$ and hence to the negation of $\phi \;\square\!\!\rightarrow\; \perp$, is a sentence true if and only if ϕ is entertainable.

We may therefore introduce into our language a pair of modal operators defined in terms of the counterfactual conditional connectives:

$$\diamondsuit\phi =^{\text{df}} \phi \;\diamondsuit\!\!\rightarrow\; \mathsf{T} \quad (\text{or, equivalently, } \sim(\phi \;\square\!\!\rightarrow\; \perp)),$$
$$\square\phi =^{\text{df}} \sim\diamondsuit\sim\phi \quad (\text{or, equivalently, } \sim\phi \;\square\!\!\rightarrow\; \perp).$$

We may read $\diamondsuit$ as '*Possibly* ____' or as '*It is entertainable that* ____'; we may read $\square$ as '*Necessarily* ____' or as '*It would be the case, no matter what, that* ____'. The two are interdefinable in the usual way: not only is $\square\phi$ definitionally equivalent to $\sim\diamondsuit\sim\phi$, as stipulated above, but also it follows that $\diamondsuit\phi$ is equivalent to $\sim\square\sim\phi$. Other definitions could be given of the two modal operators:

$$\diamondsuit\phi =^{\text{df}} \phi \;\diamondsuit\!\!\rightarrow\; \phi,$$
$$\square\phi =^{\text{df}} \sim\phi \;\square\!\!\rightarrow\; \phi,$$

for instance, are equivalent to the definitions given above.

From the truth conditions for counterfactuals and the definitions of the two modal operators, we obtain derived truth conditions for modal sentences as follows.

$\diamondsuit\phi$ is true at a world i (according to a system of spheres $) if and only if ϕ is true at some world in some sphere S in $_i$.

$\square\phi$ is true at a world i (according to a system of spheres $) if and only if ϕ is true at every world in every sphere S in $_i$.

We can also express these truth conditions in terms of the assignment to each world i of the set of worlds $\bigcup_i$: the union of all the spheres around i (that is, the set of all and only those worlds that belong to some or other sphere around i). $\bigcup_i$ is itself a sphere around i; it is the largest, or *outermost* sphere around i.

$\diamondsuit\phi$ is true at i (according to $) if and only if ϕ is true at some world in $\bigcup_i$.

$\square\phi$ is true at i (according to $) if and only if ϕ is true at every world in $\bigcup_i$.

Hence our defined modal operators turn out to be interpretable in the usual way by means of accessibility; they correspond to the assignment to each world i of the single sphere of accessibility $\bigcup \$_i$. Since they pertain to the outermost of our spheres around each world i, let us call them the *outer modalities*: outer necessity and outer possibility.

In case our system of spheres is universal, in that each $\bigcup \$_i$ is the set of all possible worlds, then our outer necessity and possibility will be ordinary logical necessity and possibility. If the system of spheres is not universal, so that at least for some worlds i the outermost sphere $\bigcup \$_i$ around i does not exhaust the set of all worlds, then our outer modalities may not be the same as any familiar modalities. They will be rather strict modalities: probably stricter than anything familiar except the logical modalities themselves.

Our reading of $\Diamond$ as '*It is entertainable that ____*' is justified by the fact that, as we have already noted, $\Diamond\phi$ is true at i if and only if ϕ is an entertainable counterfactual supposition at i. That is so, we recall, if and only if there is some ϕ-permitting sphere around i, so that counterfactuals with ϕ as antecedent can be false or non-vacuously true at i. In other words, that is so if and only if ϕ is true at some world in some sphere around i.

Our reading of $\Box$ as '*It would be the case, no matter what, that ____*' is justified by the fact that if $\Box\phi$ is true at a world i, then $\chi \Box\!\!\rightarrow \phi$ is true at i for any antecedent χ whatever. If χ is not entertainable, then $\chi \Box\!\!\rightarrow \phi$ is vacuously true; if χ is entertainable, then $\chi \Box\!\!\rightarrow \phi$ is non-vacuously true because by hypothesis ϕ is true throughout every sphere around i, and hence ϕ is true throughout some χ-permitting sphere around i, and hence $\chi \supset \phi$ is true throughout some χ-permitting sphere around i.

$\Box(\phi \supset \psi)$, the *outer strict conditional*, implies the counterfactual $\phi \Box\!\!\rightarrow \psi$; if $\phi \supset \psi$ is true throughout every sphere around i, then in particular, if there is any ϕ-permitting sphere around i, it is true throughout that. But not conversely: the counterfactual is not the outer strict conditional any more than it is any other constantly strict conditional, despite the fact that $\Box$ is defined from $\Box\!\!\rightarrow$. $\phi \Box\!\!\rightarrow \psi$ is true and $\Box(\phi \supset \psi)$ is false if $\phi \supset \psi$ is true throughout some ϕ-permitting sphere, but false somewhere in some larger ϕ-permitting sphere.

Indeed the counterfactual cannot be defined in any way whatever from the outer modalities and truth-functional connectives. Given a system of spheres, we may consider what happens to the truth values of sentences when spheres are added or deleted, but in such a way as never to change the outermost sphere around any world. The truth values at worlds of counterfactuals (with non-counterfactual antecedents and consequents) will in some cases change when non-outermost spheres are added or deleted; but such additions or deletions never could change the truth value at any world of any sentence built up from non-counterfactual sentences by means of the outer modalities and truth-functional connectives alone. Therefore some counterfactuals cannot be definitionally equivalent to any such sentences.

1.6 Impossible Antecedents

There is at least some intuitive justification for the decision to make a 'would' counterfactual with an impossible antecedent come out vacuously true. Confronted by an antecedent that is not really an entertainable supposition, one may react by saying, with a shrug: If that were so, anything you like would be true! Further, it seems that a counterfactual in which the antecedent logically implies the consequent ought always to be true; and one sort of impossible antecedent, a self-contradictory one, logically implies any consequent.

Moreover, one sometimes asserts counterfactuals by way of *reductio* in philosophy, mathematics, and even logic. (I have done so in this very chapter.) These counterfactuals are asserted in argument, and must therefore be thought true; but their antecedents deny what are thought to be philosophical, mathematical, or even logical truths, and must therefore be thought not only false but impossible. These asserted counterphilosophicals, countermathematicals, and counterlogicals look like examples of vacuously true counterfactuals.

There are other things they might be, however. They might not really be counterfactuals, but subjunctive conditionals of some other kind. More interesting, they might be non-vacuously true counterfactuals, understood in the way I have proposed; but so understood under the pretense that along with the *possible* possible worlds that differ from our world only in matters of contingent, empirical fact, there also are some *impossible* possible worlds that differ from our world in matters of philosophical, mathematical, and even logical truth. (The pretense need not be taken very seriously to explain what happens in conversation; it just might be that this part of our conversational practice is founded upon a confused fantasy.) These alternative hypotheses have the merit that they might explain how we could discriminate in truth value between different counterfactuals with impossible antecedents, whereas my theory makes all of them alike come out vacuously true.

I do not think, however, that we need to discriminate in truth value among such counterfactuals. Of course there are some we would assert and some we would not:

> *If there were a largest prime p, p!+1 would be prime.*
> *If there were a largest prime p, p!+1 would be composite.*

are both sensible things to say, but

> *If there were a largest prime p, there would be six regular solids.*
> *If there were a largest prime p, pigs would have wings.*

are not. But what does that prove? We have to explain why things we do want to assert are true (or at least why we take them to be true, or at least why we take them to approximate to truth), but we do not have to explain why things we do not want to assert are false. We have plenty of cases in which we do not want to assert counterfactuals with impossible antecedents, but so far as I know we do not want to assert their negations either. Therefore they do not have to be made false by a correct account of truth conditions; they can be truths which (for good conversational reasons) it would always be pointless to assert.

Therefore I am fairly content to let counterfactuals with impossible antecedents be vacuously true. But my reasons are less than decisive, and some might prefer a stronger 'would' counterfactual that cannot be vacuously true. We write this as $\Box\!\!\rightarrow$, and give it the following truth conditions:

> $\phi\,\Box\!\!\rightarrow\,\psi$ is true at a world i (according to a system of spheres \$) if and only if there is some sphere S in $\$_i$ such that S contains at least one ϕ-world, and $\phi \supset \psi$ holds at every world in S.

Preserving the interdefinability of 'would' and 'might' counterfactuals as before, we introduce also a weakened 'might' counterfactual $\Diamond\!\!\rightarrow$, vacuously true whenever its antecedent is impossible. It is defined by

$$\phi\,\Diamond\!\!\rightarrow\,\psi =^{\text{df}} \sim(\phi\,\Box\!\!\rightarrow\,\sim\psi),$$

and it has the following derived truth conditions:

> $\phi\,\Diamond\!\!\rightarrow\,\psi$ is true at a world i (according to a system of spheres \$) if and only if every sphere S in $\$_i$ that contains at least one ϕ-world contains at least one ϕ-world at which $\phi\,\&\,\psi$ holds.

One might perhaps motivate this weakened 'might' in much the same way as I motivated the original, weak 'would': confronted by an antecedent that is not really entertainable, one might say, with a shrug: If that were so, anything you like *might* be true!

I find $\Box\!\!\rightarrow$ and $\Diamond\!\!\rightarrow$, taken as a pair, somewhat better intuitively than $\Box\!\!\rightarrow$ and $\Diamond\!\!\rightarrow$; and the simple interdefinability of 'would' and 'might' seems plausible enough to destroy the appeal of the mixed pair of $\Box\!\!\rightarrow$ and $\Diamond\!\!\rightarrow$. There seems not to be much more to be said; perhaps ordinary usage is insufficiently fixed to force either choice, and technical convenience may favor one or the other pair depending on how we choose to formulate our truth conditions. (On the present formulation, $\square\!\!\rightarrow$ and $\diamondsuit\!\!\rightarrow$ have simpler truth conditions; on the formulation to be given in Section 2.7, $\square\!\!\rightarrow$ and $\diamondsuit\!\!\rightarrow$ have simpler truth conditions.) In any case, we have both pairs in stock; and we can get either pair from the other via the following definitions:

$$\phi \diamondsuit\!\!\rightarrow \psi =^{\mathrm{df}} (\phi \diamondsuit\!\!\rightarrow \phi) \supset (\phi \diamondsuit\!\!\rightarrow \psi),$$
$$\phi \square\!\!\rightarrow \psi =^{\mathrm{df}} (\phi \square\!\!\rightarrow \phi) \supset (\phi \square\!\!\rightarrow \psi).$$

1.7 True Antecedents

We noted at the outset that truth of the antecedent was a defect in a counterfactual, but not necessarily the sort of defect that produces automatic falsity or a truth-value gap. According to the truth conditions I have given, a counterfactual with true antecedent is true if and only if the consequent is true. This is so both for 'would' and 'might' counterfactuals (and for the strong 'would' and weak 'might' counterfactuals introduced in the previous section). In short: counterfactuals with true antecedents reduce to material conditionals.

Suppose the antecedent ϕ is true at a world i. Then there is a ϕ-permitting sphere around i, because $\{i\}$ is a sphere. If the consequent ψ is true at i, then there is a ϕ-permitting sphere around i throughout which $\phi \supset \psi$ holds, to wit $\{i\}$; so $\phi \square\!\!\rightarrow \psi$ is true at i. Also every ϕ-permitting sphere around i contains a world where $\phi \& \psi$ holds, since every sphere around i, except the empty set which is not a ϕ-permitting sphere, contains the world i itself; so $\phi \diamondsuit\!\!\rightarrow \psi$ is true at i. If, on the other hand, the consequent ψ is false at i, then there is no ϕ-permitting sphere around i throughout which $\phi \supset \psi$ holds, since it fails at the world i which belongs to every ϕ-permitting sphere; so $\phi \square\!\!\rightarrow \psi$ is false at i. Also there is a ϕ-permitting sphere containing no world where $\phi \& \psi$ holds, to wit $\{i\}$; so $\phi \diamondsuit\!\!\rightarrow \psi$ is false at i.

I can summarize the status of counterfactuals with true antecedents by noting that the following two inference-patterns are valid: that is, my truth conditions guarantee that whenever the premise is true at a world, so is the conclusion.

$$\frac{\phi \ \& \ \sim\psi}{\therefore \ \sim(\phi \square\!\!\rightarrow \psi)} \qquad \frac{\phi \ \& \ \psi}{\therefore \ \phi \square\!\!\rightarrow \psi}.$$

The validity of the first inference-pattern guarantees also the validity of the inference from a counterfactual to a material conditional and the validity of *modus ponens* from a counterfactual conditional:

$$\frac{\phi \,\square\!\!\rightarrow\, \psi}{\therefore \phi \supset \psi} \quad \text{and} \quad \begin{array}{c} \phi \,\square\!\!\rightarrow\, \psi \\ \phi \\ \hline \therefore \psi \end{array}.$$

How plausible are these consequences of my truth conditions? It is hard to test them directly. It is not much help considering a counterfactual with an antecedent known to be true, and asking whether it seems to be true or false according as the consequent is thought to be true or false. Our principal response will be not that the conditional is true or that it is false, but that it is mistaken and misleading because of its true antecedent. So it is, but that is not at issue. The false information conveyed by using a counterfactual construction with a true antecedent eclipses the falsity or truth of the conditional itself.

It is not safe to put the conditional in indicative form in order to get rid of the presupposition that the antecedent is false. Sometimes when the antecedent is thought to be probably false, so that the counterfactual construction is appropriate, the counterfactual and indicative conditionals are thought to differ in truth value. (We considered Ernest Adams's example of this in Section 1.1.) Therefore we have no right to take for granted that they have the same truth values when the antecedent is thought to be true, differing only in the presuppositions they carry.

What we must do, I think, is consider a dialog in which the participants disagree on the truth of the antecedent. The first speaker does not deliberately violate the prohibition against asserting a counterfactual with a true antecedent; rather, he asserts a counterfactual with an antecedent he takes to be false. The second speaker replies, registering disagreement with the first speaker's manifest supposition that the antecedent is false, but also expressing agreement or disagreement with the first speaker's assertion.

You say: '*If Caspar had come, it would have been a good party.*' I reply: '*That's false; for he* did *come, yet it was a rotten party.*' Or else I reply: '*That's true; for he* did, *and it* was *a good party. You didn't see him because you spent the whole time in the kitchen, missing all the fun.*' Either reply seems perfectly cogent. In each reply, I correct your false belief that Caspar was absent, manifest in your use of the counterfactual form; but I do this while expressing overall disagreement or agreement with your conditional assertion. Moreover, I justify my disagreement or agreement by giving an argument. The argument is abbreviated, but its presence is signalled by the word 'for' in my reply. The arguments I give have the forms

$$\frac{\phi \ \& \ \sim\psi}{\therefore \ \textit{That's false}} \quad \text{and} \quad \frac{\phi \ \& \ \psi}{\therefore \ \textit{That's true}}$$

respectively, where ϕ and ψ are the antecedent and consequent of the counterfactual you have just asserted, and 'that' in the conclusion refers to what you have asserted. Therefore my replies are cogent only if the inference-patterns that we want to test,

$$\frac{\phi \ \& \ \sim\psi}{\therefore \ \sim(\phi \ \square\!\!\rightarrow \psi)} \quad \text{and} \quad \frac{\phi \ \& \ \psi}{\therefore \ \phi \ \square\!\!\rightarrow \psi},$$

are valid. The replies do seem cogent; so the inference-patterns are valid; so my truth conditions for counterfactuals with true antecedents are confirmed.

I admit that this test is not quite decisive. It is just possible that my arguments to '*That's false*' and '*That's true*' are invalid with only the premises that appear explicitly in my reply, and depend also on further premises that are understood but not stated. Or it is just possible that what I refer to as 'that' in my reply, and judge false or true, is not the counterfactual you asserted, but rather some belief that I take to have been your reason for thinking the counterfactual true.

The test by dialog is evidence for my truth conditions. What can be said against them? So far as I know, only this: it would seem very odd to pick two completely unrelated truths ϕ and ψ and, on the strength of their truth, to deny the counterfactual $\phi \ \square\!\!\rightarrow \sim\psi$; and even odder to assert the counterfactual $\phi \ \square\!\!\rightarrow \psi$. What would we make of someone who saw fit to deny that if the sky were blue then grass would not be green, or to assert that if the sky were blue then grass would be green? It would be doubly odd. First, because he is using the counterfactual construction with an antecedent he takes to be true, though this construction is customarily reserved for antecedents taken to be false; second, because his assertions could serve no likely conversational purpose that would not be better served by separate assertions of ϕ and ψ. But oddity is not falsity; not everything true is a good thing to say. In fact, the oddity dazzles us. It blinds us to the truth value of the sentences, and we can make no confident judgements one way or the other. We ordinarily take no interest in the truth value of extreme oddities, so we cannot be expected to be good at judging them. They prove nothing at all about truth conditions.

I have claimed that the counterfactuals with true antecedent and false consequent are false, and that those with true antecedent and true consequent are true. I am fairly sure of both claims, but surer of the first; so it may be of interest to see what changes could be made to keep the first result but not the second.

The first is a consequence of the assumption that no world is more similar to a world i than i itself is; and that seems perfectly safe. The second is a consequence of the assumption that no other world is even *as* similar to i as i itself is; and that is not quite such a safe assumption. Perhaps our discriminations of similarity are rather coarse, and some worlds different from i are enough like i so that such small differences as there are fail to register. In that case, we would need to revise the definition of a system of spheres, weakening the original centering condition (C) which stipulated that $\{i\}$ was to be a sphere around i.

Let \$ be an assignment to each world i of a set $\$_i$ of sets of worlds. Then \$ is a *weakly centered system of spheres* if and only if, for each world i, the following conditions hold.

(W) $\$_i$ is *weakly centered* on i; that is, i belongs to every nonempty sphere around i, and there is at least one nonempty sphere around i.

(1)–(3) $\$_i$ is nested, closed under unions, and closed under (nonempty) intersections; these conditions are unchanged.

In a weakly centered system of spheres, the smallest, or *innermost*, nonempty sphere around i is the intersection of all nonempty spheres around i—that is, $\bigcap(\$_i - \{\Lambda\})$. It contains the closest worlds to i. The world i itself is one of these closest worlds to i; but there may be others as well—worlds differing negligibly from i, so that they come out just as close to i as i itself.

Having weakened our conditions on the system of spheres, we can leave the truth conditions for counterfactuals unchanged and still have the intended result: a counterfactual with true antecedent and false consequent must be false, but one with true antecedent and true consequent may be either true or false. Suppose ϕ is true at a world i; then the smallest ϕ-permitting sphere around i is the innermost nonempty sphere around i. This sphere contains i itself. It may or may not contain other worlds, now that we have (temporarily!) retreated from centering to weak centering. If it does, there may or may not be ϕ-worlds other than i among them. Suppose there are; then $\phi \mathrel{\Box\!\!\rightarrow} \psi$ holds at i if and only if the consequent ψ holds not only at i itself but also at the other ϕ-worlds in the innermost nonempty sphere around i. Thus it may happen that a counterfactual with true antecedent and consequent is false if the consequent is false at a sufficiently close antecedent-world.

When we weaken centering, then a distinction appears between truth at i itself and truth at all or some of the worlds in the innermost nonempty sphere around i. To express the latter, we may introduce a second pair of modal operators, defined ultimately in terms of the counterfactual connectives. These will pertain to the innermost nonempty sphere around each world i, so let us call them the *inner modalities:* inner necessity and inner possibility.

$$\boxdot \phi =^{df} \mathsf{T} \,\square\!\!\!\rightarrow \phi \quad \text{(or, equivalently, } \lozenge \mathsf{T} \,\&\, \mathsf{T} \,\square\!\rightarrow \phi),$$
$$\diamondsuit\!\!\!\cdot\, \phi =^{df} \mathsf{T} \,\diamondsuit\!\!\!\rightarrow \phi \quad \text{(or, equivalently, } \lozenge \mathsf{T} \supset \mathsf{T} \,\diamondsuit\!\rightarrow \phi).$$

We obtain derived truth conditions for the inner modalities as follows.

   $\boxdot \phi$ is true at i if and only if ϕ is true at every world in some nonempty sphere around i.

   $\diamondsuit\!\!\!\cdot\, \phi$ is true at i if and only if ϕ is true at some world in every nonempty sphere around i.

Given that we have an innermost nonempty sphere around i, the truth conditions can be stated more simply: the inner modalities are interpreted by means of accessibility, the appropriate assignment of spheres of accessibility being the assignment to each world i of the innermost nonempty sphere around i, that is $\bigcap(\$_i - \{\Lambda\})$, as its single sphere of accessibility. $\boxdot \phi$ is true at i if and only if ϕ holds throughout the innermost nonempty sphere around i, and thus means that ϕ holds at every maximally close world. $\diamondsuit\!\!\!\cdot\, \phi$ is true at i if and only if ϕ holds somewhere in the innermost nonempty sphere around i, and thus means that ϕ holds at some maximally close world.

   The outermost sphere includes the innermost nonempty sphere; therefore outer necessity is stricter than inner necessity. Therefore $\square \phi$ implies $\boxdot \phi$ and $\diamondsuit\!\!\!\cdot\, \phi$ implies $\lozenge \phi$.

   So long as we confine our attention to weakly centered systems of spheres, the inner modalities could be defined more simply as $\mathsf{T} \,\square\!\rightarrow \phi$ and $\mathsf{T} \,\diamondsuit\!\rightarrow \phi$ respectively. According to any weakly centered system of spheres, these definitions are exactly equivalent to those I gave, since T is true at every world and hence never fails to be entertainable. But in Section 5.1 I shall give a deontic reinterpretation of our language, on which it will be appropriate to give up even weak centering. Then there may not be any nonempty spheres around a world; in which case nothing, not even T, is entertainable and the definitions no longer will be equivalent. Then it will prove advantageous to have defined the inner modalities as I did.

   If we insist—correctly, I think—on interpreting the counterfactuals by means of a centered system of spheres, then it is pointless to consider the inner modalities. Under unweakened centering, the inner modalities are trivial: both $\boxdot\phi$ and $\diamondsuit\!\!\!\!\cdot\,\phi$ are equivalent to ϕ itself.*

We noted that the counterfactual cannot be defined from truth-functional connectives and the outer modalities; neither can it be defined from these plus the inner modalities. That is so whether we assume centering, weak centering, or neither. The reason is that we can change truth values of counterfactuals by adding or deleting spheres that are neither outermost nor innermost, but we cannot in this way change the truth value of any sentence built up from non-counterfactual sentences by means of truth-functional connectives and outer and inner modalities.

1.8 Counterfactual Fallacies

Certain inferences are correct for the material conditional, and indeed for any constantly strict conditional, but not for variably strict conditionals. The inference fails because the strictness varies between different conditionals in the premises and conclusion. Three especially important inferences that fail for variably strict conditionals may be called the *fallacy of strengthening the antecedent*, the *fallacy of transitivity*, and the *fallacy of contraposition*.‡

The fallacy of *strengthening the antecedent* is the invalid inference-pattern:

$$\frac{\phi \,\square\!\!\rightarrow\, \psi}{\therefore\ \phi \ \& \ \chi \,\square\!\!\rightarrow\, \psi}.$$

We have already noted that the premise of such an inference may be true and the conclusion false, in connection with my sequences of counterfactuals and their negated opposites with stronger and stronger antecedents and consequents alternating between a sentence and its negation. The consistency of such sequences, and therefore the invalidity of inference by strengthening the antecedent, was indeed the principal evidence I gave that counterfactuals were variably, not constantly, strict conditionals.

Adding a conjunct to an antecedent is only one among many ways to

---

* The observation that two different pairs of modalities are definable from the counterfactual, both non-trival under weak centering, is due to Sobel.

‡ These three fallacies have been discussed by Robert Stalnaker from the standpoint of a theory equivalent (as explained in Section 3.4) to a special case of mine. See Stalnaker, 'A Theory of Conditionals', in N. Rescher, *Studies in Logical Theory* (Blackwell: Oxford, 1968). An extensive survey of these and other counterfactual fallacies is given in Sobel, 'Utilitarianisms: Simple and General' (appendix).

strengthen it. A more general form of the fallacy of strengthening the antecedent is as an invalid inference-pattern with two premises:

$$\frac{\begin{array}{c}\Box(\chi \supset \phi)\\ \phi \Box\!\!\rightarrow \psi\end{array}}{\therefore \ \chi \Box\!\!\rightarrow \psi}.$$

In the special case that χ is the conjunction of ϕ and something else, the strict conditional $\Box(\chi \supset \phi)$ will hold. The inference is fallacious even if outer necessity is logical necessity, and *a fortiori* also if it is a less strict necessity. For a counterexample to inference by strengthening the antecedent, in which the strengthening is done otherwise than by adding a conjunct, consider this invalid argument.

> $\Box$ (*I started at 5 this morning $\supset$ I started before 6*)
> *If I had started before 6, I would have arrived before noon.*
>
> ∴ *If I had started at 5, I would have arrived before noon.*

Certainly the first premise is true. To see how the second premise may be true and the conclusion false, suppose that in fact I started just after 6, tried out a new shortcut that turned out to cut two hours off the usual time for the journey, and arrived at noon exactly; but suppose that if I had started at 5, I would have been too sleepy to remember to try the shortcut. (I am supposing that the later I started, in the range of times permitted by the antecedent, the closer an antecedent-world is to our actual world; this may be so, but might not be if, for instance, I planned on starting at 5 and failed to do so only because my alarm did not quite wake me up.)

The *fallacy of transitivity* is the invalid inference-pattern

$$\frac{\begin{array}{c}\chi \Box\!\!\rightarrow \phi\\ \phi \Box\!\!\rightarrow \psi\end{array}}{\therefore \ \chi \Box\!\!\rightarrow \psi}.$$

The fallacy of transitivity is a further generalization of the fallacy of strengthening the antecedent. From the strict conditional $\Box(\chi \supset \phi)$ we can correctly infer $\chi \Box\!\!\rightarrow \phi$; from that and $\phi \Box\!\!\rightarrow \psi$ we can fallaciously infer $\chi \Box\!\!\rightarrow \psi$ by transitivity. Inference by transitivity would thus justify inference by strengthening the antecedent; since we know that the latter is fallacious, so is the former. For a direct counterexample to transitivity, consider this argument:

> *If Otto had gone to the party, then Anna would have gone.*
> *If Anna had gone, then Waldo would have gone.*
>
> ∴ *If Otto had gone, then Waldo would have gone.*

The fact is that Otto is Waldo's successful rival for Anna's affections. Waldo still tags around after Anna, but never runs the risk of meeting Otto. Otto was locked up at the time of the party, so that his going to it is a far-fetched supposition; but Anna almost did go. Then the premises are true and the conclusion false. Or take this counterexample, from Stalnaker:*

> *If J. Edgar Hoover had been born a Russian, then he would have been a Communist.*
> *If he had been a Communist, he would have been a traitor.*
> ∴ *If he had been born a Russian, he would have been a traitor.*

In general, transitivity fails in the situation shown in Figure 4(A). The antecedent of the first premise must be more far-fetched than the antecedent of the second, which is the consequent of the first. Then the closest worlds where the first antecedent holds are different from—and may differ in character from—the closest worlds where the second antecedent holds. That is the situation in our examples. We must go farther from actuality to find worlds where Otto went than to find worlds where Anna went. A Communist Hoover is nowhere to be found at worlds near ours, but a Russian-born Hoover is still more remote.

In these and all other counterexamples to transitivity, the 'might' counterfactual $\phi \diamondsuit\rightarrow \sim\chi$ is true. In these examples, but not in all, we can say something stronger: the 'would' counterfactual $\phi \square\rightarrow \sim\chi$ is non-vacuously true. If Anna had gone, Otto would still not have; if Hoover had been a Communist, he would still not have been born a Russian.‡ By adding a third premise to the inference by transitivity, we may rule out all cases where transitivity fails. The inference-pattern

$$\frac{\sim(\phi \diamondsuit\rightarrow \sim\chi)}{\therefore \chi \square\rightarrow \phi} \quad \text{or, more simply,} \quad \frac{\phi \square\rightarrow \chi}{\therefore \chi \square\rightarrow \psi}$$

* 'A Theory of Conditionals'.

‡ 'Still', 'even so', etc. in the consequent, or 'even' before the antecedent, mark a presupposition that the consequent fails to contrast with something. In the cases above, it is true and so fails to contrast with the actual state of affairs; in other cases, it is false but fails to contrast with the consequent of some other counterfactual. Insofar as it is misleading to omit these contrast-marking devices when they would be appropriate, perhaps we may say that the unmarked counterfactual carries a weak presupposition that the consequent *does* contrast with something. I treat such presuppositions about the consequent, as I do the presupposed falsity of the antecedent, as matters of conversational implicature irrelevant to truth conditions.

(A) FAILURE OF TRANSITIVITY

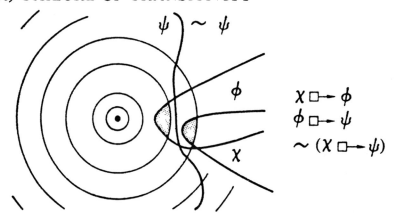

$$\chi \;\square\!\!\rightarrow\; \phi$$
$$\phi \;\square\!\!\rightarrow\; \psi$$
$$\sim (\chi \;\square\!\!\rightarrow\; \psi)$$

(B) FAILURE OF CONTRAPOSITION

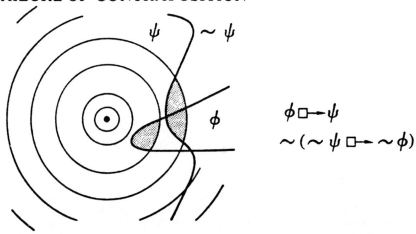

$$\phi \;\square\!\!\rightarrow\; \psi$$
$$\sim (\sim\!\psi \;\square\!\!\rightarrow\; \sim\!\phi)$$

FIGURE 4

is perfectly valid. Using this valid inference-pattern, and the fact that the requisite third premise of the form $\chi \, \& \, \phi \,\square\!\!\rightarrow\, \chi$ must be true, we can justify a valid special case of inference by transitivity:

$$\frac{\chi \,\square\!\!\rightarrow\, \chi \, \& \, \phi}{\chi \, \& \, \phi \,\square\!\!\rightarrow\, \psi}$$
$$\therefore \, \chi \,\square\!\!\rightarrow\, \psi$$

Since the inference from $\chi \,\square\!\!\rightarrow\, \phi$ to $\chi \,\square\!\!\rightarrow\, \chi \, \& \, \phi$ is valid, we can simplify this inference-pattern to:

$$\frac{\chi \,\square\!\!\rightarrow\, \phi}{\chi \, \& \, \phi \,\square\!\!\rightarrow\, \psi}$$
$$\therefore \, \chi \,\square\!\!\rightarrow\, \psi$$

Another valid inference-pattern resembling the fallacious inference by transitivity may be called inference by weakening the consequent. It is like transitivity except that the second conditional premise is a strict conditional instead of the corresponding counterfactual.

$$\frac{\chi \,\square\!\!\rightarrow\, \phi}{\square(\phi \supset \psi)}$$
$$\therefore \, \chi \,\square\!\!\rightarrow\, \psi$$

The *fallacy of contraposition* is either one of the two invalid inference-patterns

$$\frac{\phi \,\square\!\!\rightarrow\, \psi}{\therefore \, {\sim}\psi \,\square\!\!\rightarrow\, {\sim}\phi} \quad \text{and} \quad \frac{{\sim}\psi \,\square\!\!\rightarrow\, {\sim}\phi}{\therefore \, \phi \,\square\!\!\rightarrow\, \psi}$$

Obviously, both or neither are valid; let us concentrate on the first. For instance, consider this argument.

> *If Boris had gone to the party, Olga would still have gone.*
> $\therefore$ *If Olga had not gone, Boris would still not have gone.*

Suppose that Boris wanted to go, but stayed away solely in order to avoid Olga, so the conclusion is false; but Olga would have gone all the more willingly if Boris had been there, so the premise is true. In general, $\phi \,\square\!\!\rightarrow\, \psi$ may be true and its contrapositive false in the situation shown in Figure 4(B).

Note that we could use contraposition to justify the following inference-pattern involving 'might' counterfactuals:

$$\frac{\phi \,\diamondsuit\!\!\rightarrow\, \psi}{\therefore \, \psi \,\diamondsuit\!\!\rightarrow\, \phi}$$

But this inference has no plausibility at all. Note also that although contraposition of counterfactuals is invalid, nevertheless inference by *modus tollens* on a counterfactual is valid:

$$\frac{\begin{array}{c} \phi \mathrel{\Box\!\!\rightarrow} \psi \\ \sim\psi \end{array}}{\therefore\ \sim\phi}\ .$$

We cannot regard this *modus tollens* as proceeding by contraposition followed by *modus ponens*, as we can in the case of *modus tollens* on a material conditional; rather we should think of it as an inference from the counterfactual to the material conditional $\phi \supset \psi$, followed by contraposition of the material conditional, followed by *modus ponens* on the contraposed material conditional.

1.9 Potentialities

We might have occasion to complain that if the winner had not bribed the judge, then he would not have won. By this, we do not mean that the closest worlds to ours where '*The winner did not bribe the judge*' is true are worlds where '*The winner did not win*' is true. Our complaint might be true, but that construal of it certainly is false. The supposition that someone managed to win without bribing the judge—far-fetched though it might be—is entertainable; but there are no worlds at all, neither the closest worlds where that supposition holds nor any others, where anyone wins without winning. (One can win officially without 'really' winning, but that is equivocation—stick to official winning.) Our complaint therefore is not

> *The winner did not bribe the judge* $\Box\!\!\rightarrow$ *the winner did not win*.

Rather, it is *de re* with respect to 'the winner'. We are ascribing to whoever actually was the winner a counterfactual property, or *potentiality*, expressed by the formula

> *x did not bribe the judge* $\Box\!\!\rightarrow$ *x did not win*.

We are talking about what would have befallen the actual winner, not about what would have befallen whoever would have been the winner. Our supposition is that *he*—the actual winner—did not bribe the judge. It matters not that the description 'winner' we used to specify him as the one we were making suppositions about would not have fitted him (in our opinion) if the supposition had been true. The right way to symbolize what we want to say would be something like this:

> *The winner is an x such that*
> $\quad$ (*x did not bribe the judge* $\Box\!\!\rightarrow$ *x did not win*).

This symbolization reveals that the counterfactual formula and its subformulas '*x did not bribe the judge*' and '*x did not win*' are what enter into the interpretation of the sentence, whereas the seeming antecedent and consequent '*The winner did not bribe the judge*' and '*The winner did not win*' are foisted upon us by a superficial illusion of grammar.

We could treat '*is an x such that . . .*' as a structureless abstraction operator that attaches to a formula ϕ_x to make a predicate that can combine in turn with a denoting term α to make a subject-predicate sentence. (Or to make another formula, in case there are free variables besides the free x in ϕ_x.) Alternatively, we could treat '___ *is an x such that . . .*' as a quantificational matrix with two gaps suitable to receive α and ϕ_x respectively:

$$\exists x(x = \underline{\quad} \ \& \ \ldots).$$

Either way, a sentence 'α *is an x such that* ϕ_x' is true at a world i if and only if whatever is denoted at i by α satisfies ϕ_x at i (as a value of the variable x)—in other words, has the property expressed by the formula ϕ_x.*

Counterfactuals *de re* crop up in connection with countercomparatives. What if my yacht were longer than it is? The supposition is notoriously not that the seeming antecedent '*My yacht is longer than it is*' is true (in any straightforward way; but see Section 2.8). One way to handle counterfactuals with this seeming antecedent is as *de re* predications of a counterfactual potentiality to whatever is the actual length of my yacht.

The length of my yacht is an x such that
(the length of my yacht exceeds x $\square\!\!\rightarrow \ldots$)

Of course, we need an entity to have the potentiality being ascribed. It is easy enough to hypostatize lengths, but what do we make of '*If mankind were wiser . . .*'?

Potentialities expressed by counterfactual formulas are needed not only in the *de re* cases, but also for universal or existential quantifications (including the existential quantifications that arise if we take '___ *is an x such that . . .*' as a quantificational matrix). We want a way to say that any winner who would not have won if he had not bribed the judge is a knave:

$$\forall x((Wx \ \& \ (\sim Bx \ \square\!\!\rightarrow \ \sim Wx)) \supset Kx),$$

---

* On the use of abstraction operators to give a clear and unambiguous symbolization of modal predications *de re*, see Richmond Thomason and Robert Stalnaker, 'Modality and Reference', *Noûs* 2 (1968): 359–372.

using the obvious abbreviations. Or that there was at least one Roman emperor who, if only he had had gunpowder, would have conquered all of Europe:

$$\exists x(Rx \ \& \ (Gx \ \Box\!\!\rightarrow Cx)).$$

Or that a thing has disposition D if and only if, subjected to test T, it would give response R:

$$\forall x(Dx \equiv (Tx \ \Box\!\!\rightarrow Rx)).$$

(The point is not that I want to *believe* instances of the last—I am inclined not to—but that I want my theory of counterfactuals to explain what they mean.) There is nothing peculiar about the use of quantifiers in these sentences. To interpret them, and to interpret also our counterfactuals *de re*, all we need is an account of satisfaction by things of counterfactual formulas. Or, in the material mode: of possession by things of counterfactual potentialities.

It is enough to ask for conditions under which a single thing satisfies a formula $\phi_x \ \Box\!\!\rightarrow \psi_x$ with x as the only free variable. The generalization to satisfaction of formulas with arbitrarily many free variables by arbitrarily long or infinite sequences of things is routine, once we know what to do in the one-variable case. It is not required that x appear both in ϕ_x and in ψ_x. Often it does not:

The length of my yacht exceeds x $\Box\!\!\rightarrow$ *I am contented*
I am ostentatious $\Box\!\!\rightarrow$ *the length of my yacht exceeds x*

for instance, might be used in symbolizations of '*If my yacht were longer I would be contented*' and '*If I were ostentatious my yacht would be longer*'. In fact, I do not even exclude the degenerate case that x appears neither in ϕ_x nor in ψ_x.

As a first try, we could give satisfaction conditions for counterfactual formulas simply by imitating the truth conditions for counterfactual sentences, letting the thing that satisfies the formula tag along throughout. Something satisfies $\phi_x \ \Box\!\!\rightarrow \psi_x$ at a world i, on this proposal, if and only if either (1) no world where it satisfies ϕ_x belongs to any sphere around i (the vacuous case), or (2) some sphere S around i does contain at least one world where it satisfies ϕ_x, and at every world in S where it satisfies ϕ_x it also satisfies ψ_x. So, for example, if Ripov is the winner because he bribed the judge (here at our world), then he has the potentiality expressed by

x did not bribe the Judge $\Box\!\!\rightarrow$ *x did not win*

non-vacuously if and only if there is some sphere containing worlds where he did not bribe the judge, throughout which all the worlds where he did not bribe the judge are worlds where he did not win. Roughly: if and only if he did not win at the closest of the worlds where he did not bribe the judge.

The trouble is that this presumes that we have the very same Ripov active at several worlds: ours, where he bribes the judge and wins, and others, where he does not bribe the judge and does not win. What makes the inhabitant of another world, who does not bribe and does not win, identical with our Ripov? I suppose the answer must be *either* that his identity with our Ripov is an irreducible fact, not to be explained in terms of anything else, *or* that his identity with our Ripov is due to some sort of similarity to our Ripov—he is Ripov because he plays much the same role at the other world that our Ripov plays here. Neither answer pleases me. The first answer either posits trans-world identities between things arbitrarily different in character, thereby denying what I take to be some of the facts about *de re* modality, or else it makes a mystery of those facts by denying us any way to explain why there are some sorts of trans-world identities but not others. The second answer at least is not defeatist, but it runs into trouble because similarity relations lack the formal properties—transitivity, for instance—of identity.

The best thing to do, I think, is to escape the problems of trans-world identity by insisting that there is nothing that inhabits more than one world. There are some abstract entities, for instance numbers or properties, that inhabit no particular world but exist alike from the standpoint of all worlds, just as they have no location in time and space but exist alike from the standpoint of all times and places. Things that do inhabit worlds—people, flames, buildings, puddles, concrete particulars generally—inhabit one world each, no more. Our Ripov is a man of our world, who does not reappear elsewhere. Other worlds may have Ripovs of their own, but none of these is our Ripov. Rather, they are counterparts of our Ripov. What comes from trans-world resemblance is not trans-world identity, but a substitute for trans-world identity: the counterpart relation. What our Ripov cannot do in person at other worlds, not being present there to do it, he may do vicariously through his counterparts. He himself is not an honest man at any world —he is dishonest here, and nonexistent elsewhere—but he is vicariously honest through his honest counterparts.

In general: something has for *counterparts* at a given world those things existing there that resemble it closely enough in important respects of intrinsic quality and extrinsic relations, and that resemble it no less closely than do other things existing there. Ordinarily something will have one counterpart or none at a world, but ties in similarity may give it multiple counterparts. Two special cases: (1) anything is its own unique counterpart at its own world, and (2) the abstract entities that exist alike from the standpoint of all worlds, but inhabit none, are their own unique counterparts at all worlds.

I have proposed elsewhere that the counterpart relation ought to be used as a substitute for trans-world identity in explaining *de re* modality.* The realm of essence and accident is the realm of the vicarious. What something *might* have done (or might have been) is what it does (or is) vicariously; and that is what its counterparts do (or are). What is essential to something is what it has in common with all its counterparts; what it nowhere vicariously lacks. Ripov's honest counterparts make him someone who might have been honest. His lack of inanimate counterparts makes him essentially animate. In terms of satisfaction of modal formulas: something satisfies $\Box\phi_x$ at a world i if and only if any counterpart of it at any world j accessible from i satisfies ϕ_x at j; something satisfies $\Diamond\phi_x$ at a world i if and only if it has some counterpart at some world j accessible from i that satisfies ϕ_x at j. Alternatively, we can say that something *vicariously satisfies* ϕ_x at a world i if and only if it has some counterpart at i that satisfies ϕ_x at i. (At one's own world, vicarious satisfaction coincides with satisfaction.) Then we can restate the conditions in terms of vicarious satisfaction. Something satisfies $\Box\phi_x$ at i if and only if there is no world accessible from i where it vicariously satisfies $\sim\phi_x$. Something satisfies $\Diamond\phi_x$ if and only if there is some world accessible from i where it vicariously satisfies ϕ_x.‡

The method of counterparts seems to me to have many virtues as a theory of *de re* modality. (1) It has the same explanatory power as a theory of *de re* modality that employs trans-world identity based on trans-world resemblance. The facts about what things might have been and might have done are explained by our standards of similarity— that is, of the comparative importances of respects of comparison—plus facts about how things actually are. Modal facts are grounded in facts about actual character, not mysteriously independent. It is because of the way Ripov actually is that certain honest men at other worlds resemble him enough to be his counterparts, and inanimate things at other worlds do not. (2) However, we are rid of the worst burden of a theory of trans-world identity based on trans-world resemblance: the counterpart relation is not identity, so we need not try to force it to

* 'Counterpart Theory and Quantified Modal Logic', *Journal of Philosophy* 65 (1968): 113–126; 'Counterparts of Persons and Their Bodies', *Journal of Philosophy* 68 (1971): 203–211.

‡ An alternative definition of vicarious satisfaction would put the double negation in the satisfaction conditions for $\Diamond\phi_x$ instead of those for $\Box\phi_x$; but we would be stuck with it one place or other. The reason is that something with more or less than one counterpart at a world may vicariously satisfy both or neither of ϕ_x and $\sim\phi_x$, so vicariously satisfying $\sim\phi_x$ is not the same as not vicariously satisfying ϕ_x.

have the logical properties of identity. (3) Therefore we have a desirable flexibility. For instance, we can say that something might have been twins because it has twin counterparts somewhere, without claiming that it is literally identical with two things not identical to one another. (4) Since the counterpart relation is based on similarity, the vagueness of similarity infects *de re* modality. And that is all to the good. It goes a long way toward explaining why questions of *de re* modality are as difficult as we have found them to be. (5) We can plead this same vagueness to explain away seeming discrepancies among our *de re* modal opinions. For instance, consider two inhabitants of a certain world that is exactly like ours in every detail until 1888, and thereafter diverges. One has exactly the ancestral origins of our Hitler; that is so in virtue of events within the region of perfect match that ended just before his birth. In that region, it is quite unequivocal what is the counterpart of what. The other has quite different ancestral origins, but as he grows up he gradually duplicates more and more of the infamous deeds of our Hitler until after 1930 his career matches our Hitler's career in every detail. Meanwhile the first lives an obscure and blameless life. Does this world prove that Hitler might have lived a blameless life? Or does it prove that he might have had different ancestral origins? I want to be able to say either—though perhaps not both in the same breath—depending on which respects of comparison are foremost in my mind; and the method of counterparts, with due allowance for vagueness, allows me to do so. (6) There are also cases where we need to mix different counterpart relations in a single sentence in order to make sense of it as a reasonable thing to think; for instance, sentences of *de re* contingent identity. We shall see other cases in connection with counterfactuals. I see no way to get the same effect by means of trans-world identity alone, though one might get it by mixing in trans-world identity along with the counterpart relations.

Now I shall use the method of counterparts to correct my previous satisfaction conditions for counterfactual formulas. The formulation I gave will not do at all. Without the trans-world identities I reject, it leads in most cases to vacuity. We need to replace trans-world identity by the counterpart relation; that is, to replace satisfaction (in the definiens) by vicarious satisfaction. Roughly speaking, I want to say that Ripov has the potentiality expressed by

x *reforms* $\Box\!\rightarrow x$ *confesses*

—that he satisfies that formula—because the closest worlds where he vicariously reforms are worlds where he vicariously confesses. But that is not quite right, even if we forget to doubt the Limit Assumption. What if he has multiple counterparts at one of the closest worlds where he vicariously reforms? It is not enough if one reforms and another confesses; it is not even enough if one reforms and confesses, and another reforms without confessing. What we must require is that at every closest world where one of Ripov's counterparts reforms, all of those who reform also confess—that is, none reforms without confessing. The closest worlds where he vicariously reforms must be worlds where he does not vicariously both reform and not confess. (Distinguish between (1) vicariously both reforming and not confessing, both through the same counterpart, and (2) both vicariously reforming and vicariously not confessing, perhaps through different counterparts.)

In general: something satisfies $\phi_x \Box\!\!\rightarrow \psi_x$ at a world i if and only if either (1) no world where it vicariously satisfies ϕ_x belongs to any sphere around i (the vacuous case), or (2) some sphere S around i does contain at least one world where it vicariously satisfies ϕ_x, and at no world in that sphere does it vicariously satisfy $\phi_x \,\&\, \sim\!\psi_x$. Putting it in terms of the counterpart relation: something satisfies $\phi_x \Box\!\!\rightarrow \psi_x$ at a world i if and only if either (1) at no world j in any sphere around i does it have a counterpart that satisfies ϕ_x at j, or (2) some sphere S around i does contain at least one world j such that some counterpart of it at j satisfies ϕ_x at j, and every counterpart of it at any world k in S that satisfies ϕ_x at k also satisfies ψ_x at k.

The method of counterparts is needed not only to give an account of satisfaction of counterfactual formulas by things that inhabit our world alone, but also to interpret counterfactuals containing 'I', 'you', or demonstratives. These denote on any occasion of utterance such things as the speaker, his audience, the things he points to; and these are things that inhabit only the world of the utterance. So if I say '*If I had given you that, you would have broken it*', what are denoted by 'I', 'you', and 'that' are three things confined to our world. The closest antecedent-worlds are not worlds where those things reappear, suitably related—that way lies vacuity—but worlds where those things have suitably related counterparts. The counterfactual is true, roughly, if and only if the closest worlds where there is a triple $\langle a, b, c \rangle$ of counterparts of I, you, and that, respectively, such that a gives c to b, are worlds where there is no such triple in which b does not break c. We have two options. We could give special truth conditions for counterfactuals with 'I', 'you', or demonstratives, along the lines I have sketched; or we could use the satisfaction conditions just laid down for counterfactual formulas by insisting that all occurrences of 'I', 'you', or demonstratives should be taken as *de re*.

It would be a good idea to provide for more than one counterpart relation. Different counterpart relations might vary in the stringency of resemblance they require; or they might stress different respects of comparison.

We can explain the simultaneous truth of Goodman's sentences

(1) *If New York City were in Georgia, New York City would be in the South.*

and

(2) *If Georgia included New York City, Georgia would not be entirely in the South.*

by the hypothesis that both are *de re* both with respect to 'New York City' and with respect to 'Georgia', and that a less stringent counterpart relation is summoned up by the subject terms 'New York City' in (1) and 'Georgia' in (2) than by the object terms 'Georgia' in (1) and 'New York City' in (2). Then in (1) we are concerned with the closest worlds to ours where a not-too-close counterpart of our New York is in a close counterpart of our Georgia, and hence is in (a counterpart of?) the South; whereas in (2) we are concerned with the closest worlds to ours where a not-too-close counterpart of our Georgia includes a close counterpart of our New York City, and hence is not entirely included in the South.*

For a familiar illustration of the need for counterpart relations stressing different respects of comparison, take '*If I were you . . .*'. The antecedent-worlds are worlds where you and I are vicariously identical; that is, we share a common counterpart. But we want him to be in *your* predicament with *my* ideas, not the other way around. He should be your counterpart under a counterpart relation that stresses similarity of predicament; mine under a different counterpart relation that stresses similarity of ideas.

---

* Alternatively, perhaps each is *de re* with respect to one of the two names—perhaps the subject in both, perhaps the object in both—and we are seeing a difference in stringency between a counterpart relation involved in satisfaction of counterfactual formulas and a counterpart relation involved in determining the denotation at other worlds of a proper name originally bestowed by an episode of naming that involved some inhabitant of our world.

2. Reformulations

2.1 Multiple Modalities

There are various ways to formulate my analysis of counterfactuals as variably strict conditionals based on comparative similarity of worlds. Let us look at some of the alternative formulations. Some are exactly equivalent to my first formulation by means of systems of spheres; others are equivalent only to special cases thereof.

Suppose there are no more than a certain finite number n of non-empty spheres around any world. Then we can number the spheres around each world i in order of increasing size. We begin with S_i^0, the empty set; then comes S_i^1, the innermost nonempty sphere (assuming centering, S_i^1 is $\{i\}$); then S_i^2, the next smallest; and so on out to S_i^n, the largest sphere around i. (In case i has fewer than its full complement of n distinct nonempty spheres, we give all the left-over numbers to the outermost sphere. If there are only $n-2$ nonempty spheres around a certain world i, for instance, the outermost of them counts as S_i^{n-2}, as S_i^{n-1}, and as S_i^n.) We introduce a family of increasingly strict necessity operators $\Box_1, \ldots, \Box_n$, together with the corresponding possibility operators $\Diamond_1, \ldots, \Diamond_n$. For any number m from 1 through n, $\Box_m \phi$ is to be true at a world i if and only if ϕ holds throughout S_i^m; and $\Diamond_m \phi$ is to be true at i and if only if ϕ holds at some world in S_i^m. In other words, the spheres S_i^m are the spheres of accessibility for the mth pair of modal operators, $\Box_m$ and $\Diamond_m$.*

Given such a family of modalities, the counterfactual connectives are definable.

$$\phi \;\Box\!\!\rightarrow\; \psi =^{\mathrm{df}} (\Diamond_1 \phi \ \& \ \Box_1 (\phi \supset \psi)) \lor \ldots \lor$$
$$(\Diamond_n \phi \ \& \ \Box_n (\phi \supset \psi)) \lor \sim\!\Diamond_n \phi,$$

$$\phi \;\Diamond\!\!\rightarrow\; \psi =^{\mathrm{df}} (\Diamond_1 \phi \supset \Diamond_1 (\phi \ \& \ \psi)) \ \& \ldots \&$$
$$(\Diamond_n \phi \supset \Diamond_n (\phi \ \& \ \psi)) \ \& \ \Diamond_n \phi.$$

---

* Such a system of multiple modalities is discussed in M. K. Rennie, 'Models for Multiply Modal Systems', *Zeitschrift für mathematische Logik und Grundlagen der Mathematik* **16** (1970): 175–186, and in L. F. Goble, 'Grades of Modality', *Logique et Analyse* **51** (1970): 323–334.

More generally, if we were willing to assume that there are no infinite descending sequences of smaller and smaller spheres around any one world, we could number the spheres around each world by ordinals, including perhaps transfinite ordinals. We could then introduce an infinite family of increasingly strict necessity operators, together with the corresponding possibility operators, indexed by ordinals and thereby placed in correspondence with the spheres around each world. We could then define the counterfactual connective by an infinite disjunction (for □→) or an infinite conjunction (for ◇→) of disjuncts or conjuncts like those in the finite definitions above.

2.2 Propositional Quantification

Infinite disjunctions or conjunctions often can be replaced by existential or universal quantifications. They can be thus replaced in this case; and as a bonus we can drop the restriction against infinite descending sequences of smaller and smaller spheres around a world. We could quantify over modalities themselves;* instead of a disjunction or conjunction of parallel clauses involving different modalities, we could have a definiens in which an initial quantifier over suitable modalities binds a modal-operator-variable in its scope. But for our present purposes we need nothing so exotic. Propositional quantification will serve as well.

Suppose that our language has the following resources: (1) propositional variables, grammatically interchangeable with sentences; (2) existential and universal quantifiers ∃ and ∀ that may be used to bind these variables; (3) the operators □ and ◇ of outer necessity and possibility; (4) the truth-functional connectives; and (5) a special one-place sentential operator ○, called the *sphericality* operator. A sentence ○ϕ is to be true at a world i if and only if there is some sphere S around i such that ϕ is true at all and only the worlds in S. More precisely, since ϕ may be an open sentence with free propositional variables: ○ϕ is true at i, relative to a given assignment of values to its free propositional variables (if any), if and only if there is some sphere S around i such that ϕ is true, relative to that assignment of values, at all and only the worlds in S.‡

Now we are ready to define the counterfactual connectives. We have

---

* A system that permits quantification over modalities is given in Richard Montague, 'Universal Grammar', *Theoria* **36** (1970): 373–398; reprinted in Montague, *Formal Philosophy*.

‡ Alternatively, suppose we are given the logical modalities rather than tne outer modalities; then we may begin by defining the outer modalities using the given apparatus.

only to copy their truth conditions into the object language. We no longer assume any special restrictions on the system of spheres.

$$\phi \,\square\!\!\rightarrow\, \psi \;=^{\mathrm{df}}\; \Diamond\phi \supset \exists\xi(\bigcirc\xi \;\&\; \Diamond(\xi \;\&\; \phi) \;\&\; \square(\xi \;\&\; \phi.\supset \psi)),$$
$$\phi \,\Diamond\!\!\rightarrow\, \psi \;=^{\mathrm{df}}\; \Diamond\phi \;\&\; \forall\xi(\bigcirc\xi \;\&\; \Diamond(\xi \;\&\; \phi).\supset \Diamond(\xi \;\&\; \phi \;\&\; \psi)).$$

Here ξ is any variable that does not occur in ϕ or ψ.

The values of propositional variables are, of course, called *propositions*. It does not much matter what propositions are, so long as (1) they are entities that can be true or false at worlds, and (2) there are enough of them. They must have truth values at worlds so that an open sentence consisting of a propositional variable standing alone will have truth values at worlds, relative to an assignment of a value to the variable: the truth value of the sentence is the truth value of the proposition assigned as value to the variable. For every proposition, as for every sentence, there is a set of the worlds where it is true. Conversely, for each set of worlds, there should be a proposition true at all and only the worlds in that set. Otherwise we cannot safely transform quantification over sets of worlds in the metalanguage into propositional quantification in the object language, as we did to obtain our definitions of the counterfactual operators.

For the sake of definiteness, we may take sets of worlds to *be* propositions.* A proposition P is true at a world i if and only if i belongs to the proposition—the set—P. There is a proposition for every set of worlds because the set itself is the proposition true at all and only the worlds

---

* As is done in much recent work in possible-world semantics. (Sometimes with a trivial difference: propositions are taken to be the characteristic functions of sets of worlds rather than the sets themselves.) The idea goes back at least to Clarence I. Lewis, 'The Modes of Meaning', *Philosophy and Phenomenological Research* 4 (1944): 236–249, in which the set of worlds is called the 'comprehension' of the proposition; and to Rudolf Carnap, *Meaning and Necessity* (University of Chicago Press: Chicago, 1947), in which propositions are taken as sets of state descriptions, and state descriptions are said to 'represent Leibniz' possible worlds or Wittgenstein's possible states of affairs'. No theory can fit all that philosophers have said about 'propositions'—they have said too much—but the identification of propositions with sets of worlds captures a good part of the tradition. Propositions so understood are non-linguistic entities capable of being true or false. They exist eternally, non-contingently, and independently of us. One proposition may be expressed by many sentences, in one language or in many, or by non-verbal means of communication; on the other hand, there may be propositions that we have no way to express. Two sentences that are logically equivalent, or that do not differ in truth value at any world for whatever reason, express the same proposition. But one part of the tradition about propositions must be given up: propositions understood as sets of worlds cannot serve as the meanings of sentences that express them, since there are sentences—for instance, all the logical truths—that express the same proposition but do not, in any ordinary sense, have the same meaning.

in the set. For any sentence ϕ, let $[\![\phi]\!]$ be the set of worlds where ϕ is true. $[\![\phi]\!]$, being a set of worlds, is a proposition; call it the proposition *expressed* by the sentence ϕ. Then a sentence ϕ is true at a world i if and only if the proposition $[\![\phi]\!]$ expressed by ϕ is true at i; that is, if and only if i belongs to the proposition $[\![\phi]\!]$. All the tautologies express the same proposition: the *necessary proposition*, in other words the set of all worlds. All contradictions express the same proposition: the *impossible proposition*, in other words the empty set. A proposition expressed by some or other sentence of a language is said to be *expressible* in that language. We cannot safely assume that every proposition is expressible in our language, or indeed in any practical enrichment thereof. There are apt to be too many propositions and too few sentences. (I shall argue in Section 4.1 that there are more worlds than sets of sentences. *A fortiori* there are more propositions than sentences.) That is why we need to quantify over propositions. Quantification over sentences—in effect, over expressible propositions—could not substitute for meta-linguistic quantification over sets of worlds.

If sets of worlds are propositions, the truth conditions for many sentential connectives and operators can be restated by means of an algebra of propositions. With an n-place connective we associate an n-place operation on propositions, so that the proposition expressed by a compound sentence is obtained by applying the operation to the propositions expressed by the sentences whence it was compounded. Negation corresponds to complementation relative to the set I of all worlds; conjunction to intersection; disjunction to union; and so on for the other truth functions. Then the truth conditions for compound sentences are given by propositional equations:

$$[\![\sim\phi]\!] = I - [\![\phi]\!],$$
$$[\![\phi \ \& \ \psi]\!] = [\![\phi]\!] \cap [\![\psi]\!],$$
$$[\![\phi \ \lor \ \psi]\!] = [\![\phi]\!] \cup [\![\psi]\!].$$

Our counterfactual connective $\Box\!\!\rightarrow$ corresponds to a more complicated two-place operation on propositions; call it the *counterfactual operation*. Given as arguments two sets of worlds P and Q, this operation yields as value the set of all worlds i such that if P overlaps any sphere around i, then P overlaps some sphere S around i such that the intersection $P \cap S$ is included in Q. We can now state the truth conditions for counterfactuals by saying that, for any ϕ and ψ, the proposition $[\![\phi \ \Box\!\!\rightarrow \ \psi]\!]$ is the result of applying this counterfactual operation to the propositions $[\![\phi]\!]$ and $[\![\psi]\!]$. We can say that the connective *expresses* the operation. If we want to give the connective an entity to be its meaning, the operation can serve the purpose.

2.3 Comparative Similarity

Our system of spheres is nothing but a convenient device for carrying information about the comparative similarity of worlds. We could do away with the spheres, and give the truth conditions for counterfactuals directly in terms of comparative similarity of worlds, together with accessibility. Let us introduce the notation

$$j \leqslant_i k$$

to mean that the world j is at least as similar to the world i as the world k is; also

$$j <_i k \quad \text{(defined as: it is not the case that } k \leqslant_i j)$$

to mean that j is more similar to i than k is. We may posit an assignment to each world i of two items: a two-place relation $\leqslant_i$ among worlds, regarded as the ordering of worlds in respect of their comparative similarity to i, and a set S_i of worlds, regarded as the set of worlds accessible from i. Call such an assignment a (*centered*) *comparative similarity system* if and only if, for each world i, the following six conditions hold.

(1) The relation $\leqslant_i$ is *transitive*; that is, whenever $j \leqslant_i k$ and $k \leqslant_i h$, then $j \leqslant_i h$.
(2) The relation $\leqslant_i$ is *strongly connected*; that is, for any worlds j and k, either $j \leqslant_i k$ or $k \leqslant_i j$. (Equivalently: if $j <_i k$ then $j \leqslant_i k$.)
(3) The world i is *self-accessible*; that is, i belongs to S_i.
(4) The world i is *strictly* $\leqslant_i$-*minimal*; that is, for any world j different from i, $i <_i j$.
(5) Inaccessible worlds are $\leqslant_i$-*maximal*; that is, if k does not belong to S_i, then for any world j, $j \leqslant_i k$.
(6) Accessible worlds are more similar to i than inaccessible worlds: if j belongs to S_i and k does not, then $j <_i k$.

A relation that is transitive and strongly connected is called a *weak ordering* or a (*total*) *preordering*.* We can state the six conditions concisely as follows: each $\leqslant_i$ is a weak ordering of the worlds, with i alone at the bottom and all the worlds inaccessible from i, if there are any, together at the top above all the accessible worlds. All inaccessible

---

* 'Weak' because, unlike a *strong* (or *linear*) *ordering*, ties are permitted: two different things can stand in the relation to each other, and thus be tied in the ordering. 'Preordering' because if we take equivalence classes under the relation of being thus tied, the induced ordering of the equivalence classes is a strong ordering. Familiar weak orderings are the relations of being at least as tall as, at least as far north as, etc. When I speak simply of an *ordering*, I shall mean a weak ordering; we shall be little concerned with strong orderings.

worlds are equally dissimilar to i; if j and k both are outside S_i, then $j \leqslant_i k$ and $k \leqslant_i j$. If there are no worlds inaccessible from i, then it may be that there are remoter and remoter accessible worlds without end, or it may be that some of the accessible worlds are maximally remote from i.

We may now give the truth conditions for the 'would' counterfactual in terms of a comparative similarity system, as follows.

$\phi \ \square\!\!\rightarrow \psi$ is true at a world i (according to a given comparative similarity system) if and only if either
(1) no ϕ-world belongs to S_i (the vacuous case), or
(2) there is a ϕ-world k in S_i such that, for any world j, if $j \leqslant_i k$ then $\phi \supset \psi$ holds at j.

The counterfactual is true at i if and only if, if there is an antecedent-world accessible from i, then the consequent holds at every antecedent-world at least as close to i as a certain accessible antecedent-world.

The present formulation is exactly equivalent to the original formulation by means of spheres, without any restrictive assumptions. Recalling the way in which systems of spheres are supposed to carry information about comparative similarity, it is easily seen that we can put systems of spheres in one-to-one correspondence with comparative similarity systems, in such a way that the corresponding systems agree on the truth value at every world of every counterfactual. Starting with a comparative similarity system that assigns to each world i the relation $\leqslant_i$ and the set S_i, let $ be the assignment to each world i of the set $_i containing all and only those subsets S of S_i such that, whenever j belongs to S and k does not, $j <_i k$. Then it is easy to show (1) that $ is a system of spheres, and (2) that a counterfactual is true at a world according to the defined system of spheres $ if and only if it is true at that world according to the original comparative similarity system. Call $ the system of spheres *derived from* the original comparative similarity system. To go the other way, suppose we start with a system of spheres $. For each world i, let $j \leqslant_i k$ if and only if every sphere S in $_i that contains k also contains j; and let S_i be $\bigcup\!_i. Then it is easy to show (1) that the assignment to each world i of the relation $\leqslant_i$ and the set S_i so defined is a comparative similarity system, and (2) that a counterfactual is true at a world according to this defined comparative similarity system if and only if it is true at that world according to the original system of spheres $. Say that this comparative similarity system is *derived from* the system of spheres $. We can show, finally, that for any comparative similarity system and system of spheres, the latter is derived from the former if and only if the former is derived from the latter. The assignment to each world i of the sphere of accessibility S_i is the accessibility assignment corresponding to the outer necessity operator. It seems clumsy to assign the two separate items $\leqslant_i$ and S_i to each world i, but S_i is independent of $\leqslant_i$. If there are no $\leqslant_i$-maximal worlds, we know that S_i must be the whole set of worlds; but if there are some $\leqslant_i$-maximal worlds, we do not know from $\leqslant_i$ alone whether these are inaccessible worlds, to be left out of consideration in determining whether a counterfactual is true at i, or maximally remote accessible worlds. An alternative method* would be to let $\leqslant_i$ be an ordering not of all worlds, but only of accessible worlds, so that S_i could be defined as the field of the relation $\leqslant_i$; but this method is even clumsier.

There is something to be said for a philosophic conscience untroubled by possible worlds, but troubled by sets. After all, possible worlds have not led into paradox. The owner of such a conscience should prefer the present formulation to the original formulation involving an assignment to each world of a set of sets of worlds. He should regard a comparative similarity system, however, not as an assignment to each world of a two-place comparative similarity relation and a set of worlds regarded as accessible, but rather as a single three-place comparative similarity relation and a single two-place accessibility relation; or better still, as the two predicates '____ *is at least as similar to - - - as . . . is*' and '____ *is accessible from . . .*'.

2.4 Similarity Measures

I have sometimes spoken informally of *degrees* of similarity, as if similarity of worlds could be measured numerically; but I have not assumed that it could be. I have not used any quantitative concept of similarity, but only a comparative concept. One world is more similar than another to a third; but we need never say how much more, and the question how much more need not make sense.

Suppose, however, that we did have a quantitative concept of the similarity of worlds, so that we could speak sensibly of the degree of similarity, measured numerically, of one world to another. Then the truth conditions of 'would' counterfactuals would be as follows: $\phi \,\square\!\!\rightarrow\, \psi$ is true at a world i if and only if either (1) no ϕ-world is similar to i to a degree greater than zero, or (2) for some positive number d, there are ϕ-worlds similar to i to degree at least d, and ψ holds at every ϕ-world similar to i to degree at least d. (Worlds too unlike i to be considered—those that we previously regarded as lying outside all the spheres around i—are now assigned zero degree of similarity to i.)

* Followed in my 'Completeness and Decidability of Three Logics of Counter-factual Conditionals', *Theoria* **37** (1971): 74–85.

What additional assumptions do we make about comparative similarity orderings if we assume that they can be obtained from a numerical measure of similarity?

For one thing, we limit the number of gradations of similarity to the number of numbers, and we limit the order type of the comparative similarity ordering to the order types of orderings of numbers. Every similarity ordering with only countably many distinct gradations of similarity can be represented as derived from a numerical measure. Not every similarity ordering with more than countably many distinct gradations can be so represented; and no ordering with more distinct gradations than there are real numbers can be. This limitation hardly seems serious.

If we measure similarity numerically, and make uninhibited use of the analogy of similarity 'distance' between worlds to spatial distance between places, we are liable to make a much more serious and questionable assumption: that the degree of similarity of i to j equals the degree of similarity of j to i.* This assumption of symmetry for the similarity measure implies a constraint on similarity orderings derived from that measure: if $j <_i k$ and $k <_j i$, then $j <_k i$. But that constraint would be unjustified if we suppose that the facts about a world i help to determine which respects of similarity and dissimilarity are important in comparing other worlds in respect of similarity to the world i. The colors of things are moderately important at our world, so similarities and dissimilarities in respect of color contribute with moderate weight to the similarity or dissimilarity of other worlds to ours. But there are worlds where colors are much more important than they are at ours; for instance, worlds where the colors of things figure in fundamental physical laws. There are other worlds where colors are much less important than they are at ours; for instance, worlds where the colors of things are random and constantly changing. Similarities or dissimilarities in color will contribute with more or less weight to the similarity or dissimilarity of a world to one of those worlds where color is more important or less important. Thus it can happen that j is more similar than k to i in the respects of comparison that are important at i; k is more similar than i to j in the respects of comparison that are important at j; yet i is more similar than j to k in the respects of comparison that are important at k.

This assumption of symmetry is, of course, not an inevitable consequence of assuming that similarity of worlds admits of numerical measurement. We could have an asymmetric similarity measure. It

---

* Sobel, in 'Utilitarianisms: Simple and General', formulates essentially my analysis of counterfactuals by means of a numerical similarity measure, and does make this assumption.

would give us the degree of similarity of j to i, from the standpoint of i; that might not equal the degree of similarity of i to j, from the standpoint of j, because the relative importances of respects of comparison might differ from the standpoints of the two different worlds. (Having gone that far, we might as well have a function of three arguments that gives the degree of similarity of i to j from the standpoint of k, whether or not k is the same as i or j.) But why bother? The appeal of a numerical similarity measure comes from the analogy between similarity 'distance' and spatial distance. To the extent that the analogy breaks down, the point of having a numerical measure is lost.

2.5 Comparative Possibility

Ordinarily we think of possibility as an all-or-nothing matter. Something is possible or it is not, and the only way for it to be more possible that ϕ than that ψ is for it to be possible that ϕ but not possible that ψ. Given the notion of comparative overall similarity of worlds, however, there is a natural comparative concept of possibility. It is more possible for a dog to talk than for a stone to talk, since some worlds with talking dogs are more like our world than is any world with talking stones. It is more possible for a stone to talk than for eighteen to be a prime number, however, since stones do talk at some worlds far from ours, but presumably eighteen is not a prime number at any world at all, no matter how remote.

We may introduce into our language three comparative possibility operators:

$$\leqslant$$

read as '*It is at least as possible that* ____ *as it is that . . .*', or as '*It is no more far-fetched that* ____ *than that . . .*', or as '*It is no more remote from actuality that* ____ *than that . . .*';

$$\prec$$

read as '*It is more possible that* ____ *than that . . .*', or as '*It is less far-fetched (less remote from actuality) that* ____ *than that . . .*'; and

$$\approx$$

read as '*It is equally possible (equally far-fetched, equally remote from actuality) that* ____ *and that . . .*'. The pair of $\leqslant$ and $\prec$ are interdefinable, and $\approx$ is definable from $\leqslant$, as follows:

$$\phi \leqslant \psi =^{\mathrm{df}} \sim(\psi \prec \phi),$$
$$\phi \prec \psi =^{\mathrm{df}} \sim(\psi \leqslant \phi),$$
$$\phi \approx \psi =^{\mathrm{df}} \phi \leqslant \psi \ \& \ \psi \leqslant \phi.$$

Let us take $\leqslant$ as primitive and the other two as defined. The truth conditions for $\leqslant$ are given thus:

$\phi \leqslant \psi$ is true at a world i (according to a system of spheres $) if and only if, for every sphere S in $_i$, if S contains any ψ-world then S contains a ϕ-world.

We thence obtain derived truth conditions for the defined operators $\prec$ and $\approx$:

$\phi \prec \psi$ is true at i (according to $) if and only if some sphere in $_i$ contains a ϕ-world but no ψ-world.

$\phi \approx \psi$ is true at i (according to $) if and only if all and only those spheres in $_i$ that contain ϕ-worlds contain ψ-worlds.

The outer and inner modalities, previously defined from the counterfactual, may now be redefined in terms of comparative possibility. The following definitions give the same derived truth conditions as the original ones. For the outer modalities:

$$\Diamond\phi =^{df} \phi \prec \bot,$$
$$\Box\phi =^{df} {\sim}\Diamond {\sim} \phi \quad \text{(or, directly, } \bot \approx {\sim}\phi\text{)}.$$

For any ϕ, $\phi \leqslant \bot$ is everywhere true; thus the everywhere-false sentence $\bot$ is minimally possible. Outer possibility, then, is more-than-minimal possibility—possibility at least exceeding that of $\bot$. For the inner modalities:

$$\diamondsuit\phi =^{df} \phi \approx \top,$$
$$\boxdot\phi =^{df} {\sim}\diamondsuit {\sim} \phi \quad \text{(or, directly, } \top \prec {\sim}\phi\text{)}.$$

For any ϕ, $\top \leqslant \phi$ is everywhere true; thus the everywhere-true sentence $\top$ is maximally possible. Inner possibility, then, is maximal possibility—possibility equal to that of $\top$. In a centered system of spheres, all and only truths are maximally possible; as we noted before, the inner modalities are trivial in this case.

Now we can reintroduce our counterfactual operators by definition from comparative possibility (and outer possibility, defined in turn from comparative possibility). The following definitions give the correct truth conditions.

$$\phi \,\Box\!\!\rightarrow \psi =^{df} (\phi \,\&\, \psi) \prec (\phi \,\&\, {\sim}\psi),$$
$$\phi \,\Diamond\!\!\rightarrow \psi =^{df} {\sim}(\phi \,\Box\!\!\rightarrow {\sim}\psi) \quad \text{(or, directly, } (\phi \,\&\, \psi) \leqslant (\phi \,\&\, {\sim}\psi)\text{)},$$
$$\phi \,\boxdot\!\!\rightarrow \psi =^{df} \Diamond\phi \supset \phi \,\Box\!\!\rightarrow \psi,$$
$$\phi \,\diamondsuit\!\!\rightarrow \psi =^{df} {\sim}(\phi \,\boxdot\!\!\rightarrow {\sim}\psi) \quad \text{(or, } \Diamond\phi \,\&\, \phi \,\diamondsuit\!\!\rightarrow \psi\text{)}.$$

We can just as well go the other way. Taking $\Box\!\!\rightarrow$ again as primitive, and defining $\Diamond\!\!\rightarrow$ and $\Box\!\!\rightarrow$ from it as in Section 1.6 (or taking one of the latter as primitive), we can introduce comparative possibility, with the correct derived truth conditions, by either of the following definitions. If we want to introduce $\leqslant$ first,

$$\phi \leqslant \psi =^{\mathrm{df}} (\phi \vee \psi) \Diamond\!\!\rightarrow \phi;$$

if we prefer to introduce $\prec$ first,

$$\phi \prec \psi =^{\mathrm{df}} (\phi \vee \psi) \Box\!\!\rightarrow \sim\!\psi.$$

We now have six alternative primitives: all of $\Box\!\!\rightarrow$, $\Diamond\!\!\rightarrow$, $\Box\!\!\rightarrow$, $\Diamond\!\!\rightarrow$, $\leqslant$, and $\prec$ can be defined from any one of them.

So far, I have only been introducing new operators into the language to be interpreted. Truth conditions for sentences with this new vocabulary have been given by means of the same system of spheres already used to give truth conditions for counterfactuals. When we consider taking $\leqslant$ rather than $\Box\!\!\rightarrow$ as our primitive, however, it becomes convenient to give truth conditions not by means of the system of spheres but by means of relations of comparative possibility among propositions (sets of worlds). Let us write

$$P \leqslant_i Q$$

to mean that the proposition P is at least as possible, at the world i, as the proposition Q; let us write

$$P \prec_i Q \quad \text{(defined as: it is not the case that } Q \leqslant_i P)$$

to mean that P is more possible at i than Q; and let us write

$$P \approx_i Q \quad \text{(defined as: } P \leqslant_i Q \text{ and } Q \leqslant_i P)$$

to mean that P and Q are equally possible at i. The symbols $\leqslant$, $\prec$, and $\approx$ thus lead a double life, but there is no danger of confusion: unsubscripted, they are sentential connectives of the object language; subscripted, they are terms of the metalanguage denoting relations between propositions.

We may posit an assignment to each world i of a two-place relation $\leqslant_i$ among propositions, regarded as the ordering of propositions in respect of their comparative possibility from the standpoint of the world i. Call such an assignment a (*centered*) *comparative possibility system* if and only if, for each world i, the following five conditions hold.

(1) The relation $\leqslant_i$ is transitive; that is, whenever $P \leqslant_i Q$ and $Q \leqslant_i R$, then $P \leqslant_i R$.

(2) The relation $\leqslant_i$ is strongly connected; that is, for any propositions P and Q, either $P \leqslant_i Q$ or $Q \leqslant_i P$. (Equivalently: if $P \prec_i Q$ then $P \leqslant_i Q$.)

(3) All and only truths are maximally possible; that is, the world i itself belongs to a proposition P if and only if, for every proposition Q, $P \leqslant_i Q$. (Equivalently: if i belongs both to a proposition P and to a proposition Q, then $P \approx_i Q$; if i belongs to P but not to Q, then $P \prec_i Q$.)

(4) The union of a set of propositions is the greatest lower bound of the set. Let $\mathfrak{S}$ be a set of propositions and let $\bigcup \mathfrak{S}$ be the proposition containing all and only the worlds contained in members of the set $\mathfrak{S}$. Then $Q \leqslant_i P$ for every P in $\mathfrak{S}$ if and only if $Q \leqslant_i \bigcup \mathfrak{S}$. (If $\mathfrak{S}$ is finite, this means that $\bigcup \mathfrak{S}$ is as possible as the most possible member of $\mathfrak{S}$.)

(5) A singleton proposition that is more possible than every member of a set of propositions is also more possible than the union of the set. Let $\mathfrak{S}$ and $\bigcup \mathfrak{S}$ be as in (4) and let $\mathfrak{S}$ be nonempty; then if $\{j\} \prec_i P$ for every P in $\mathfrak{S}$, $\{j\} \prec_i \bigcup \mathfrak{S}$.

A comparative possibility system thus assigns to each world i a weak ordering of all propositions, with the propositions true at i itself—that is, containing i—together at the bottom. It follows from (4) that whenever Q is a subset of P, $P \leqslant_i Q$. From that it follows further that for any proposition P, $P \leqslant_i \Lambda$, where Λ is the empty set—in other words, the proposition true at no world, expressed by $\bot$ or any contradiction. As we shall see, the five conditions are required by the connection we intend between comparative possibility of propositions and comparative similarity of worlds.

It is easy to give the truth conditions for comparative possibility sentences according to a given comparative possibility system:

$\phi \leqslant \psi$ is true at i if and only if $[\![\phi]\!] \leqslant_i [\![\psi]\!]$.

(Recall that for any sentence ϕ, $[\![\phi]\!]$ is the set of worlds where ϕ is true, or in other words the proposition expressed by ϕ.) The derived truth conditions for $\prec$ and $\approx$ are similar:

$\phi \prec \psi$ is true at i if and only if $[\![\phi]\!] \prec_i [\![\psi]\!]$,

$\phi \approx \psi$ is true at i if and only if $[\![\phi]\!] \approx_i [\![\psi]\!]$.

The derived truth conditions for modal sentences and counterfactuals can simply be read off from the definitions of these in terms of the connectives of comparative possibility. For instance:

$\Diamond \phi$ is true at i if and only if $[\![\phi]\!] \prec_i \Lambda$.

$\phi \: \Box\!\!\rightarrow \psi$ is true at i if and only if, if $[\![\phi]\!] \prec_i \Lambda$,

then $[\![\phi]\!] \cap [\![\psi]\!] \prec_i [\![\phi]\!] - [\![\psi]\!]$.

The present formulation by means of comparative possibility is exactly equivalent to the original formulation by means of spheres, with no restrictive assumptions. We can put systems of spheres in one-to-one correspondence with comparative possibility systems, in such a way that the corresponding systems agree on the truth value at every world of all counterfactuals and comparative possibility sentences. Starting with a comparative possibility system that assigns to each world i the relation $\leqslant_i$, let \$ be the assignment to each world i of the set $\$_i$ of all and only those sets S of worlds such that, whenever a proposition P overlaps S and a proposition Q does not, then $P \prec_i Q$. Then it is easy to show (1) that \$ is a system of spheres, and (2) that a counterfactual or comparative possibility sentence is true at a world according to the defined system of spheres \$ if and only if it is true at that world according to the original comparative possibility system. Call \$ the system of spheres *derived from* the comparative possibility system. Starting rather with a system of spheres \$, let $P \leqslant_i Q$ if and only if every sphere S in $\$_i$ that overlaps Q also overlaps P. Then it is easy to show (1) that the assignment to each world i of the relation $\leqslant_i$ so defined is a comparative possibility system, and (2) that a counter-factual or comparative possibility sentence is true at a world according to this defined comparative possibility system if and only if it is true at that world according to the original system of spheres \$. Say that the comparative possibility system is *derived from* the system of spheres. Then we can show that for any comparative possibility system and system of spheres, the latter is derived from the former if and only if the former is derived from the latter.

Since comparative possibility systems and comparative similarity systems both can be put into one-to-one truth-preserving correspon-dence with systems of spheres, it follows that they can also be put into one-to-one truth-preserving correspondence with each other. This correspondence is quite simple: a comparative similarity ordering of worlds is, essentially, the corresponding comparative possibility ordering of singleton propositions, and accessible worlds are worlds that are more than minimally possible. More precisely: if the com-parative similarity system that assigns to each world i the similarity ordering $\leqslant_i$ of worlds and the sphere of accessibility S_i corresponds to the comparative possibility system that assigns to each world i the ordering $\leqslant_i$ of propositions, then (1) $j \leqslant_i k$ if and only if $\{j\} \leqslant_i \{k\}$, and (2) j belongs to S_i if and only if $\{j\} \prec_i \Lambda$.

2.6 Cotenability

In order to compare my theory with most previous theories of counter-factuals (this will be done in Sections 3.1–3.3) it will be helpful to reformulate my truth conditions in terms of relations of logical implication and of 'cotenability' between sentences.

Let us say that χ is *cotenable* with ϕ at a world i (according to a system of spheres \$) if and only if either (1) χ holds throughout $\bigcup\$_i$, or (2) χ holds throughout some ϕ-permitting sphere in $\$_i$. In other words: if and only if either (1) χ holds at all worlds accessible from i, or (2) some ϕ-world is closer to i than any $\sim\chi$-world. A necessary truth (in the sense of outer necessity) is cotenable with anything; a falsehood is cotenable with nothing; between these limits, cotenability is a matter of comparative possibility. If ϕ is entertainable at i, χ is cotenable with ϕ at i if and only if $[\![\phi]\!] \prec_i [\![\sim\chi]\!]$.

A counterfactual $\phi \;\square\!\!\rightarrow\; \psi$ is true at i (according to my truth conditions) if and only if the premise ϕ and some auxiliary premise χ, cotenable with ϕ at i, logically imply ψ. Proof: Suppose there is some such premise χ. Perhaps there is no ϕ-permitting sphere around i, in which case $\phi \;\square\!\!\rightarrow\; \psi$ is vacuously true at i. Otherwise there is a ϕ-permitting sphere throughout which χ holds; since ϕ and χ jointly imply ψ, $\phi \supset \psi$ also holds throughout this sphere; so $\phi \;\square\!\!\rightarrow\; \psi$ is true. Conversely, suppose $\phi \;\square\!\!\rightarrow\; \psi$ is true at i. Either there is no ϕ-permitting sphere around i, in which case $\sim\phi$ is a premise, cotenable with ϕ at i, which together with ϕ implies ψ; or else there is a ϕ-permitting sphere throughout which $\phi \supset \psi$ holds, in which case $\phi \supset \psi$ is a premise, cotenable with ϕ at i, which together with ϕ implies ψ. Q.E.D.

If each of $\chi_1, \ldots, \chi_n$ is cotenable with ϕ, then so is their conjunction; so we can also say that $\phi \;\square\!\!\rightarrow\; \psi$ is true at i if and only if ϕ together with finitely many premises $\chi_1, \ldots, \chi_n$, each cotenable with ϕ at i, logically imply ψ.

That would be the customary way to give truth conditions by means of cotenability, but there is an easier way: $\phi \;\square\!\!\rightarrow\; \psi$ is vacuously true at i if and only if $\sim\phi$ is cotenable with ϕ at i, non-vacuously true at i if and only if $\phi \supset \psi$ is cotenable with ϕ at i.

2.7 Selection Functions

The simplest and most direct formulation of the idea that a counter-factual is true if and only if the consequent holds at the closest antecedent-worlds depends, unfortunately, on the objectionable Limit Assumption. Suppose we are given a system of spheres \$ that satisfies the Assumption (for antecedents in our language). That means, we recall, that for every world i and antecedent ϕ (in our language) that is entertainable at i, there is a smallest ϕ-permitting sphere around i. The ϕ-worlds in that sphere are the closest ϕ-worlds to i. If an antecedent ϕ is not entertainable at i, then the set of closest ϕ-worlds to i is empty.

We may define a function f which selects, for any sentence ϕ and world i, the set $f(\phi, i)$ of closest ϕ-worlds to i. Let

$$f(\phi, i) = \begin{cases} \text{the set of } \phi\text{-worlds belonging to every } \phi\text{-permit-} \\ \quad \text{ting sphere in } \$_i, \text{ if there is any } \phi\text{-permitting} \\ \quad \text{sphere in } \$_i, \\ \text{the empty set otherwise.} \end{cases}$$

We call f a *selection function* (or a *set-selection function*, when we wish to compare these with Stalnaker's world-selection functions to be considered in Section 3.4). We will say that f is *derived from* the given system of spheres $\$$. We have already seen how to give the truth conditions for counterfactuals under the Limit Assumption. In terms of the selection function: the 'would' counterfactual $\phi \,\square\!\!\rightarrow\, \psi$ is true at a world i if and only if ψ is true at every world in $f(\phi, i)$. Similarly the 'might' counterfactual $\phi \,\diamondsuit\!\!\rightarrow\, \psi$ is true at i if and only if ψ is true at some world in $f(\phi, i)$.*

When f is derived from a system of spheres $\$$ that satisfies the Limit Assumption, then these truth conditions will agree with my original truth conditions given in terms of the system of spheres. But if $\$$ does not satisfy the Limit Assumption, then there will be disagreement. Sometimes $f(\phi, i)$, as I have defined it, will be empty because, although there are ϕ-permitting spheres around i, yet there is no ϕ-world that belongs to every ϕ-permitting sphere. Then $\phi \,\square\!\!\rightarrow\, \psi$ will incorrectly come out as vacuously true at i for any consequent ψ, contrary to my original truth conditions in terms of the system of spheres.

We may call a function f from sentences and worlds to sets of worlds a *(centered) (set-) selection function* if and only if, for all sentences ϕ and ψ and for each world i, the following four conditions hold.

(1) If ϕ is true at i, then $f(\phi, i)$ is the set $\{i\}$ having i as its only member.
(2) $f(\phi, i)$ is included in $[\![\phi]\!]$.
(3) If $[\![\phi]\!]$ is included in $[\![\psi]\!]$ and $f(\phi, i)$ is nonempty, then $f(\psi, i)$ also is nonempty.
(4) If $[\![\phi]\!]$ is included in $[\![\psi]\!]$ and $[\![\phi]\!]$ overlaps $f(\psi, i)$, then $f(\phi, i)$ is the intersection of $[\![\phi]\!]$ and $f(\psi, i)$.

* The use of set-selection functions in this way to give an analysis of counterfactuals has been suggested by John Vickers, and further studied by Peter Woodruff in 'Notes on Conditional Logic' (duplicated, May 1969, University of California at Irvine).

Such selection functions turn out to be all and only the selection functions derived from (centered) systems of spheres satisfying the Limit Assumption. If f is derived from some such system of spheres, then it is easily verified that conditions (1)–(4) are satisfied. Conversely, suppose f satisfies conditions (1)–(4). Let $ be the assignment to each world i of the set $_i$ of all and only those sets S of worlds such that, first, every world in S belongs to some $f(\phi, i)$; and, second, whenever $[\![\phi]\!]$ overlaps $S, f(\phi, i)$ is included in S. Then it is easily verified that $ is a system of spheres satisfying the Limit Assumption. It remains to show that f is derived from $. Proof: first consider the case that there is no ϕ-permitting sphere in $_i$. The union of the sets $f(\psi, i)$ for all sentences ψ—including ϕ—is obviously a sphere in $_i$; if this sphere is not ϕ-permitting although it includes $f(\phi, i)$, then $f(\phi, i)$ must be empty, so in this case $f(\phi, i)$ agrees with the selection function derived from $. Next consider the case that there is some ϕ-permitting sphere in $_i$. By (2) and the definition of $, $f(\phi, i)$ is included in the intersection of $[\![\phi]\!]$ and any ϕ-permitting sphere; so to show that in this case also $f(\phi, i)$ agrees with the selection function derived from $, it suffices to find a sphere S in $_i$ such that the intersection of $[\![\phi]\!]$ and S is exactly $f(\phi, i)$. Take S to be the union of the sets $f(\psi, i)$, for all sentences ψ such that $[\![\phi]\!]$ is included in $[\![\psi]\!]$. Whenever $[\![\chi]\!]$ overlaps S, $[\![\chi]\!]$ overlaps some $f(\psi, i)$ such that $[\![\phi]\!]$ is included in $[\![\psi]\!]$. $[\![\phi]\!]$ is included also in $[\![\chi \vee \psi]\!]$, so $f(\chi \vee \psi, i)$ is included in S. $[\![\chi]\!]$ overlaps $f(\chi \vee \psi, i)$; if not, it would follow by (2)–(4) that $f(\psi, i)$ and $f(\chi \vee \psi, i)$ are the same, contradicting the fact that $[\![\chi]\!]$ does overlap $f(\psi, i)$. It now follows by (4) that $f(\chi, i)$ is included in $f(\chi \vee \psi, i)$, and hence in S; so S is a sphere. The intersection of $[\![\phi]\!]$ and S is the union of all intersections of $[\![\phi]\!]$ with a set $f(\psi, i)$ such that $[\![\phi]\!]$ is included in $[\![\psi]\!]$. By (4), each such intersection is either the empty set or $f(\phi, i)$; and by (2), one such intersection—that of $[\![\phi]\!]$ with $f(\phi, i)$—is $f(\phi, i)$; so the intersection of $[\![\phi]\!]$ and the sphere S is exactly $f(\phi, i)$, as desired. Q.E.D.

The truth-preserving correspondence between systems of spheres satisfying the Limit Assumption and the selection functions derived from them is not, in general, one-to-one. Given a system of spheres $ satisfying the Limit Assumption, we may be able to add a new sphere S around some world i in such a way that S does not become the smallest ϕ-permitting sphere around i for any sentence ϕ. Let $' be the new system of spheres obtained by the addition of S; then $' also satisfies the Limit Assumption, and $ and $' yield the same derived selection function. This means that systems of spheres sometimes carry more information about comparative similarity than is needed to determine the truth values at all worlds of all counterfactuals. The same is true of comparative similarity and comparative possibility systems since these, as we have seen, stand in one-to-one truth-preserving correspondence with systems of spheres.

My conditions (2)–(4) imply that if $[\![\phi]\!]$ and $[\![\psi]\!]$ are the same—if ϕ and ψ are different sentences expressing the same proposition—then $f(\phi, i)$ and $f(\psi, i)$ are the same. Therefore instead of taking the first arguments of selection functions to be sentences, as I did, I could just as well have taken them to be propositions expressible by sentences.

Instead of taking a single function f of two arguments, I could just as well have taken an assignment to each world i of a function f_i of one argument—a sentence or a proposition, according to taste. Instead of $f(\phi, i)$ we then have $f_i(\phi)$ or $f_i([\![\phi]\!])$. If we take the arguments to be propositions rather than sentences, and if we let $\mathcal{U}_i$ be the set of expressible propositions A such that $f_i(A)$ is nonempty, then each $\langle\mathcal{U}_i, f_i\rangle$ is what Bengt Hansson has called a *choice structure*.*

We might also reformulate a selection function as a family, indexed by sentences or by propositions, of assignments to worlds of spheres of accessibility; or, more traditionally, as a family, indexed by sentences or by propositions, of accessibility relations between worlds. A world j is *accessible$_\phi$* (or *accessible$_{[\phi]}$* if we prefer) from a world i if and only if j is in $f(\phi, i)$. For any fixed antecedent ϕ, we can regard $\phi\,\Box\!\!\rightarrow$ and $\phi\Diamond\!\!\rightarrow$ as if they were a pair of one-place modal operators, interpreted as usual by means of accessibility$_\phi$. $\phi\,\Box\!\!\rightarrow\psi$ is true at i if and only if ψ holds at every world accessible$_\phi$ from i; $\phi\Diamond\!\!\rightarrow\psi$ is true at i if and only if ψ holds at some world accessible$_\phi$ from i. My analysis of variably strict conditionals, as restricted by the Limit Assumption, can thus be subsumed as a special case under a general theory of sententially or propositionally indexed modalities.‡ My analysis in its full generality, on the other hand, cannot be thus subsumed—the Limit Assumption is essential.

* 'Choice Structures and Preference Relations', *Synthese* 18 (1968): 443–458. We saw that every selection function is derived from a system of spheres; this could have been obtained as a corollary of Hansson's theorem that whenever $\langle\mathcal{U}, f\rangle$ is a choice structure such that $\mathcal{U}$ is closed under finite unions, there is a weak ordering R *underlying* $\langle\mathcal{U}, f\rangle$—that is, for each A in $\mathcal{U}$, $f(A)$ is the set of members of A that bear R to every member of A. In this case, the ordering underlying $\langle\mathcal{U}_i, f_i\rangle$ is the comparative similarity ordering $\leq_i$.

‡ A general account of propositionally indexed modalities is to be found in Brian F. Chellas, 'Basic Conditional Logic', *Journal of Philosophical Logic* 4 (1975): 133–153.

2.8 The Selection Operator

If we tolerate the Limit Assumption and use a selection function to interpret the counterfactual, we can express the selection function by an operator in the object language. We can define the counterfactual connectives from that operator, plus other logical apparatus.

Introduce a one-place sentential operator f, called the *selection operator*. We may read it as '*Things are the way they would be if it were the case that* _____'. The sentence $f\phi$ is to be true at all and only the selected, closest ϕ-worlds given by our selection function f. The counterfactual may (provisionally) be defined thus:

$$\phi \mathbin{\Box\!\!\rightarrow} \psi = ^{\mathrm{df}} \Box(f\phi \supset \psi).$$

This definition makes the counterfactual into a strict conditional after all; however the antecedent ϕ of the counterfactual is not the same as the antecedent $f\phi$ of the strict conditional. According to this definition the counterfactual is true if and only if ψ holds at all $f\phi$-worlds—that is, at all of the selected, closest ϕ-worlds.

That is more or less what we want, but the account so far is incomplete. The $f\phi$-worlds are the 'selected, closest ϕ-worlds'. Selected from, and closest to, what world? A selection function has *two* arguments. I said that $f\phi$ was to be true at all and only the worlds in $f(\phi, i)$—but without specifying which world is i.

Lennart Åqvist, in first proposing the use of a selection operator, specified that the selection was to be done always from the standpoint of our actual world.* That is, $f\phi$ was to be true at all and only the closest ϕ-worlds to ours—all and only the worlds in $f(\phi, i)$ where i is our actual world. Since Åqvist selects always from the standpoint of a single world, ours, his selection functions have no need of a second argument.

That will do so long as we care only to say how the *actual* truth values of counterfactuals depend on the truth values at various worlds of their antecedents and consequents. But we have been more ambitious hitherto. Counterfactuals are, for the most part, contingent. We have been trying to give their truth conditions in general: to say how the truth value of a counterfactual at *any* world depends on the truth values at various worlds of its antecedent and consequent. Even if we are ultimately interested only in the actual truth values of sentences, still we must consider the truth values of counterfactuals at other worlds than ours to obtain the actual truth values of sentences in

* 'Modal Logic with Subjunctive Conditionals and Dispositional Predicates', *Journal of Philosophical Logic* 2 (1973): 1–76.

which counterfactuals are embedded inside other counterfactuals. For instance, Åqvist's method cannot be made to account for the truth of the sentence

> (*I look in my pocket* $\Box\!\!\rightarrow$ *I find a penny*) & (*There is no penny in my pocket* $\Box\!\!\rightarrow$ $\sim$(*I look in my pocket* $\Box\!\!\rightarrow$ *I find a penny*)).

In order to make proper use of the selection operator, we must recognize that there are sentences that cannot naturally be assessed simply for truth or falsehood at a world, but rather call for a three-place truth relation: truth *of* a sentence ϕ *at* a world i *with reference to* a world j. For instance, '*Things are better*' is true at i with reference to j if and only if things are better at i than at j, but there is no natural way to assess '*Things are better*' for truth at a world without some reference world to serve as a standard of comparison. Similarly, we cannot give a satisfactory general account of the truth conditions for the selection operator by means simply of the two-place truth-at relation. We should rather use the three-place truth relation and say that $f\phi$ is true at a world i with reference to a world j if and only if i belongs to $f(\phi, j)$—that is, if and only if i is a closest ϕ-world to j.

What shall we do when we need to mix these special sentences that require the three-place truth relation with ordinary sentences that can be treated adequately by means of the two-place truth relation? Although it is unsatisfactory to treat special sentences as though they were ordinary, it is harmless to treat ordinary sentences as though they were special. Let us call an ordinary sentence true at i with reference to any j if and only if it is true at i. Given this stipulation, we can explain the difference between ordinary and special sentences by saying that an ordinary sentence is true at a world with reference to all worlds or none, whereas a special sentence is sometimes true at a world with reference to some worlds but not others.

Just as the truth conditions for ordinary sentences are formulated in terms of the two-place truth relation, so parallel truth conditions for special sentences—or for ordinary sentences treated as special in order to compound them with special sentences—may be given in terms of the three-place truth relation. The reference world tags along throughout. For instance, a material conditional is true at i with reference to j if and only if either the consequent is true at i with reference to j or the antecedent is false at i with reference to j. A sentence $\Box\phi$ is true at i with reference to j if and only if ϕ is true with reference to j at every world accessible from i; the appropriate accessibility assignment for outer modality is given in terms of the selection function by specifying that a world is accessible from i if and only if it belongs to some $f(\chi, i)$ or other.

Suppose ϕ and ψ are ordinary sentences. Then the strict conditional $\Box(f\phi \supset \psi)$ that we took provisionally to define $\phi \,\Box\!\!\rightarrow\, \psi$ is in many cases a special sentence. It is true at a world i with reference to a world j if and only if $f\phi \supset \psi$ is true with reference to j at every world accessible from i; that is, if and only if ψ is true with reference to j at every world accessible from i where $f\phi$ is true with reference to j; that is, if and only if ψ is true at every world in $f(\phi, j)$ that is accessible from i. Taking j as i, the accessibility restriction becomes redundant. Thus $\Box(f\phi \supset \psi)$ is true at i with reference to i itself if and only if ψ is true at every world in $f(\phi, i)$; that is, if and only if $\phi \,\Box\!\!\rightarrow\, \psi$ is true at i.

That is good enough to explain our success with actual truth values, but it is not quite right. We want to define $\phi \,\Box\!\!\rightarrow\, \psi$ by an ordinary sentence that will be true at a world i if and only if our provisional definiens $\Box(f\phi \supset \psi)$ is true at i with reference to i. We must provide a new operator $\dagger$ with truth conditions as follows: $\dagger\chi$ is an ordinary sentence true at i if and only if χ is true at i with reference to i. (When χ is ordinary, $\dagger\chi$ has the same truth conditions as χ itself.) Prefixing the $\dagger$-operator to our provisional definens, we obtain the correct definition.* With it we have a parallel definition for the 'might' counterfactual.

$$\phi \,\Box\!\!\rightarrow\, \psi =^{\mathrm{df}} \dagger\Box(f\phi \supset \psi),$$
$$\phi \,\Diamond\!\!\rightarrow\, \psi =^{\mathrm{df}} \dagger\Diamond(f\phi \,\&\, \psi).$$

We could go instead in the other direction and define the selection operator from the counterfactual, using propositional quantification and another special operator for the three-place truth relation. Let $\downarrow\chi$ be true at i with reference to j if and only if χ is true at j with reference to j; a sentence $\downarrow\chi$ will in most cases be special. Now we may define f thus:

$$f\phi =^{\mathrm{df}} \forall\xi(\downarrow(\phi \,\Box\!\!\rightarrow\, \xi) \supset \xi).$$

(Here ξ is to be any propositional variable that does not occur in ϕ.) Intuitively, the definiens says that whatever *would* hold, if ϕ did, *does* hold.‡

---

* Correct on the assumption that the antecedent and consequent are ordinary. But we might want to drop that assumption. For instance, if we want to handle countercomparatives like '*If my yacht were longer, things would be better*' without quantifying in, we will want to take the antecedent and consequent as special sentences. But if we want to use the object-language selection operator in the presence of special antecedents and consequents, then we must consider extra-special sentences that require a four-place truth relation—and so on up.

‡ The $\downarrow$-operator and the $\dagger$-operator, or rather their temporal analogs, were first introduced by Hans Kamp and Frank Vlach, respectively. They are needed for symbolizing such sentences as '*Jones is going to remember (simultaneously) everyone now living*' and '*Jones was once going to remember (simultaneously)*

everyone then living' in a language without overt quantification over times. 'Now' or 'then' is ↓, 'once' is †. See Kamp, 'Formal Properties of "Now"', *Theoria* 37 (1971): 227–273; and Vlach, '"Now" and "Then": a Formal Study in the Logic of Tense and Anaphora' (Ph.D. dissertation, 1973, University of California at Los Angeles). Åqvist, in an appendix to 'Modal Logic with Subjunctive Conditionals and Dispositional Predicates' (written subsequently to the body of the work) has adopted my suggestion to use the †-operator along with a selection operator that yields special rather than ordinary sentences.

3. Comparisons

3.1 The Metalinguistic Theory: Implicit Premises

It is not to be expected that an adequate new theory of counterfactuals will be entirely unlike previous theories. I hope I have improved on them, but it is incumbent on me to show that, to the considerable extent that other theories succeed, my new theory has enough in common with them to share in their success and to explain it.

Most previous theories of counterfactuals are *metalinguistic*: a counter-factual is true, or assertable, if and only if its antecedent, together with suitable further premises, implies its consequent.* Thus a counter-factual $\phi \mathbin{\square\!\!\rightarrow} \psi$ is somehow backed by a valid argument:

$$\frac{\phi, \chi_1, \ldots, \chi_n}{\therefore \psi}.$$

Either the counterfactual is a sentence meaning that some such argument exists, or—as in Mackie's version—it is itself an elliptical pre-sentation of such an argument.‡ On the former version, the counter-factual can be evaluated as true or false according as there do or do not exist suitable premises $\chi_1, \ldots, \chi_n$ which, together with ϕ, imply ψ. On the latter version, it cannot be evaluated as true or false, but only—after

---

* Such theories of counterfactuals are given, for instance, in Roderick Chisholm, 'The Contrary-to-fact Conditional', *Mind* 55 (1946): 289–307; Nelson Goodman, 'The Problem of Counterfactual Conditionals', *Journal of Philosophy* 44 (1947): 113–128; John L. Mackie, 'Counterfactuals and Causal Laws', in R. J. Butler, *Analytical Philosophy* (Blackwell: Oxford, 1962): 66–80; and Nicholas Rescher, *Hypothetical Reasoning* (North-Holland: Amsterdam, 1964).

‡ There is an analogous disagreement about sentences of the form

$$\psi \text{ because } \phi.$$

Morton White, in *Foundations of Historical Knowledge* (Harper & Row: New York, 1965): 56–84, regards the sentence as meaning that there exists some correct explanatory argument from ϕ and other premises to ψ; whereas Carl Hempel, in *Aspects of Scientific Explanation* (The Free Press: New York, 1965): 415, regards it as being itself an elliptical presentation of such an argument.

the omitted premises $\chi_1, \ldots, \chi_n$ have been restored—as valid or invalid. The latter version has the drawback common to all theories that make do with conditions for assertability rather than truth conditions: it gives no account of the meaning of compounds with embedded conditionals that are not themselves asserted, such as a material conditional with a counterfactual as its antecedent.

Note that metalinguistic theorists are so-called because they hold that linguistic entities—arguments and their premises—enter prominently into the truth conditions or assertability conditions of counterfactuals. That is not to say that counterfactuals are *about* linguistic entities. A metalinguistic theorist may well insist that a counterfactual is about whatever its antecedent and consequent are about. Indeed, a metalinguistic theorist like Mackie, who regards a counterfactual as an elliptical argument with its antecedent as one premise and its consequent as conclusion, could scarcely say anything else.

On any metalinguistic theory, the principal problem is to specify which further premises $\chi_1, \ldots, \chi_n$ are suitable to be used with a given antecedent and which are not. The metalinguistic theorist uses his further premises in much the same way as I have used the system of spheres representing comparative similarity of worlds: to rule out of consideration many of the various ways the antecedent could hold, especially the more bizarre ways. $\phi \;\square\!\!\rightarrow\; \psi$ is true or assertable on a metalinguistic theory if and only if ψ holds at all ϕ-worlds of a certain sort: ϕ-worlds at which some further premises, suitable for use with the antecedent ϕ, hold.

Whence come the further premises? A metalinguistic theorist might hold that some of them, at least, are implicitly understood. The antecedent that is explicitly spoken is not the whole antecedent that the parties to a conversation have in mind, but only an elliptical sketch of it. The rest is understood. Each party to a conversation has in mind, more or less consciously, a way to spell out the antecedent in full; and each supposes that the others have in mind the same expansion of the antecedent, each supposes that each supposes this, and so on. Or the rest of the antecedent fails to be understood, on occasion; but then more and more of it can be spelled out until the rest is understood. Thus we account for such pairs of counterfactuals as Quine's

> *If Caesar had been in command [in Korea] he would have used the atom bomb.*

versus

> *If Caesar had been in command he would have used catapults.*

If in doubt, we ask the propounder of the counterfactual supposition that Caesar was in command whether he has in mind a modernized or an unmodernized Caesar. We thus ask him to make explicit part of his antecedent that was left implicit in his antecedent-sketch '*If Caesar had been in command . . .*'.

I would not mind agreeing that sometimes the real, conversationally understood antecedent is an expansion of the explicit part of the antecedent. I would then say that my theory applies to counterfactuals in a conversational context (as opposed to counterfactuals considered in isolation) only after any part of the antecedent that had been left implicit has been restored.

I am not forced to agree to this, however. I could get the same effect another way. In dealing with Quine's opposed counterfactuals about Caesar, context must of course be consulted somehow. But instead of using context to restore the real antecedent from the explicit part of the antecedent, I could say that the explicit antecedent *is* the real antecedent and call on context rather to resolve part of the vagueness of comparative similarity in a way favorable to the truth of one counterfactual or the other. In one context, we may attach great importance to similarities and differences in respect of Caesar's character and in respect of regularities concerning the knowledge of weapons common to commanders in Korea. In another context we may attach less importance to these similarities and differences, and more importance to similarities and differences in respect of Caesar's own knowledge of weapons. The first context resolves the vagueness of comparative similarity in such a way that some worlds with a modernized Caesar in command come out closer to our world than any with an unmodernized Caesar. It thereby makes the first counterfactual true. The second context resolves the vagueness in the opposite direction, making the second counterfactual true. Other contexts might resolve the vagueness in other ways. A third context, for instance, might produce a tie between the closest worlds with modernized Caesars and the closest worlds with unmodernized Caesars. That context makes both counterfactuals false.

It matters little how we divide up the influence of context between (1) resolution of the vagueness of comparative similarity, and (2) expansion of the explicit antecedent to the real, conversationally understood antecedent. My inclination, however, is to explain the influence of context entirely as the resolution influence. Better one sort of influence of context than two different sorts; we are stuck with the resolution influence whether or not we also admit the expansion influence; but given the resolution influence we do not need to admit the expansion influence as well.

3.2 The Metalinguistic Theory: Factual Premises

A metalinguistic theorist cannot be content only with the sort of further premises we have considered so far: those that spell out parts of the understood antecedent that originally were left implicit. Counterfactuals are usually contingent. The truth value of a counterfactual may depend on matters of empirical fact, unknown to the parties in a conversation. Even when they understand perfectly what antecedent it is that they are concerned with, and how any implicit parts of it are to be spelled out, they may yet be in doubt or disagreement about the truth of the counterfactual. Consider this counterfactual:

If I had looked in my wallet, I would have found a penny.

I may say this, and someone else may doubt it. There may be some work to do on reaching agreement about the antecedent I have in mind: I may have to explain that I meant that if I had looked *just now, carefully,* in the wallet *in my pocket* I would have found a penny. But this legitimate expansion of the antecedent does not settle the question whether the counterfactual is true. That still depends on whether there was a penny there to be found. Of course, if I expanded the antecedent to '*If I had looked and there had been a penny . . .*' or to '*If I had looked and there had been no penny . . .*' I would thereby obtain an uncontroversial (but still contingent) counterfactual. But neither expansion merely makes explicit what was already present implicitly in the original counterfactual supposition, as understood by the parties to the conversation.

The premise that there was a penny may or may not be a 'suitable further premise' in this case. But whether it is cannot depend on whether it was implicitly understood; for it definitely was not. Rather, it depends principally on whether there was a penny in my wallet. It is another kind of premise, eligible to enter the argument that backs the counterfactual (if it is eligible) not because it is implicitly understood but because it is true. Call it a *factual premise.*

Not any old truth will do as a factual premise; the negation of a false antecedent is a truth, but ordinarily not eligible to enter into the argument that backs a counterfactual with that antecedent. I shall use Goodman's term 'cotenability' for the present, simply to name whatever relation it is that must obtain between a truth and an antecedent to make that truth eligible to enter into a backing argument with that antecedent.

Let us recapitulate the metalinguistic theory. A counterfactual $\phi \;\square\!\!\rightarrow\; \psi$ is *backed*, on a given occasion, by an argument

$$\frac{\phi, \chi_1, \ldots, \chi_n}{\therefore \; \psi}$$

if and only if the argument is valid, and each of the premises $\chi_1, \ldots, \chi_n$ added to ϕ is either (1) understood, on that occasion, as an implicit part of the counterfactual supposition being made, or (2) true, and cotenable with the counterfactual supposition (ϕ plus implicit premises, if any) being made on that occasion. A counterfactual is true on an occasion if and only if there exists an argument backing it; or it is assertable if and only if a backing argument is thought to exist; or it is an elliptical presentation of some particular backing argument.

On a metalinguistic theory of truth conditions, most counterfactuals express contingent propositions about the world. They can do so because it is a contingent matter of fact what truths cotenable with the antecedent there are. On my theory also, most counterfactuals express contingent propositions about the world. It may seem that they are about other worlds than ours; so they are, but they are about our actual world as well. The truth of a counterfactual at our world depends on the character of the closest antecedent-worlds to ours. Which worlds those are depends on which world is ours. It is a fact about a town that it is situated near to one city rather than another, and in the same way it is a fact about our world that its character is such as to make some antecedent-worlds be similar to it, and others not. It is just such contingent facts about our world that make some counterfactuals true at it, and others false. It is the fact that there was a penny in my wallet that makes some of the worlds where I looked and found a penny be closer to ours than any of the worlds where I looked and found no penny. If this were one of the worlds with no penny, it would be the other way around. Such worlds are situated in other neighborhoods than ours.

What is cotenability? That is the problem of counterfactuals for a metalinguistic theorist, and counterfactuals remain mysterious to him just to the extent that cotenability remains mysterious. I suggested an answer to his problem in Section 2.6. Say that χ is cotenable with an entertainable antecedent ϕ at a world i if and only if χ holds throughout some ϕ-permitting sphere around i; say also that χ is cotenable with ϕ at i if χ holds throughout every sphere around i, whether or not ϕ is entertainable. We saw in Section 2.6 that the metalinguistic theory of truth conditions obtained by using this definition of cotenability is exactly equivalent to my theory.

Other definitions of cotenability also would yield metalinguistic theories equivalent to my theory. We might simply say that χ is cotenable with ϕ at i if and only if χ is true at i and $\phi \,\square\!\!\rightarrow \chi$ is true (according to my theory) at i. But I think that my definition of cotenability, unlike this one, captures the intentions of metalinguistic theorists. On my definition, a cotenable premise is not only true, but also necessary to some extent. The strictness of its necessity is the least strictness that will not rule the antecedent out as impossible, provided that the antecedent is entertainable so that some such strictness exists. In terms of comparative possibility: the denial of a cotenable premise is less possible than the counterfactual antecedent itself, unless the antecedent is already minimally possible.*

Of course, anyone who holds a metalinguistic theory is likely to do so partly because he does not like such things as possible worlds and comparative similarity relations among them. Then my definition of cotenability will be almost useless to him because of its suspect commitments. But perhaps not quite useless. We know better what it is to be inspired by a muse for knowing the myth of the muses, even though we reject the mythical analysis that says that someone is inspired by a muse if and only if there exists a muse who inspires him. Likewise a metalinguistic theorist who rejects the foundations of my definition of cotenability may yet find that the definition offers some guidance about which premises are cotenable with which antecedents.

A metalinguistic theorist who is content to give conditions of assertability for counterfactuals, rather than a metalinguistic theory of truth conditions, need not face the problem of saying when a premise actually *is* cotenable with an antecedent. His problem is rather: when is a premise *thought to be* cotenable with an antecedent? Some metalinguistic theorists propose to solve this problem by means of thought experiments.‡ Imagine that you somehow came to know the antecedent for certain and reorganized your system of beliefs under the impact of this new knowledge; the beliefs you would retain are the ones you regard as cotenable with the antecedent. The problem of cotenability then reduces, as Mackie observes, to the familiar problem of induction:

* The doctrine of modal categories in Rescher, *Hypothetical Reasoning*, is an approach to cotenability by way of something like comparative possibility. But since Rescher is principally concerned with conditions of assertability or acceptability for counterfactuals, rather than with truth conditions, I shall not pursue the comparison further.

‡ For instance Chisholm, 'The Contrary-to-fact Conditional'; Mackie, 'Counterfactuals and Causal Laws'; and Rescher, *Hypothetical Reasoning*. F. P. Ramsey, in *Foundations* ·(Routledge & Kegan Paul: London, 1978): 143, mentions such thought experiments, but he seems to have in mind assertability conditions for indicative conditionals rather than counterfactuals.

how should one's system of beliefs change under the impact of an exogenous piece of new knowledge.

But the method of thought experiments is wrong. Return to Ernest Adams's example about Oswald and Kennedy, used for another purpose in Section 1.1. I am a moderate Warrenite. I think it quite probable that Oswald killed Kennedy, that he was working alone, and that there was no second killer waiting. But I think it slightly probable that Oswald was innocent, and that someone else killed Kennedy. I think it overwhelmingly probable that one or other of these two hypotheses is true; and negligibly probable, for instance, that Kennedy was not killed at all. Then what happens when I make the thought experiment of adding '*Oswald did not kill Kennedy*' to my stock of beliefs as if it were an item of new knowledge? Clearly I continue to believe that Kennedy was killed (perhaps not with quite as much certainty as before, but still very strongly indeed), and give up the belief that there was no killer but Oswald. That is: when my most probable hypothesis is ruled out, most of the probability goes to what was my next-most-probable hypothesis. According to the method of thought experiments, this means that '*Kennedy was killed*' is cotenable for me with the supposition that Oswald did not kill him, and '*No one but Oswald killed Kennedy*' is not. I should therefore assert such counterfactuals as

> If Oswald had not killed Kennedy, someone else would have.

rather than

> If Oswald had not killed him, Kennedy would not have been killed.

But that is just backward from the truth. Actually I assert the second and deny the first. Further, I regard '*No one but Oswald killed Kennedy*' as cotenable with the supposition that Oswald did not kill him, and I regard '*Kennedy was killed*' as not cotenable with that supposition. The reason is plain. According to my actual system of beliefs—beliefs that have not really been revised under the impact of new knowledge—probably I inhabit one of the worlds where Oswald did kill Kennedy, working alone, with no other killer waiting. These worlds (except for some with negligible probability according to my beliefs) are worlds where the second counterfactual is true and the first is false. That is because they are worlds to which worlds with no killing are closer than worlds with a different killer. Therefore the second counterfactual is probably true, according to my beliefs, and the first is probably false. Therefore I assert the second and deny the first. To summarize: there is no reason at all why my most probable antecedent-worlds should be the same as the antecedent-worlds closest to my most probable worlds. The method of thought experiments gives me the character of the former worlds, but the assertability of counterfactuals depends on the character of the latter worlds.*

Perhaps I have considered the wrong thought experiment; the right one is to add the antecedent to your system of beliefs not as if it were an item of new knowledge, but simply *as a counterfactual supposition*. That is the right thing to do, I agree, but it is unhelpful to say so. For what is the thought experiment of adding ϕ to your beliefs as a counterfactual supposition? I suppose it is nothing else than the exercise of deciding which counterfactuals with the antecedent ϕ you believe.

3.3 The Metalinguistic Theory: Laws of Nature

Metalinguistic theorists commonly give a special place among cotenable factual premises to laws of nature. A law is thought to be cotenable with any antecedent, except an antecedent that is logically inconsistent with that law, or perhaps with some other law. On this view, if the antecedent of a counterfactual, together with some laws, implies the consequent, and if the antecedent is logically consistent with all laws, then the counterfactual is true. (Or: if that is thought to be the case, then the counterfactual is assertable.) On this view also, there can be no true counterfactual saying that if so-and-so particular state of affairs were to hold, then such-and-such law would be violated.

I could, if I wished, incorporate this special status of laws into my theory by imposing the following constraint on systems of spheres: the set of all and only those worlds that do not violate the laws prevailing at

---

* Perhaps the method of thought experiments gives the proper conditions of assertability not for counterfactuals but for *indicative* conditionals. Let P be a subjective probability function representing your system of beliefs, and let P_ϕ likewise represent the revised belief system that would result under the new item of knowledge ϕ. According to standard Bayesian confirmation theory, $P_\phi(\psi) = P(\psi/\phi) =^{\text{df}} P(\psi \,\&\, \phi)\,/\,P(\phi)$, provided that the denominator $P(\phi)$ is nonzero. Ernest Adams has observed that $P(\psi/\phi)$ seems also to measure the assertability of the indicative conditional '*If ϕ, then ψ*' according to the belief system P; see his 'The Logic of Conditionals', *Inquiry* 8 (1965): 166–197. For instance, I do assert that if Oswald did not kill Kennedy, then someone else did; I do so because P (*Someone else did / Oswald did not*) is high. And I deny that if Oswald did not kill Kennedy, then Kennedy was not killed; that is because P(*Kennedy was not killed / Oswald did not kill him*) is low. (The indicatives are thus opposite in assertability to the corresponding counterfactuals.) Adams's observation about the *assertability* conditions for indicative conditionals is compatible with various alternative views about their *truth* conditions, or lack thereof. I favor the view that the indicative conditional '*If ϕ, then ψ*' has the truth conditions of the material conditional $\phi \supset \psi$; its assertability is measured by $P(\psi / \phi)$ rather than $P(\phi \supset \psi)$ because if the latter is high and the former is low, then $P(\sim\phi)$ is almost as high as $P(\phi \supset \psi)$ and it is pointless and misleading to assert $\phi \supset \psi$ rather than $\sim\phi$.

a world i is one of the spheres around i. Equivalently, in terms of comparative similarity: whenever the laws prevailing at i are violated at a world k but not at a world j, j is closer than k to i. This would mean that any violation of the laws of i, however slight, would outweigh any amount of difference from i in respect of particular states of affairs.

I have not chosen to impose any such constraint. I doubt that laws of nature have as much of a special status as has been thought. Such special status as they do have, they need not have by fiat. I think I can explain, within the theory already given, why laws tend to be cotenable, unless inconsistent, with counterfactual suppositions.

I adopt as a working hypothesis a theory of lawhood held by F. P. Ramsey in 1928: that laws are 'consequences of those propositions which we should take as axioms if we knew everything and organized it as simply as possible in a deductive system'.* We need not state Ramsey's theory as a counterfactual about omniscience. Whatever we may or may not ever come to know, there exist (as abstract objects) innumerable true deductive systems: deductively closed, axiomatizable sets of true sentences. Of these true deductive systems, some can be axiomatized more *simply* than others. Also, some of them have more *strength*, or *information content*, than others. The virtues of simplicity and strength tend to conflict. Simplicity without strength can be had from pure logic, strength without simplicity from (the deductive closure of) an almanac. Some deductive systems, of course, are neither simple nor strong. What we value in a deductive system is a properly balanced combination of simplicity and strength—as much of both as truth and our way of balancing will permit. We can restate Ramsey's 1928 theory of lawhood as follows: a contingent generalization is a *law of nature* if and only if it appears as a theorem (or axiom) in each of the true deductive systems that achieves a best combination of simplicity and strength.‡ A generalization is a law at a world i, likewise, if and only if it appears as a theorem in each of the best deductive systems true at i.

In science we have standards—vague ones, to be sure—for assessing

---

* See 'Universals of Law and Fact', in Ramsey, *Foundations*. (R. B. Braithwaite kindly permitted me to see this note in manuscript.) Ramsey regarded it as superseded by 'General Propositions and Causality', also in *Foundations*. He there alludes to his previous theory of 1928 in the words I have quoted (page 138); rejects it on the ground that we never will know everything; and goes on to develop a different theory. See also Braithwaite's mention of the 1928 note in his editorial introduction, *The Foundations of Mathematics*: xiii.

‡ I doubt that our standards of simplicity would permit an infinite ascent of better and better systems; but if they do, we should say that a law must appear as a theorem in all sufficiently good true systems.

the combinations of strength and simplicity offered by deductive systems. We trade off these virtues against each other and against probability of truth on the available evidence. If we knew everything, probability of truth would no longer be a consideration. The false systems would drop out, leaving the true ones to compete in simplicity-cum-strength. (Imagine that God has decided to provide mankind with a *Concise Encyclopedia of Unified Science,* chosen according to His standards of truthfulness and our standards of simplicity and strength.) Our standards of simplicity and strength, and of the proper balance between them, apply—though we who are not omniscient have no occasion so to apply them—to the set of all true deductive systems. Thus it makes sense to speak of the best true systems, and of the theorems common to all the best true systems.

I adopt Ramsey's 1928 theory of lawhood, glossed as above, because of its success in explaining some facts about laws of nature. (1) It explains why lawhood is not just a matter of the generality, syntactically or semantically defined, of a single sentence. It may happen that two true sentences are alike general, but one is a law of nature and the other is not. That can happen because the first does, and the second does not, fit together with other truths to make a best system. (2) It explains why lawhood is a contingent property. A generalization may be true as a law at one world, and true but not as a law at another, because the first world but not the second provides other truths with which it makes a best system. (3) It therefore explains how we can know by exhausting the instances that a generalization—say, Bode's 'Law'—is true, but not yet know if it is a law. (4) It explains why *being* a law is not the same as being regarded as a law—being projected, and so forth—and not the same as being regarded as a law and also being true. It allows there to be laws of which we have no inkling. (5) It explains why we have reason to take the theorems of well-established scientific theories provisionally as laws. Our scientific theorizing is an attempt to approximate, as best we can, the true deductive systems with the best combination of simplicity and strength. (6) It explains why lawhood has seemed a rather vague and difficult concept: our standards of simplicity and strength, and of the proper balance between them, are only roughly fixed. That may or may not matter. We may hope, or take as an item of faith, that our world is one where certain true deductive systems come out as best, and certain generalizations come out as laws, by *any* remotely reasonable standards—but we might be unlucky.

On the working hypothesis that the laws of a world are the generalizations that fit into the best deductive systems true there, we can also say that the laws are generalizations which (given suitable companions) are highly informative about that world in a simple way. Such generalizations are important to us. It makes a big difference to the character of a world which generalizations enjoy the status of lawhood there. Therefore similarity and difference of worlds in respect of their laws is an important respect of similarity and difference, contributing weightily to overall similarity and difference. Since a difference in laws would be a big difference between worlds, we can expect that worlds with the same laws as a world *i* will tend to be closer to *i* than worlds at which the laws of *i* hold only as accidental generalizations, or are violated, or—worse still—are replaced by contrary laws. In other words, the laws of *i* will hold throughout many of the spheres around *i*, and thus will tend to be cotenable with counterfactual suppositions. That is so simply because laws are especially important to us, compared with particular facts or true generalizations that are not laws.

Though similarities or differences in laws have some tendency to outweigh differences or similarities in particular facts, I do not think they invariably do so. Suppose that the laws prevailing at a world *i* are deterministic, as we used to think the laws of our own world were. Suppose a certain roulette wheel in this deterministic world *i* stops on black at a time *t*, and consider the counterfactual antecedent that it stopped on red. What sort of antecedent-worlds are closest to *i*? On the one hand, we have antecedent-worlds where the deterministic laws of *i* hold without exception, but where the wheel is determined to stop on red by particular facts different from those of *i*. Since the laws are deterministic, the particular facts must be different at all times before *t*, no matter how far back. (Nor can we assume that the differences of particular fact diminish as we go back in time. Assume for the sake of argument that *i* and its laws are such that any antecedent-world where the laws hold without exception differs more and more from *i* as we go back.) On the other hand, we have antecedent-worlds that are exactly like *i* until *t* or shortly before; where the laws of *i* hold *almost* without exception; but where a small, localized, inconspicuous miracle at *t* or just before permits the wheel to stop on red in violation of the laws. Laws are very important, but great masses of particular fact count for something too; and a localized violation is not the most serious sort of difference of law. The violated deterministic law has presumably not been replaced by a contrary law. Indeed, a version of the violated law, complicated and weakened by a clause to permit the one exception, may still be simple and strong enough to survive as a law. Therefore some of the antecedent-worlds where the law is violated may be closer to *i* than any of the ones where the particular facts are different at all times before *t*. At least, this seems plausible enough to deter me from decreeing the opposite. I therefore proceed on the assumption that the preeminence of laws of nature among cotenable factual premises is a matter only of degree.

My example of the deterministic roulette wheel raises a problem for me: what about differences of particular fact at times *after t*? Among the antecedent worlds I prefer—those where the wheel stops on red by a minor miracle and the particular facts are just as they are at *i* until *t* or shortly before—there are two sorts. There are some where the deterministic laws of *i* are unviolated after *t* and the particular facts after *t* diverge more and more from those of *i*. (I now assume that the deterministic laws are deterministic both forward and backward, so that they do not permit a reconvergence.) There are others where a second minor miracle occurs just after *t*, erasing all traces of the first miracle, so that we have two violations of law instead of one but the particular facts from that time on are just as they are at *i*. If I have decided that a small miracle *before t* makes less of a difference from *i* than a big difference of particular fact at all times *before t*, then why do I not also think that a small miracle *after t* makes less of a difference from *i* than a big difference of particular fact at all times *after t*? That is not what I do think: the worlds with no second miracle and divergence must be regarded as closer, since I certainly think it true (at *i*) that if the wheel had stopped on red at *t*, all sorts of particular facts afterward would have been otherwise than they are at *i*. The stopping on red would have plenty of traces and consequences from that time on.

Perhaps it is just brute fact that we put more weight on earlier similarities of particular fact than on later ones. Divergence of particular fact throughout the past might make more of a difference than a small violation of law, but a small violation of law might make more of a difference than divergence of particular fact throughout the future. Then the closest antecedent-worlds to *i* would be those with a miracle and with no difference of particular fact before *t*, but with no miracle and with divergence of particular fact after *t*. Such discrimination between the two directions of time seems anthropocentric; but we are understandably given to just such anthropocentric discrimination, and it would be no surprise if it turns out to infect our standards of comparative similarity and our truth conditions for counterfactuals.

But perhaps my standards are less discriminatory than they seem. For some reason—something to do with the *de facto* or nomological asymmetries of time that prevail at *i* if *i* is a world something like ours—it seems to take less of a miracle to give us an antecedent-world exactly like *i* in the past than it does to give us one exactly like *i* in the future. For the first, all we need is one little miraculous shove, applied to the wheel at the right moment. For the second, we need much more. All kinds of traces of the wheel's having stopped on red must be falsified. The rest position of the wheel; the distribution of light, heat, and sound in the vicinity; the memories of the spectators—all must be changed to bring about a reconvergence of particular fact between the antecedent-world and *i*. One shove will not do it; many of the laws of *i* must be violated in many ways at many places. Small wonder if the closest antecedent-worlds to *i* are worlds where the particular facts before *t* are preserved at the cost of a small miracle, but the particular facts after *t* are not preserved at the cost of a bigger, more complicated miracle.

3.4 Stalnaker's Theory

The previous theory closest to mine is not any sort of metalinguistic theory, but rather the theory of conditionals put forth by Robert Stalnaker and developed formally by Stalnaker and Richmond Thomason.* According to Stalnaker's theory, a counterfactual $\phi \mathbin{\square\!\!\rightarrow} \psi$ (he writes it as $\phi > \psi$) is true at a world *i* if and only if either (1) ϕ is true at no world accessible from *i* (the vacuous case), or (2) ψ is true at the ϕ-world closest to *i*.

Stalnaker's theory depends for its success not only on the Limit Assumption that there never are closer and closer ϕ-worlds to *i* without end, but also on a stronger assumption: that there never are two equally close closest ϕ-worlds to *i*, but rather (if ϕ is true at any world accessible from *i*) there is exactly *one* closest ϕ-world. Otherwise there would be no such thing as *the* closest ϕ-world to *i*, and counterfactuals that certainly ought to be true—say, $\phi \mathbin{\square\!\!\rightarrow} \phi$—would turn out false.

Stalnaker's formal apparatus consists of three things. The first is an *accessibility relation*. Only those worlds that are accessible from *i* need be considered in determining the truth value at *i* of a counterfactual, given the truth values at all worlds of the antecedent and consequent. The second (and principal) one is a *selection function f*. Given any antecedent ϕ and world *i* such that some ϕ-world is accessible from *i*, *f* picks out a single world $f(\phi, i)$: one of the ϕ-worlds accessible from *i*, regarded as the one closest to *i*. The third item is the *absurd world* where everything whatever is true; it is the value of $f(\phi, i)$ if, but only if, there is no ϕ-world accessible from *i*.

Two further formal constraints are imposed, without which we could not regard *f* as making a selection based on comparative similarity. (1) Whenever *i* itself is a ϕ-world, $f(\phi, i)$ is *i*. (2) Whenever ψ holds at $f(\phi, i)$ and ϕ holds at $f(\psi, i)$, $f(\phi, i)$ and $f(\psi, i)$ are the same world.

* Stalnaker, 'A Theory of Conditionals'; Stalnaker and Thomason, 'A Semantic Analysis of Conditional Logic', *Theoria* **36** (1970): 23–42; and Thomason, 'A Fitch-Style Formulation of Conditional Logic', *Logique et Analyse* **52** (1970): 397–412.

The truth conditions for counterfactuals are very simple: $\phi \,\square\!\!\rightarrow\, \psi$ is true at i if and only if ψ is true at $f(\phi, i)$.

Stalnaker's absurd world is a technical convenience not to be taken seriously. To do without it, we could simply say that when no ϕ-world is accessible from i, $f(\phi, i)$ is undefined and $\phi \,\square\!\!\rightarrow\, \psi$ is true for any consequent ψ. Also it is unnecessary to introduce the accessibility relation independently. It will suffice to say that j is accessible from i if and only if, for any ϕ that holds at j, $f(\phi, i)$ is defined (otherwise than as the absurd world).

Stalnaker's theory is equivalent to a special case of mine. Consider those systems of spheres that satisfy the following condition, which we may call *Stalnaker's Assumption*: for every world i and antecedent ϕ (in our language) that is entertainable at i, there is a sphere around i containing exactly one ϕ-world. Stalnaker's Assumption implies but is not implied by the Limit Assumption: one such sphere is the smallest ϕ-permitting sphere around i, and the one ϕ-world in it is the closest ϕ-world to i. $\phi \,\square\!\!\rightarrow\, \psi$ is true at i, under my truth conditions, if and only if ψ holds at this closest ϕ-world to i. So if we define a selection function

$$f(\phi, i) = \begin{cases} \text{the only } \phi\text{-world in the smallest } \phi\text{-permitting} \\ \quad \text{sphere around } i, \text{ if there is any } \phi\text{-permitting} \\ \quad \text{sphere around } i, \\ \text{the absurd world (or undefined) otherwise,} \end{cases}$$

then it is easy to show (1) that f meets Stalnaker's conditions for a selection function, and (2) that a counterfactual is true at a world according to Stalnaker's truth conditions involving the derived selection function f if and only if it is true there according to my truth conditions involving the system of spheres.

Going the other way, let f be any selection function meeting Stalnaker's conditions. The function f selects single worlds; but we can convert it into a set-selection function of the sort we considered in Section 2.7. Let f' be derived from f as follows: whenever $f(\phi, i)$ is j (and j is not the absurd world), let $f'(\phi, i)$ be $\{j\}$; whenever $f(\phi,i)$ is the absurd world (or undefined) let $f'(\phi, i)$ be the empty set. It is easy to show (1) that f' is a set-selection function according to my definition in Section 2.7, and (2) that a counterfactual is true at a world according to my truth conditions involving f' if and only if it is true there according to Stalnaker's truth conditions involving f. We know, further, that since f' is a set-selection function, it is derived from a system of spheres $\$$: that is, for any entertainable antecedent ϕ and world i, $f'(\phi, i)$ is the set of ϕ-worlds belonging to every ϕ-permitting sphere in $\$_i$. It follows (1) that $\$$ satisfies Stalnaker's Assumption, and (2) that a counterfactual is true at a world according to my truth conditions involving the system of spheres $ if and only if it is true there according to Stalnaker's truth conditions involving the selection function f.

As we saw in Section 2.3, systems of spheres stand in one-to-one truth-preserving correspondence with comparative similarity systems. Accordingly, Stalnaker's selection functions also can be placed in truth-preserving correspondence (not in general one-to-one) with a certain class of comparative similarity systems: those such that, for any sentence ϕ and world i, if there is some ϕ-world in the sphere of accessibility S_i, then there is exactly one ϕ-world j such that, for every other ϕ-world $k, j <_i k$. Taking this world j as $f(\phi, i)$, and taking $f(\phi, i)$ as the absurd world (or undefined) in case there is no ϕ-world in S_i, f is a Stalnaker selection function and agrees with the given comparative similarity system on the truth value at every world of every counterfactual. Given a selection function f, on the other hand, we may let S_i, for each world i, be the set of (non-absurd) values of $f(\phi, i)$ for all sentences ϕ; and we may let $j \leqslant_i k$ if and only if either k does not belong to S_i or, for some sentence ϕ holding both at j and at k, j is $f(\phi, i)$. We thus derive a comparative similarity system meeting the condition above, and it agrees with the given selection function on the truth value at every world of every counterfactual.

If all propositions were expressible in our language (or if we had taken selection functions defined not on sentences but on all propositions) we could describe the appropriate class of comparative similarity systems more simply as those such that, for every world i, $\leqslant_i$ is a *well-ordering* of S_i: that is, a linear ordering such that every nonempty set has a lowest member.

The principal virtue and the principal vice of Stalnaker's theory is that it makes valid the law of *Conditional Excluded Middle*:

$$(\phi \;\square\!\!\rightarrow \psi) \lor (\phi \;\square\!\!\rightarrow \sim\!\psi).$$

Both disjuncts are true in the vacuous case; otherwise exactly one is, since by the ordinary law of excluded middle exactly one of ψ and $\sim\!\psi$ is true at any one world, and in particular at the single world $f(\phi, i)$.

The law of Conditional Excluded Middle is plausible because it explains why we do not distinguish, in ordinary language, between the external negation of a whole conditional

$$\sim\!(\phi \;\square\!\!\rightarrow \psi)$$

and the internal negation of the consequent

$$\phi \;\square\!\!\rightarrow \sim\!\psi.$$

The latter implies the former, except in the vacuous case, both on

Stalnaker's theory and on mine; given Conditional Excluded Middle, the former also implies the latter.

Given Conditional Excluded Middle, we cannot truly say such things as this:

> *It is not the case that if Bizet and Verdi were compatriots, Bizet would be Italian; and it is not the case that if Bizet and Verdi were compatriots, Bizet would not be Italian; nevertheless, if Bizet and Verdi were compatriots, Bizet either would or would not be Italian.*

That is:

$$\sim(\phi \;\square\!\!\rightarrow\; \psi) \;\&\; \sim(\phi \;\square\!\!\rightarrow\; \sim\psi) \;\&\; (\phi \;\square\!\!\rightarrow\; \psi \vee \sim\psi).$$

I want to say this, and think it probably true; my own theory was designed to make it true. But offhand, I must admit, it does sound like a contradiction. Stalnaker's theory does, and mine does not, respect the opinion of any ordinary language speaker who cares to insist that it is a contradiction.

But the cost of respecting this offhand opinion is too much. However little there is to choose for closeness between worlds where Bizet and Verdi are compatriots by both being Italian and worlds where they are compatriots by both being French, the selection function still must choose. I do not think it *can* choose—not if it is based entirely on comparative similarity, anyhow. Comparative similarity permits ties, and Stalnaker's selection function does not.

Another manifestation of Stalnaker's Assumption is that, except in the vacuous case, the difference between 'would' and 'might' counterfactuals is lost. Given my definition of $\diamond\!\!\rightarrow$ (namely, $\phi \;\diamond\!\!\rightarrow\; \psi =^{df} \sim(\phi \;\square\!\!\rightarrow\; \sim\psi)$), it is a consequence of Conditional Excluded Middle that $\phi \;\diamond\!\!\rightarrow\; \psi$ implies $\phi \;\square\!\!\rightarrow\; \psi$; and $\phi \;\square\!\!\rightarrow\; \psi$ implies $\phi \;\diamond\!\!\rightarrow\; \psi$, except in the vacuous case, both on Stalnaker's theory and on mine. Hence $\phi \;\square\!\!\rightarrow\; \psi$ and $\phi \;\diamond\!\!\rightarrow\; \psi$ cannot differ in truth value, for Stalnaker, except in the vacuous case. But surely English 'would' and 'might' counterfactuals do sometimes differ in truth value, and not only in the vacuous case. Stalnaker therefore cannot define the 'might' counterfactual as I have done.

How else could he define it? Four candidates come to mind: $\diamond(\phi \;\&\; \psi)$, $\diamond(\phi \;\square\!\!\rightarrow\; \psi)$, $\phi \;\square\!\!\rightarrow\; \diamond\psi$, and $\phi \;\square\!\!\rightarrow\; \diamond(\phi \;\&\; \psi)$. But none will do. Take ϕ as '*I looked in my pocket*' and ψ as '*I found a penny*'; suppose I did not look, suppose there was no penny to be found, and make commonplace assumptions about relevant matters of fact. Then '*If I had looked, I might have found a penny*' is plainly false, but all four candidate symbolizations are true. $\phi \;\&\; \psi$ is false, but only contingently so; hence $\diamond(\phi \;\&\; \psi)$ is true. $\phi \;\square\!\!\rightarrow\; \psi$ is false, but again only contingently so; hence $\Diamond(\phi \,\square\!\!\!\rightarrow \psi)$ is true. If I had looked, ψ and $(\phi \,\&\, \psi)$ would have been false, but again only contingently so; hence $\phi \,\square\!\!\!\rightarrow \Diamond\psi$ and $\phi \,\square\!\!\!\rightarrow \Diamond(\phi \,\&\, \psi)$ are true. Nor would it help to exchange the outer possibility operator $\Diamond$ for some other sort of possibility operator, since the contingencies I have noted persist for other sorts of possibility also. (Exception: if I had looked, I would have known that I had found no penny; ψ and $\phi \,\&\, \psi$ would not have been epistemically possible. But change the example so that if I had looked I would not have known whether I had found a penny or not, so that ψ and $\phi \,\&\, \psi$ would have been epistemically possible; yet the original English 'might' counterfactual remains false.)

The obvious revision of Stalnaker's theory, for one who cannot accept Conditional Excluded Middle because he thinks there might be more than one equally close closest antecedent-world, is the theory based on set-selection functions that we considered in Section 2.7. If we have a function that selects a set of closest antecedent-worlds to a world i, the set *may* contain a single world, but it may rather contain finitely or infinitely many. (Or none, in case the antecedent is not entertainable at i; a set-selection function selects the empty set when a world-selection function selects the absurd world, or is undefined.) The theory of set-selection functions does away with Stalnaker's Assumption, but still depends on the Limit Assumption. I argued that the Limit Assumption also was unjustified, but at least it is safer than Stalnaker's Assumption.

Be that as it may; if we are prepared to tolerate the Limit Assumption but not Stalnaker's Assumption, then there is another way to revise Stalnaker's theory, preserving more of its original character. We can stick to world-selection functions of Stalnaker's sort while denying that the choice of one of them is fully determined by comparative similarity of worlds. We are required to pick an *admissible* world-selection function—that being one such that, for any antecedent ϕ and world i (provided there is some ϕ-world accessible from i) the selection function gives us *one* of the closest ϕ-worlds to i. If Stalnaker's Assumption fails and we sometimes have more than one closest ϕ-world to i, then we will have more than one admissible selection function. If so, the choice of one of these admissible selection functions is arbitrary.

Stalnaker's truth conditions, taken over unchanged, tell us about truth relative to any one particular arbitrary choice of an admissible selection function. But we are not much interested in what happens under any one arbitrary choice. Rather we are interested in what is common to all the choices. Call a sentence *true* at a world if it is true there relative to all admissible selection functions; *false* if it is false there relative to all admissible selection functions; *arbitrary* or *neuter* there if it is true there relative to some admissible selection functions but false there relative to others. It is truth *simpliciter*—not truth relative to some particular arbitrary choice—that makes a sentence worthy of assertion.

So far as the truth conditions for counterfactuals go, it is just as if we had gone over to set-selection functions: $\phi \:\square\!\!\rightarrow\: \psi$ is true at i relative to all admissible selection functions—that is, true at i—if and only if ψ is true at every closest ϕ-world to i, if there are any. But when we turn to falsity conditions for counterfactuals, and truth conditions for negations or other truth-functional compounds of counterfactuals, we find differences. Assume that the closest worlds to ours where Bizet and Verdi are compatriots are divided into worlds where both are French and worlds where both are Italian. '*If they were compatriots, they would be French*' is simply false on my theory; and its negation is true. But on the revised version of Stalnaker's theory that we are examining, this counterfactual and its negation both are neither true nor false, since they vary from one admissible selection function to another. Their truth value is arbitrary. ('*If they were compatriots, they would be German*', on the other hand, is false on either theory; and its negation is true on either theory.) '*Either if they were compatriots they would be French or if they were compatriots they would be Italian*' is false on my theory, being a disjunction of two falsehoods. But on the revision of Stalnaker's theory, it is true although both disjuncts are not true but arbitrary; for since every admissible selection function makes one disjunct or the other true, every admissible selection function makes the disjunction true. For the same reason, Conditional Excluded Middle is valid: every admissible selection function makes one of the disjuncts $\phi \:\square\!\!\rightarrow\: \psi$ and $\phi \:\square\!\!\rightarrow\: \sim\!\psi$ true, though it may be that they do not all make the same one true. More generally: *any* sentence schema valid on the original version of Stalnaker's theory is valid still on the revised version.*

This revision of Stalnaker's theory overcomes one defect of the original version: no longer does the theory depend for its success on the implausible assumption that we never have two or more tied closest antecedent-worlds. Two major problems remain. First, the revised version still depends for success on the Limit Assumption. If ever there were closer and closer antecedent-worlds without end, there would be no admissible selection functions at all. Second, the revised version still

---

* The strategy followed to obtain this half-way house between Stalnaker's theory and mine is Bas van Fraassen's method of supervaluations. See van Fraassen, 'Singular Terms, Truth–Value Gaps and Free Logic', *Journal of Philosophy* 63 (1966): 481–495. Stalnaker suggested the revision I have outlined (personal communication, 1968) and discusses it further in 'A Defense of Conditional Excluded Middle', in W. L. Harper *et al.*, *Ifs* (D. Reidel: Dordrecht, 1981); Thomason makes a similar proposal in 'A Fitch-Style Formulation of Conditional Logic'.

gives us no 'might' counterfactual. My definition is still ruled out because, except in the vacuous case, $\phi \;\square\!\!\rightarrow\; \psi$ and $\phi \;\diamondsuit\!\!\rightarrow\; \psi$ are still equivalent. (They are both true, both false, or both arbitrary; moreover, they have the same truth value relative to any admissible selection function.) Nor does the revision help us to find an alternative definition.*

* Except that *my* 'might' counterfactual, and with it my 'would' counterfactual, can be defined on the revised version of Stalnaker's theory, with the aid of certain special operators. For instance, suppose we have an operator that attaches to any sentence ϕ to make a sentence that is true if ϕ is true, false if ϕ is either false or arbitrary. By prefixing this operator to $\phi \;\square\!\!\rightarrow\; \psi$ we recover my 'would' counterfactual, and from there we can get to my 'might' counterfactual as usual. But why bother? If you like my theory, there are easier ways to formulate it; if you prefer Stalnaker's you will not wish to introduce my 'might' and 'would' counterfactuals into it.

4. Foundations

4.1 Possible Worlds

It is time to face the fact that my analysis rests on suspect foundations. Doubly so: possible worlds are widely regarded with suspicion, and so is similarity even among entities not themselves suspect. If the common suspicion of possible worlds and of similarity were justified, then my analysis could have little interest: only the interest of connecting mysteries to other mysteries. I shall argue, however, that the suspicions are not well justified.

I believe that there are possible worlds other than the one we happen to inhabit. If an argument is wanted, it is this. It is uncontroversially true that things might be otherwise than they are. I believe, and so do you, that things could have been different in countless ways. But what does this mean? Ordinary language permits the paraphrase: there are many ways things could have been besides the way they actually are. On the face of it, this sentence is an existential quantification. It says that there exist many entities of a certain description, to wit 'ways things could have been'. I believe that things could have been different in countless ways; I believe permissible paraphrases of what I believe; taking the paraphrase at its face value, I therefore believe in the existence of entities that might be called 'ways things could have been'. I prefer to call them 'possible worlds'.

I do not make it an inviolable principle to take seeming existential quantifications in ordinary language at their face value. But I do recognize a presumption in favor of taking sentences at their face value, unless (1) taking them at face value is known to lead to trouble, and (2) taking them some other way is known not to. In this case, neither condition is met. I do not know any successful argument that my realism about possible worlds leads to trouble, unless you beg the question by saying that it already *is* trouble. (I shall shortly consider some unsuccessful arguments.) All the alternatives I know, on the other hand, do lead to trouble.

If our modal idioms are not quantifiers over possible worlds, then what else are they? (1) We might take them as unanalyzed primitives; this is not an alternative theory at all, but an abstinence from theorizing. (2) We might take them as metalinguistic predicates analyzable in terms of consistency: '*Possibly* ϕ' means that ϕ is a consistent sentence. But what is consistency? If a consistent sentence is one that could be true, or one that is not necessarily false, then the theory is circular; of course, one can be more artful than I have been in hiding the circularity. If a consistent sentence is one whose denial is not a theorem of some specified deductive system, then the theory is incorrect rather than circular: no falsehood of arithmetic is possibly true, but for any deductive system you care to specify either there are falsehoods among its theorems or there is some falsehood of arithmetic whose denial is not among its theorems. If a consistent sentence is one that comes out true under some assignment of extensions to the non-logical vocabulary, then the theory is incorrect: some assignments of extensions are impossible, for instance one that assigns overlapping extensions to the English terms 'pig' and 'sheep'. If a consistent sentence is one that comes out true under some possible assignment of extensions, then the theory is again circular. (3) We might take them as quantifiers over so-called 'possible worlds' that are really some sort of respectable linguistic entities: say, maximal consistent sets of sentences of some language. (Or maximal consistent sets of atomic sentences, that is *state-descriptions*; or maximal consistent sets of atomic sentences in the language as enriched by the addition of names for all the things there are, that is *diagrammed models*.) We might call these things 'possible worlds', but hasten to reassure anyone who was worried that secretly we were talking about something else that he likes better. But again the theory would be either circular or incorrect, according as we explain consistency in modal terms or in deductive (or purely model-theoretic) terms.

I emphatically do not identify possible worlds in any way with respectable linguistic entities; I take them to be respectable entities in their own right. When I profess realism about possible worlds, I mean to be taken literally. Possible worlds are what they are, and not some other thing. If asked what sort of thing they are, I cannot give the kind of reply my questioner probably expects: that is, a proposal to reduce possible worlds to something else.

I can only ask him to admit that he knows what sort of thing our actual world is, and then explain that other worlds are more things of *that* sort, differing not in kind but only in what goes on at them. Our actual world is only one world among others. We call it alone actual not because it differs in kind from all the rest but because it is the world we inhabit. The inhabitants of other worlds may truly call their own worlds actual, if they mean by 'actual' what we do; for the meaning we give to 'actual' is such that it refers at any world i to that world i itself. 'Actual' is indexical, like 'I' or 'here', or 'now': it depends for its reference on the circumstances of utterance, to wit the world where the utterance is located.*

My indexical theory of actuality exactly mirrors a less controversial doctrine about time. Our present time is only one time among others. We call it alone present not because it differs in kind from all the rest, but because it is the time we inhabit. The inhabitants of other times may truly call their own times 'present', if they mean by 'present' what we do; for the meaning we give to 'present' is such that it is indexical, and refers at any time t to that time t itself.

I have already said that it would gain us nothing to identify possible worlds with sets of sentences (or the like), since we would need the notion of possibility otherwise understood to specify correctly which sets of sentences were to be identified with worlds. Not only would it gain nothing: given that the actual world does not differ in kind from the rest, it would lead to the conclusion that our actual world is a set of sentences. Since I cannot believe that I and all my surroundings are a set of sentences (though I have no argument that they are not), I cannot believe that other worlds are sets of sentences either.

What arguments can be given against realism about possible worlds? I have met with few arguments—incredulous stares are more common. But I shall try to answer those that I have heard.

It is said that realism about possible worlds is false because only our own world, and its contents, actually exist. But of course unactualized possible worlds and their unactualized inhabitants do not *actually* exist. To actually exist is to exist and to be located here at our actual world—at this world that we inhabit. Other worlds than ours are not our world, or inhabitants thereof. It does not follow that realism about possible worlds is false. Realism about unactualized possibles is exactly the thesis that there are more things than actually exist. Either the argument tacitly assumes what it purports to prove, that realism about possibles is false, or it proceeds by equivocation. Our idioms of existential quantification may be used to range over everything without exception, or they may be tacitly restricted in various ways. In particular, they may be restricted to our own world and things in it. Taking them as thus restricted, we can truly say that there exist nothing but our own world and its inhabitants; by removing the restriction we pass illegitimately from that truth to the conclusion that realism about possibles is false. It would be convenient if there were one idiom of

* For more on this theme, see my 'Anselm and Actuality', *Noûs* 4 (1970): 175–188.

quantification, say *'there are . . .'*, that was firmly reserved for un-restricted use and another, say *'there actually exist . . .'*, that was firmly reserved for the restricted use. Unfortunately, even these two idioms of quantification can be used either way; and thus one can pass indecisively from equivocating on one to equivocating on another. All the same, there are the two uses (unless realism about possibles is false, as has yet to be shown) and we need only keep track of them to see that the argument is fallacious.

Realism about possible worlds might be thought implausible on grounds of parsimony, though this could not be a decisive argument against it. Distinguish two kinds of parsimony, however: qualitative and quantitative. A doctrine is qualitatively parsimonious if it keeps down the number of fundamentally different *kinds* of entity: if it posits sets alone rather than sets and unreduced numbers, or particles alone rather than particles and fields, or bodies alone or spirits alone rather than both bodies and spirits. A doctrine is quantitatively parsimonious if it keeps down the number of instances of the kinds it posits; if it posits 10^{29} electrons rather than 10^{37}, or spirits only for people rather than spirits for all animals. I subscribe to the general view that qualitative parsimony is good in a philosophical or empirical hypothesis; but I recognize no presumption whatever in favor of quantitative parsimony. My realism about possible worlds is merely quantitatively, not qualitatively, unparsimonious. You believe in our actual world already. I ask you to believe in more things of that kind, not in things of some new kind.

Quine has complained that unactualized possibles are disorderly elements, well-nigh incorrigibly involved in mysteries of individuation.* That well may be true of any unactualized possibles who lead double lives, lounging in the doorways of two worlds at once. But I do not believe in any of those. The unactualized possibles I do believe in, confined each to his own world and united only by ties of resemblance to their counterparts elsewhere (see Section 1.9) do not pose any special problems of individuation. At least, they pose only such problems of individuation as might arise within a single world.

Perhaps some who dislike the use of possible worlds in philosophical analysis are bothered not because they think they have reason to doubt the existence of other worlds, but only because they wish to be told more about these supposed entities before they know what to think. How many are there? In what respects do they vary, and what is common to them all? Do they obey a non-trivial law of identity of indiscernibles? Here I am at a disadvantage compared to someone who

---

* Willard V. Quine, 'On What There Is', in *From a Logical Point of View* (Harvard University Press: Cambridge, Mass., 1953): 4.

pretends as a figure of speech to believe in possible worlds, but really does not. If worlds were creatures of my imagination, I could imagine them to be any way I liked, and I could tell you all you wish to hear simply by carrying on my imaginative creation. But as I believe that there really are other worlds, I am entitled to confess that there is much about them that I do not know, and that I do not know how to find out.

One comes to philosophy already endowed with a stock of opinions. It is not the business of philosophy either to undermine or to justify these preexisting opinions, to any great extent, but only to try to discover ways of expanding them into an orderly system. A metaphysician's analysis of mind is an attempt at systematizing our opinions about mind. It succeeds to the extent that (1) it is systematic, and (2) it respects those of our pre-philosophical opinions to which we are firmly attached. Insofar as it does both better than any alternative we have thought of, we give it credence. There is some give-and-take, but not too much: some of us sometimes change our minds on some points of common opinion, if they conflict irremediably with a doctrine that commands our belief by its systematic beauty and its agreement with more important common opinions.

So it is throughout metaphysics; and so it is with my doctrine of realism about possible worlds. Among my common opinions that philosophy must respect (if it is to deserve credence) are not only my naive belief in tables and chairs, but also my naive belief that these tables and chairs might have been otherwise arranged. Realism about possible worlds is an attempt, the only successful attempt I know of, to systematize these preexisting modal opinions. To the extent that I am modally opinionated, independently of my philosophizing, I can distinguish between alternative versions of realism about possible worlds that conform to my opinions and versions that do not. Because I believe my opinions, I believe that the true version is one of the former. For instance, I believe that there are worlds where physics is different from the physics of our world, but none where logic and arithmetic are different from the logic and arithmetic of our world. This is nothing but the systematic expression of my naive, pre-philosophical opinion that physics could be different, but not logic or arithmetic. I do not know of any non-circular argument that I could give in favor of that opinion; but so long as that *is* my firm opinion nevertheless, I must make a place for it when I do metaphysics. I have no more use for a philosophical doctrine that denies my firm, unjustified modal opinions than I have for one that denies my firm, unjustified belief in chairs and tables.

Unfortunately, though, I am not opinionated enough. There are too many versions of realism about worlds that would serve equally well to systematize my modal opinions. I do not know which to believe; unless

I become more opinionated, or find unsuspected connections between my opinions I may never have any way to choose. But why should I think that I ought to be able to make up my mind on every question about possible worlds, when it seems clear that I may have no way whatever of finding out the answers to other questions about noncontingent matters—for instance, about the infinite cardinals?

Quine has suggested one way to seek fixation of belief about possible worlds by proposing that worlds might be put into correspondence with certain mathematical structures representing the distribution of matter in space and time.* Suppose, for simplicity, that we are concerned with worlds where space-time is Euclidean and four-dimensional, and where there is only one kind of matter and no fields. (Quine calls these *Democritean* worlds.) We can represent any such world by a mapping from all quadruples $\langle x, y, z, t \rangle$ of real numbers to the numbers 0 and 1. We are to think of the quadruples as coordinates, in some coordinate system, of space-time points; and we are to think of the quadruples mapped onto 0 as coordinates of points unoccupied by matter, and of quadruples mapped onto 1 as coordinates of points occupied by matter. Thus the entire mapping represents a possible distribution of uniform matter over Euclidean space-time. Since there are many different coordinate systems—differing in the location of the $\langle 0, 0, 0, 0 \rangle$ point, the length of the units of spatial and of temporal distance, and the directions of the spatial axes—there are many different mappings (differing by a transformation of coordinates) that we regard as representing the same distribution of matter. To overcome this dependence of the mapping on an arbitrary choice of coordinates, we take not the mappings themselves, but equivalence classes of mappings under transformations of coordinates. We get a perfectly well-defined, well-understood set of mathematical entities, exactly one for every different possible distribution of matter.

Of course, this is a simplified example. The construction must be generalized in several ways to cover possibilities so far overlooked. Space-time might be non-Euclidean; there might be scalar, vector, or tensor fields independent of the distribution of matter; there might be more than one kind of matter, or more or less density of matter, even in the small. We would have to go on generalizing as long as we could think of possibilities not yet taken into account. But generalizing Quine's simplified example is easy mathematical work. We can hope that soon we will reach the end of the generalizations required and permitted by our opinions about what is possible, and then we will have a well-defined set of mathematical entities of a familiar and

* Willard V. Quine, 'Propositional Objects', in *Ontological Relativity* (Columbia University Press: New York, 1969): 147–155.

well-understood sort, corresponding one-to-one in a specified way with
the possible worlds.

I do not, of course, claim that these complicated mathematical
entities *are* the possible worlds. I cannot believe (though I do not know
why not) that our own world is a purely mathematical entity. Since I
do not believe that other worlds are different in kind from ours, I do not
believe that they are either. What is interesting is not the reduction of
worlds to mathematical entities, but rather the claim that the possible
worlds stand in a certain one-to-one correspondence with certain
mathematical entities. Call these *ersatz possible worlds*. Any credible
correspondence claim would give us an excellent grip on the real
possible worlds by their ersatz handles. It would answer most of our
questions about what the possible worlds are like.*

We already have a good grip, in this way, on at least *some* of the
possible worlds: those that correspond to mathematical ersatz worlds
constructed at the highest level of generality that our modal opinions
clearly require and permit. It is only because there may be higher levels
of generality that we have failed to think of, and because our modal
opinions are indecisive about whether there really are possibilities
corresponding to some of the levels of generality we have thought of
(what about letting the number of spatial dimensions vary? what about
letting there be entities that are temporally but not spatially located?
what about letting the distinction between space and time be local rather
than global, like the distinction between up and down?), that we fail to
have a good grip on all the worlds.

The mathematical construction of ersatz worlds may seem to depend
too much on our current knowledge of physics. We know that we must
generalize enough to include non-Euclidean worlds, for instance, just
because the physicists have found reason to believe that we live in one.
But physics is contingent. If we look to physics to tell us what is possible,
will we get all possible worlds? Or only the physically possible worlds,
according to current physics?

More, at least, than the latter. We will certainly construct ersatz
worlds that disobey currently accepted physical laws; for instance,

* Even the indefinite correspondence claim that *some* generalization of Quine's
simplified example is right is enough to answer one important question about the
possible worlds. How many are there? Answer: at least $\beth_2$, the infinite cardinal
of the set of all subsets of the real numbers. It can easily be shown that this is the
number of ersatz worlds in Quine's original construction. Indeed, it is the number
of ersatz worlds at any level of generality that seems to me clearly called for.
Here is another reason why possible worlds are not sets of sentences of a language.
If we take 'language' at all literally, so that sentences are finite strings over a
finite alphabet, there are not enough sets of sentences to go around. There are at
most $\beth_1$, the infinite cardinal of the set of all real numbers.

ersatz worlds where mass-energy is not conserved. Still, we cannot be sure of getting all possible worlds, since we cannot be sure that we have constructed our ersatz worlds at a high enough level of generality. If we knew only the physics of 1871, we would fail to cover some of the possibilities that we recognize today. Perhaps we fail today to cover possibilities that will be recognized in 2071. Our modal opinions do change, and physicists do a lot to change them. But this is *not* to say that we can argue from the contingent results of empirical investigation to conclusions about what possibilities there are. It is only to say that when we find it hard to locate our actual world among the possibilities that we recognize, we may reasonably be stimulated to reconsider our modal opinions. We may try to think of credible possibilities hitherto overlooked, and we may consider whether we are still as sure as we were about those of our modal opinions that have turned out to be restrictive. It is this reconsideration of modal opinions that may influence our construction of ersatz worlds, not the results of empirical investigation itself. We are concerned not with physics proper, but with the preliminary metaphysics done by physicists.

4.2 Similarity

It may be said that even if possible worlds are tolerable, still the notion of comparative overall similarity of worlds is hopelessly unclear, and so no fit foundation for the clarification of counterfactuals or anything else. I think the objection is wrong. 'Unclear' is unclear: does it mean 'ill-understood' or does it mean 'vague'? Ill-understood notions are bad primitives because an analysis by means of them will be an ill-understood analysis. (It may yet be better than no analysis at all.) But comparative similarity is not ill-understood. It is vague—very vague—in a well-understood way. Therefore it is just the sort of primitive that we must use to give a correct analysis of something that is itself undeniably vague.

Overall similarity consists of innumerable similarities and differences in innumerable respects of comparison, balanced against each other according to the relative importances we attach to those respects of comparison. Insofar as these relative importances differ from one person to another, or differ from one occasion to another, or are indeterminate even for a single person on a single occasion, so far is comparative similarity indeterminate. As Goodman says,* 'Importance is a highly

---

* Nelson Goodman, 'Seven Strictures on Similarity', in L. Foster and J. W. Swanson, *Experience and Theory* (University of Massachusetts Press: 1970): 27.

volatile matter, varying with every shift of context and interest, and quite incapable of supporting the fixed distinctions that philosophers so often seek to rest upon it.'

All this is not special to the comparative similarity of worlds that appears in my analysis of counterfactuals. It is the same sort of vagueness that arises if I say that Seattle resembles San Francisco more closely than it resembles Los Angeles. Does it? That depends on whether we attach more importance to the surrounding landscape, the architecture, the dominant industries, the political temper, the state of the arts, the climate, the public transportation system, the form of the city government, or what. Possible worlds are bigger than cities (sometimes), and are capable of differing in a greater variety of respects. They are also capable of being more alike than any two actual cities. Still, any problems posed by my use of comparative similarity differ only in degree, not in kind, from problems about similarity that we would be stuck with no matter what we did about counterfactuals. Somehow, we *do* have a familiar notion of comparative overall similarity, even of comparative similarity of big, complicated, variegated things like whole people, whole cities, or even—I think—whole possible worlds. However mysterious that notion may be, if we can analyze counterfactuals by means of it we will be left with one mystery in place of two.

I am not one of those philosophers who seek to rest fixed distinctions upon a foundation quite incapable of supporting them. I rather seek to rest an unfixed distinction upon a swaying foundation, claiming that the two sway together rather than independently. The truth conditions for counterfactuals are fixed only within rough limits; like the relative importances of respects of comparison that underlie the comparative similarity of worlds, they are a highly volatile matter, varying with every shift of context and interest.

It often happens that two vague concepts are vague in a coordinated way: firmly connected to each other, if to nothing else. The border between blue and green is not well fixed, so 'blue' and 'green' are both vague. But their relation to each other is fixed: one begins where the other leaves off, with no gap and no overlap. They are vague in a coordinated way, not independently. A single roughly fixed parameter serves to delineate both the border of blue (on the side facing green) and the border of green (on the side facing blue). If we wish to give truth conditions for sentences containing the vague terms 'blue' and 'green', there are two things to do. First we can give precise conditions of truth *relative to* any given value of this delineating parameter (and others, such as the one that delineates the border between green and yellow). Then we can go on to say roughly what the values of the delineating parameters are supposed to be, thereby removing the relativity and giving imprecise conditions of truth *simpliciter*.* In easy cases, such as the vagueness of 'many' or 'hot', the delineating parameter need be nothing more than a single number. In other cases, it will have to be something more complicated—several numbers, for instance, or a surface through the color solid.

The delineating parameter for the vagueness of counterfactuals is the comparative similarity relation itself: the system of spheres, comparative similarity system, selection function, or whatever other entity we use to carry information about the comparative similarity of worlds. I have stated precise truth conditions relative to any given value of this roughly fixed parameter. My formal statements of truth conditions in Section 1.3 took the form: $\phi \mathbin{\Box\!\!\rightarrow} \psi$ is true at a world *i according to a system of spheres* $ if and only if. . . . To get down to truth at a world *simpliciter*, I had to remove the relativity at the cost of introducing vagueness by saying that the system of spheres was supposed to be based on comparative similarity. Thus I fixed the delineating parameter $ within a fuzzily bounded range of values.

The border delineating blue from green is only roughly fixed, but it is at least roughly fixed. Not anything goes. We can find a color that is blue according to some quite permissible delineations and green according to others, and therefore indeterminate between blue and green. But it is not indeterminate whether the sky is blue or green. No delineation is at all permissible, under our conventions of language, relative to which it is anything but blue. Likewise the relative importances of respects of comparison, and thereby the comparative similarity of worlds, are at least roughly fixed. Not anything goes. It can happen that a counterfactual is true (at a world) according to some permissible systems of spheres but not according to others, so that its truth value will be indeterminate by reason of vagueness. But it can happen also, and often does, that a counterfactual has the same truth value according to all permissible systems of spheres, and so is definitely true or definitely false.

There might be a man who was inclined to deny that if he had stepped out of his window he would have fallen to the ground; to deny this not—as we might expect—because he had eccentric factual opinions, but rather because he attached eccentric relative importances to respects of comparison of worlds and therefore favored a system of spheres unlike systems that others would favor. He is not entitled to give in to his inclination to deny this, at least not without giving warning of his eccentric notions. If he denies it without warning he lies; if he denies it with warning, he temporarily changes the conventional meaning of his words. There is a rough consensus about the importances of respects

* This treatment of vagueness is discussed further in my 'General Semantics'.

of comparison, and hence about comparative similarity. Our standards of importance and similarity do vary; but mostly within a certain range, narrow by comparison with the range of variation permitted by the formal constraints in my definition of a system of spheres. We mostly stay within that comparatively narrow range, expect each other to stay within it, expect each other to expect each other to stay within it, and so on. It is natural that we should have vocabulary conventionally reserved for use within that mutually expected range. If special interests or eccentricity lead us outside the mutually expected range of variation, we have no right to take our conventionally reserved vocabulary with us. For if we do (unless we serve notice), we will deceive those of our listeners who justifiably suppose that our standards of importance and similarity are more or less the usual ones.

. I conclude that the limited vagueness of similarity accounts nicely for the limited vagueness of counterfactuals. It accounts for the fact that some sensitive counterfactuals are so vague as to be unsuitable for use in serious discourse; that others have definite truth values only when context serves to narrow their range of vagueness; and that many more have quite definite truth values (in worlds of the sort we think we inhabit), insensitive to small shifts in our standards of comparative similarity.

It is tempting to try to define some exact measure of the similarity 'distance' among worlds, using the mathematical ersatz worlds introduced in Section 4.1. Assume, for instance, that the worlds stand in one-to-one correspondence with Quine's Democritean ersatz worlds. These, we recall, are equivalence classes, under certain transformations of coordinates, of mappings from the set of all quadruples of real numbers to 0 (for the quadruples which are the coordinates of points unoccupied by matter) and 1 (for the coordinates of occupied points). We might define the distance between any two of these mappings as the hypervolume of the set of quadruples on which the two mappings differ in value; and we might next define the distance between any two sets of these mappings—in particular, between any two ersatz worlds—as the greatest lower bound on the distances between a mapping in one set and a mapping in the other. It remains only to equate the similarity 'distance' between two worlds with the defined distance between the two corresponding ersatz worlds.

The Democritean ersatz worlds are not constructed at a high enough level of generality. We could, however, define exact distance measures in much the same way for more adequate constructions of ersatz worlds. At worst, we might need a few numerical parameters. For instance, we might define one similarity measure for distribution of matter and another for distribution of fields, and we would then need to choose a weighting parameter to tell us how to combine these in arriving at the overall similarity of two worlds. All this would be easy work for those who like that sort of thing, and would yield an exact measure of *something*—something that we might be tempted to regard as the similarity 'distance' between worlds.

We must resist temptation. The exact measure thus defined cannot be expected to correspond well to our own opinions about comparative similarity. Some of the similarities and differences most important to us involve idiosyncratic, subtle, Gestalt properties. It is impossible in practice, and perhaps in principle, to express these respects of comparison in terms of the distribution of matter over space-time (or the like), even if the distribution of matter suffices to determine them.

Consider a similar proposal to measure the visual similarity of faces. Any face can be represented by a matrix of dots, some black and some white. (I ignore color for simplicity.) With enough dots, nothing perceptible is lost: any two faces that yield the same matrix of dots look exactly alike to the (color-blind) eye. There is an easy way to measure the 'distance' between two matrices of dots (with the same number of rows and columns). Take the number of dots that are black in the first matrix but white in the second, or black in the second but white in the first, as a fraction of the total number of dots. Let the measure of the difference between two faces be the distance, so defined, between their representations by matrices of dots.

Various refinements come to mind. Vertical and horizontal shifts should not affect the measure of distance, so take the minimum distance that can be obtained by vertical and horizontal shifting. Likewise for rotation, for change of scale, for change of average darkness, and for change of contrast (within limits).

When all this is done, we may have a measure that will be right at the extremes. When we think two faces are very similar, they will be very similar according to the measure; when we think two faces are very different, they will be very different according to the measure. Between the extremes, however, the measure will miss features that we consider important. Not many dots need to be switched between black and white to go from an Oriental face to a Caucasian face; from a male face to a female face; from an open, friendly face to a face with a sinister leer. So we will have defined a precise measure of something, but it will not be a measure of the overall similarity of faces according to any ordinary standards. The same goes, I fear, for any humanly possible attempt at a precise definition of comparative similarity of worlds. Not only would we go wrong by giving a precise analysis of an imprecise concept; our precise concept would not fall within—or even near—the permissible range of variation of the ordinary concept.

5. Analogies

5.1 Conditional Obligation

Our understanding of modality has been much improved by the exploitation of formal analogies between modal logic and other branches of intensional logic: deontic logic, tense logic, and recently Prior's 'egocentric logic'. It therefore behooves us to see whether counterfactuals likewise bear formal analogies to anything else. They do: there are variably strict conditionals to be found also in deontic logic, tense logic, and egocentric logic. These turn out to be familiar concepts, with an interest independent of their analogy to counterfactuals.

We may base a system of spheres not on comparative similarity of possible worlds, but rather on comparative goodness of worlds. Suppose we have a preference ordering of the worlds, perhaps different from the standpoints of different worlds. As is the custom in deontic logic, I shall say nothing definite about the source and significance of this ordering. Perhaps the worlds are ordered according to their total net content of pleasure, measured by some hedonic calculus; or their content of beauty, truth, and love; or their content of some simple, non-natural quality. Perhaps they are ordered according to the extent that their inhabitants obey the law of God, of Nature, or of man. Perhaps according to how well they measure up to some sort of standards of objective morality, if such there be; perhaps according to someone's personal taste in possible worlds; perhaps according to the tastes we would have if we attained a superhuman capacity for calm, sympathetic, impartial contemplation of alternative possibilities. It does not matter. We can build in the same way on any of these foundations, or on others.

   Suppose we have also an assignment to each world i of a sphere of accessibility, or *evaluability*. We may leave a world out of i's sphere of evaluability if we want to exclude it from consideration, from the standpoint of i—say, because the standards of evaluation that give rise to the ordering cannot be applied to that world.

Let a sphere around a world i now be any set S of worlds evaluable from i such that any world in S is better than any world outside S, in our ordering from the standpoint of i. If the preference ordering (from the standpoint of any world i) has the properties of a weak ordering, then a world j is better than a world k if and only if some sphere contains j but not k. The system of spheres so obtained is nested, closed under unions, and closed under nonempty intersections.

In contrast to systems of spheres based on comparative similarity, however, these systems of spheres based on comparative goodness will not generally be centered, or even weakly centered. Centering means that for each world i, $\{i\}$ is a sphere around i; and that would mean now that each world is, from its own standpoint, the best of all possible worlds. Weak centering means that each world i belongs to the innermost nonempty sphere around i; and that would mean now that each world is, from its own standpoint, at least one of the best worlds. It is quite clear, no matter what (within reason) is the source of our preference ordering, that ours is nowhere near being one of the best possible worlds!

Let us restate the definition of a system of spheres in a general form, without the previous clauses for centering or weak centering. Let \$ be an assignment to each world i of a set $\$_i$ of sets of worlds. Then \$ is called a *system of spheres*, and the members of each $\$_i$ are called *spheres around i*,* if and only if, for each world i, the following conditions hold.

(1) $\$_i$ is nested; that is, whenever S and T belong to $\$_i$, either S is included in T or T is included in S.

(2) $\$_i$ is closed under unions; that is, whenever S is a subset of $\$_i$ and $\bigcup S$ is the set of all worlds j such that j belongs to some member of S, $\bigcup S$ belongs to $\$_i$.

(3) $\$_i$ is closed under (nonempty) intersections; that is, whenever S is a nonempty subset of $\$_i$ and $\bigcap S$ is the set of all worlds j such that j belongs to every member of S, $\bigcap S$ belongs to $\$_i$.

The Limit Assumption may fail for spheres based on comparative goodness, just as for spheres based on comparative similarity. If there is a ϕ-permitting sphere around i, there may be a smallest ϕ-permitting sphere around i, containing exactly those ϕ-worlds that are best from the standpoint of i; or there may be no smallest ϕ-permitting sphere, and better and better ϕ-worlds without end. (That is not to say that the goodness of ϕ-worlds is unbounded; there may also be worlds better than any of the ϕ-worlds.) That could happen in a way parallel to failures of the Limit Assumption for spheres based on comparative

---

* 'Around' is rather a misnomer without centering, but we shall keep using it nonetheless.

similarity. Suppose that the goodness of certain worlds increases according to the value of some continuously variable magnitude, and let ϕ be true at all and only those worlds of the proper kind where the value of the magnitude is strictly less than some upper bound. Then there are no best ϕ-worlds.

Previously, centering (or weak centering) guaranteed us one special case of the Limit Assumption, at least: a smallest ϕ-permitting sphere around i whenever ϕ was true at i. This was the innermost nonempty sphere around i; in other words, the intersection of all nonempty spheres around i, which was itself nonempty because it contained i. Now that special case is no more defensible than the Limit Assumption in general. We might have an infinite ascent to better and better worlds, and no innermost sphere containing best worlds of all. For every world, there would be a sphere small enough to exclude it, so the intersection of all nonempty spheres would be empty.

For our systems of spheres based on comparative goodness, the analog of Stalnaker's Assumption is implausible in the extreme. By any reasonable standards of evaluation, there are respects of difference among worlds that are wholly irrelevant to their comparative goodness. Worlds differing only in such respects would be tied in the preference order. Further ties would occur if relevant differences balanced out. If any of the respects of comparison admit of continuous variation, ties by balancing seem inevitable. (Previously, we had only ties by balancing. No differences are irrelevant to comparative similarity, so we had no ties by irrelevance.)

There are three conditions we might wish to impose, however, beyond those that are definitive of a system of spheres.

Normality. Call a world i *abnormal* if there are no nonempty spheres around i, so that $\bigcup \$_i$ is empty; otherwise *normal*. The system of spheres $\$$ is normal if and only if all worlds are normal. Previously we had normality as a consequence of centering (or weak centering), but there is nothing in the general definition of a system of spheres to rule out the abnormality of some—or even all—worlds. We shall see that abnormal worlds are deservedly so-called. Peculiar things happen there. Nothing is obligatory; everything is permissible. In what would otherwise be reasonable senses of 'necessary' and 'possible', everything is necessary, even contradictions, and nothing is possible, not even tautologies. We might choose to rule out these objectionable consequences by imposing a prohibition against abnormal worlds.

What shall we do, then, if our preference ordering from the standpoint of any world i depends on some contingent feature of i, and there are certain worlds where this feature is either missing or somehow unsuited to determine a preference ordering? For instance, let the worlds be ordered, from the standpoint of a world *i*, according to the extent that their inhabitants obey the laws promulgated by the ruling god of *i*. Then what shall we do when we have no ordering from the standpoint of a certain world *i* because *i* is not ruled by any law-promulgating god? We can have no distinctions in comparative goodness from the standpoint of *i*, so there are only two options. (1) Let there be no nonempty spheres around *i*, making *i* abnormal; or (2) let the set of all worlds be the one and only nonempty sphere around *i*. If we have decided to impose a requirement of normality, we must choose the second option.

Universality. As before, call $ universal if and only if each $\bigcup \$_i$ is the set of all worlds. The worlds left out of $\bigcup \$_i$ are the worlds, if any, that are not evaluable from *i*. To assume universality is therefore to do away with evaluability restrictions. I am not sure whether evaluability restrictions are needed (just as I was previously not sure whether accessibility restrictions were needed for the counterfactual case). It would be a simplification if they could be dropped.* Universality implies normality, but if we do not wish to prohibit abnormal worlds, we still might want to impose a condition requiring *normal universality*: each $\bigcup \$_i$ is the set of all worlds unless *i* is abnormal. That would be to assume that evaluability of *j* from *i* may be blocked by a defect in *i*, but never by a defect in *j*.

Absoluteness. Call $ *absolute* if and only if $\$_i$ is the same for all worlds *i*. That is so if we have the same preference ordering from the standpoint of every world. Then one world is better than another *simpliciter*, better from the standpoint of every world; or else it is better from the standpoint of none. (Obviously we never have the same order of comparative similarity to different worlds, so that absoluteness was out of the question for the counterfactual case. Indeed, absoluteness is incompatible with centering unless there is only one world.) Clearly the assumption of absoluteness is correct for some preference orderings and wrong for others. An ordering of worlds according to their net content of pleasure or whatnot is the same from the standpoint of any world, so it yields an absolute system of spheres. But an ordering of worlds according to the extent that their inhabitants obey the law of God will differ from the standpoints of different worlds ruled by different gods who promulgate different laws, so the system of spheres will not be absolute.

* I left the question of universality open in the counterfactual case partly in order not to exaggerate my disagreements with Stalnaker's theory. Stalnaker, like me, does not assume universality but does not make a case against it. Similarly, I leave the question open in this case partly in order not to multiply disagreements with van Fraassen's treatment of conditional obligation, discussed below.

The truth conditions for our variably strict conditionals, inner and outer modalities, and comparative possibility operators (according to a system of spheres $) remain as before. The interdefinitions of the operators continue to give the correct derived truth conditions.

The variably strict conditionals $\square\rightarrow$ and $\square\Rightarrow$ may now be regarded as versions of the *conditional obligation* operator of deontic logic, commonly written as $O(../..)$.* Either $\phi\,\square\rightarrow\psi$ or $\phi\,\square\Rightarrow\psi$ may be read as '*Given that ϕ, it is obligatory that ψ*' or—better—as '*Given that ϕ, it ought to be that ψ*'. Roughly (under the Limit Assumption) if there are ϕ-worlds evaluable from a world i, then $\phi\,\square\rightarrow\psi$ and $\phi\,\square\Rightarrow\psi$ are true at i if and only if ψ holds at all the best ϕ-worlds, according to the ordering from the standpoint of i. More precisely: if there are ϕ-worlds evaluable from i, then they are true at i if and only if some $(\phi\ \&\ \psi)$-world is better, from the standpoint of i, than any $(\phi\ \&\ \sim\psi)$-world. $\phi\,\square\rightarrow\psi$ and $\phi\,\square\Rightarrow\psi$ diverge only when ϕ is impossible—true nowhere, except perhaps at inevaluable worlds that are left out of consideration—in which case $\phi\,\square\rightarrow\psi$ is vacuously true and $\phi\,\square\Rightarrow\psi$ is automatically false, regardless of ψ. It is hard to summon up any opinion about whether everything or nothing ought to come out as obligatory under an impossible condition.

$\diamondsuit\rightarrow$ and $\diamondsuit\Rightarrow$ are the corresponding versions of the *conditional permission* operator, commonly written as $P(../..)$. Either $\phi\,\diamondsuit\rightarrow\psi$ or $\phi\,\diamondsuit\Rightarrow\psi$ may be read as '*Given that ϕ, it is permissible that ψ*'. Roughly, if there are ϕ-worlds evaluable from a world i, then $\phi\,\diamondsuit\rightarrow\psi$ and $\phi\,\diamondsuit\Rightarrow\psi$ are true at i if and only if ψ holds at some of the best ϕ-worlds, from the standpoint of i. More precisely: if there are ϕ-worlds evaluable from i, then they are true if and only if, for any $(\phi\ \&\ \sim\psi)$-world, there is some $(\phi\ \&\ \psi)$-world at least as good, from the standpoint of i. If there are no ϕ-worlds evaluable from i, then $\phi\,\diamondsuit\rightarrow\psi$ is false and $\phi\,\diamondsuit\Rightarrow\psi$ is true, regardless of ψ; again, there seems little to choose.

The inner modalities $\boxdot$ and $\diamondsuit$ are versions of the basic deontic operators of (*unconditional*) *obligation* and *permission*, commonly written as O and P. $\boxdot\phi$ may be read as '*It is obligatory that ϕ*' or as '*It ought to be that ϕ*'; $\diamondsuit\phi$ may be read as '*It is permissible that ϕ*'. If there is an innermost nonempty sphere around each world i, containing the best of all worlds from the standpoint of i, then $\boxdot$ and $\diamondsuit$ may be treated as ordinary necessity and possibility operators, interpreted by assigning the set of best worlds to i as its sphere of accessibility. $\boxdot\phi$ is true at i if and only if ϕ holds at all worlds that are best from the stand-

---

* 'Obligation' is here used in a special, impersonal sense. What is obligatory (conditionally or unconditionally) is what ought to be the case, whether or not anyone in particular is obligated to see to it. Personal obligations may or may not follow from these impersonal obligations.

point of i; $\diamondsuit \phi$ is true at i if and only if ϕ holds at some world that is best from the standpoint of i. If there is no nonempty sphere around some world i, however, there is no way to interpret $\boxdot$ and $\diamondsuit$ by means of an accessibility assignment. If there are no best worlds from the standpoint of i, but rather there is an infinite ascent to better and better worlds, then $\boxdot \phi$ is true at i if and only if ϕ holds throughout all sufficiently good worlds; and $\diamondsuit \phi$ is true at i if and only if there continue to be some ϕ-worlds no matter how high we ascend. If i is an abnormal world—say, a world with no god to promulgate laws that would determine a preference ordering from the standpoint of i—then $\boxdot \phi$ is false and $\diamondsuit \phi$ is true, at i, for any ϕ whatever. Deontic distinctions collapse: nothing is obligatory, everything is permissible.*

The outer modalities $\square$ and $\diamondsuit$ are the logical modalities if we assume universality. Otherwise they are nothing familiar. In general, $\square \phi$ is true at i if and only if ϕ holds at every world evaluable from i; $\diamondsuit \phi$ is true at i if and only if ϕ holds at some world evaluable from i. If we want to regard the outer modalities as expressing necessity and possibility, in any more or less ordinary sense, then we must insist on normality. At an abnormal world, if such there be, the outer modalities go vacuous: $\square \phi$ is true and $\diamondsuit \phi$ is false, for any ϕ whatever. Even contradictions are 'necessary'; even tautologies are not 'possible'.

The comparative possibility operators now express comparative permissibility—that is, comparative goodness-at-best. We may read $\phi \prec \psi$ as '*It is better that ϕ than that ψ*; it is true at i if and only if, from the standpoint of i, some evaluable ϕ-world is better than any ψ-world. This is not instrumental or intrinsic betterness of any familiar sort, but rather *maximax betterness*. Roughly, we are comparing ϕ-at-its-best with ψ-at-its-best, and ignoring the non-best ways for ϕ and ψ to hold. Nothing is better than the truth of a tautology (at its best). It is better that either I drink cyanide or I drink beer than that I drink water, since any disjunction is as good-at-best as its best disjunct. As for the other operators: $\phi \preccurlyeq \psi$ may be read as '*It is at least as good that ϕ as that ψ*' in a similar maximax sense, and is true at i if and only if, from the standpoint of i, no evaluable ψ-world is better than every ϕ-world. $\phi \approx \psi$ may be read as '*It is just as good that ϕ as that ψ*', and is true at i if and only if, from the standpoint of i, neither is there an evaluable ϕ-world better than every ψ-world nor vice versa. Most simply, it is true if the best ϕ-worlds and the best ψ-worlds are equally good. It can also be true in another way: if, for instance, the ϕ-worlds have goodnesses of .9, .99, .999, . . . and the ψ-worlds have goodnesses of .8, .98,

---

* If we had defined the inner modalities as $\top \square \rightarrow$ and $\top \diamondsuit \rightarrow$, rather than as $\top \square \rightarrow$ and $\top \diamondsuit \rightarrow$, the collapse at abnormal worlds would have gone the wrong way: everything obligatory, nothing permissible.

.998, . . . (pretending momentarily that we have some sort of numerical scale).

Operators of conditional obligation and permission were introduced into deontic logic in order to handle cases in which, given that ϕ, it ought to be that ψ, but it (unconditionally) ought not to be that ψ and it ought not to be that ϕ. For instance, let ϕ be '*Jesse robs the bank*' and let ψ be '*Jesse confesses and gives back the loot*'. It ought not to be that ϕ. Also it ought not to be that ψ, since what really ought to be the case—what is the case at the best of worlds—is that Jesse has nothing to confess and no loot to give back. But it ought to be that ψ, given that ϕ. Analyses of '*Given that ϕ, it ought to be that ψ*' by means of the unconditional obligation operator—our $\boxdot$, or something similar—do not work. $\boxdot(\phi \supset \psi)$ fails because this follows simply from $\boxdot \sim \phi$, whatever ψ may be: given that Jesse robs the bank, it ought to be that he shoots up the town afterward, or that the cow jumps over the moon. $\phi \supset \boxdot\psi$, or the corresponding counterfactual or logical strict conditional, fails because $\boxdot\psi$ is false even if ϕ is true.* Since these analyses fail, and no better way comes to mind of expressing conditional obligation in terms of unconditional obligation, the conditional obligation operator has to be provided as a primitive.

Several axiomatic or semantic treatments of conditional obligation are open to serious criticism because they validate inferences from '*Given that ϕ_1, it ought to be that ψ*' to '*Given that ϕ_1 & ϕ_2, it ought to be that ψ*', or conversely.‡ Neither direction ought to be valid, since it seems that we can have consistent alternating sequences like this:

Given that ϕ_1, it ought to be that ψ,
Given that ϕ_1 & ϕ_2, it ought to be that $\sim\psi$,
Given that ϕ_1 & ϕ_2 & ϕ_3, it ought to be that ψ,
$$\vdots$$

along with all their negated opposites.§ For instance: '*Given that Jesse robbed the bank, he ought to confess; but given in addition that his confession would send his ailing mother to an early grave, he ought not to;*

---

* There is a natural way to construe '*It ought to be that ψ*' so that it does become true when Jesse robs the bank. It can be taken as tacitly conditional, meaning something like '*Given those actual circumstances that now cannot be helped, it ought to be that ψ*'. But this tacitly conditional and time-dependent construal is not the appropriate one when '*It ought to be that ψ*' is used as a reading for the unconditional obligation operator of standard tenseless deontic logic.

‡ Such criticisms may be found in Bengt Hansson, 'An Analysis of Some Deontic Logics', *Noûs* 3 (1969): 373–398, and in Bas van Fraassen, 'The Logic of Conditional Obligation', *Journal of Philosophical Logic* 1 (1972): 417–438.

§ We have the negated opposites, rather than conflicting obligations, because we are dealing not with *prima facie* obligations but with what ought on balance to be the case.

but given in addition that an innocent man is on trial for the crime, he ought to after all. . . '. This alternating sequence is analogous to those I gave in Section 1.2 as evidence that the counterfactual is a variably strict conditional. It has a parallel explanation by means of my proposal that conditional obligation is a variably strict conditional based on comparative goodness of worlds.

Bengt Hansson and Bas van Fraassen have given analyses of conditional obligation expressly designed to permit such appearances and disappearances of conditional obligation as are found in my alternating sequence.* I have based my analysis on theirs, but with various changes.

Hansson, for his principal system **DSDL3**, posits a preference ordering of worlds and specifies that a sentence $O(\psi / \phi)$ is to be true if and only if ψ holds at the best ϕ-worlds, if such there be. These would be my truth conditions for $\phi \,\square\!\!\rightarrow \psi$ under the Limit Assumption, stated directly in terms of the preference ordering. Hansson imposes the Limit Assumption in this form: if a sentence ϕ without deontic operators is true at any world, then there are some best ϕ-worlds. Hansson declines to consider sentences having deontic operators within the scope of deontic operators. Hence he does not need to evaluate the truth of any sentence $O(\psi / \phi)$ at other worlds than our actual world in order to evaluate the actual truth value of any of the sentences he considers. He thus avoids the question of absoluteness: whether his preference ordering of worlds is the ordering from the standpoint of our world only, or from the standpoint of every world. He assumes universality, and consequently also normality, in positing a preference ordering of all worlds.‡

Van Fraassen posits a preference ordering not of worlds themselves but of *values* (items of unspecified character) that are *realized* at worlds. He specifies that a sentence $O(\psi / \phi)$ is true at a world i if and only if, from the standpoint of i, some value realized at some (ϕ & ψ)-world is better than any value realized at any (ϕ & $\sim\psi$)-world. Compare my truth conditions for $\phi \,\square\!\!\rightarrow \psi$: it is true at i if and only if, from the standpoint of i, some evaluable (ϕ & ψ)-world is better than any (ϕ & $\sim\psi$)-world. Given van Fraassen's preference ordering of values realized at worlds, we may derive a preference ordering of the worlds themselves (from the standpoint of any world i) as follows. Let the

* Hansson, 'An Analysis of Some Deontic Logics'; van Fraassen, 'The Logic of Conditional Obligation'.

‡ More precisely: of all *state descriptions*, these being maximal logically consistent sets of negated and unnegated atomic formulas. Unless the language is such that every state description is possible, he may be assuming *more* than universality by including not only state descriptions representing all possible worlds but also state descriptions representing impossible worlds.

evaluable worlds be those where values are realized; and let one evaluable world be better than another if and only if some value realized at the first is better than any realized at the second. Provided that, for any evaluable world, there is a best value among the values realized there, my truth conditions for $\phi \,\Box\!\!\rightarrow \psi$ and van Fraassen's for $O(\psi \,/\, \phi)$ will then agree.

But if at some world there is no best value, but rather an infinite ascent to better and better values, then the truth conditions may not agree. For instance, suppose that from the standpoint of some world i (1) the values are the integers, under their usual ordering, (2) some $(\phi \,\&\, \psi)$-world j is assigned the set of all integers as its set of values, (3) every other ϕ-world is assigned only finitely many integers as values, and (4) every integer is realized as a value not only at j but at some $(\phi \,\&\, \sim\!\psi)$-world as well. Then $\phi \,\Box\!\!\rightarrow \psi$ is true at i according to my truth conditions, but $O(\psi \,/\, \phi)$ is false at i according to van Fraassen's truth conditions. Thus my analysis (with $\Box\!\!\rightarrow$ as the conditional obligation operator) is equivalent to a special case of van Fraassen's.*

Van Fraassen assumes normality, in the form of a requirement that, from the standpoint of any world, some value is realized at some world. He does not assume universality: there may be worlds where no value is realized, and these are left out of consideration. He does not assume absoluteness: the values, their preference ordering, and their assignment to worlds may be completely different from the standpoint of different worlds.

5.2 'When Next' and 'When Last'

Contingent sentences have different truth values at different worlds; many sentences likewise have different truth values at different moments of time. In fact, most of our sentences depend for their truth values on a bundle of coordinates: world, time, place, and many more. We have so far been concerned with dependence on world. To avoid distraction, I have tried (with imperfect success) to keep the other dimensions of variation out of sight by sticking to examples where they may be held fixed. Let us, for a change, now isolate dependence on time, tacitly holding the world and the other coordinates fixed. Moments of time now play the same role as possible worlds hitherto. Sentences are true at them; propositions are sets of them; and systems of spheres are sets of sets of them.

* It can be shown that van Fraassen's truth conditions are equivalent to mine minus the requirement that systems of spheres are closed under nonempty intersections, and plus the normality condition.

There is one big difference between worlds and times: times come with a natural linear order. I shall assume that it *is* linear, ignoring the possibility of branches or loops, but I shall not assume anything else about it. As for relativity, let us stick to some one definite inertial frame.

I shall use the usual notation for intervals. Letting $\leqslant$ and $<$ signify the linear order of time:

$$[i, j] =^{\text{df}} \text{ the set of times } k \text{ such that } i \leqslant k \leqslant j,$$
$$[i, j) =^{\text{df}} \text{ the set of times } k \text{ such that } i \leqslant k < j,$$
$$(i, j] =^{\text{df}} \text{ the set of times } k \text{ such that } i < k \leqslant j,$$
$$(i, j) =^{\text{df}} \text{ the set of times } k \text{ such that } i < k < j$$
$$[i, \infty) =^{\text{df}} \text{ the set of times } k \text{ such that } i \leqslant k,$$
$$(i, \infty) =^{\text{df}} \text{ the set of times } k \text{ such that } i < k,$$
$$(-\infty, i] =^{\text{df}} \text{ the set of times } k \text{ such that } k \leqslant i,$$
$$(-\infty, i) =^{\text{df}} \text{ the set of times } k \text{ such that } k < i.$$

There are not really times ∞ and $-\infty$; they are a notational pretense. Note that (i, i), $[i, i)$, $(i, i]$, and any interval with the beginning (left-hand) endpoint later than the ending (right-hand) endpoint are all the empty interval.

We shall be concerned with four systems of spheres, all based on the order of time. The *future temporal system of spheres* $\$^F$ assigns to each time i the set $\$^F_i$ of all intervals $(i, j]$, (i, j), or (i, ∞) beginning at i but not including i itself; that is, all intervals beginning immediately after i and extending into the future (and the empty interval). The *past temporal system of spheres* $\$^P$ assigns to each time i the set $\$^P_i$ of all intervals $[j, i)$, (j, i), or $(-\infty, i)$ ending at i but not including i. The *semi-future temporal system of spheres* $\$^f$ assigns to each time i the set $\$^f_i$ of all intervals $[i, j]$, $[i, j)$, or $[i, \infty)$ beginning at i and including i itself, as though the present were the first moment of the future. The *semi-past temporal system of spheres* $\$^p$ assigns to each time i the set $\$^p_i$ of all intervals $[j, i]$, $(j, i]$, or $(-\infty, i]$ ending at i and including i.

The semi-future and semi-past systems of spheres are centered; they are not universal or absolute except in the trivial case that there is only one moment of time. Thus they are analogous to centered systems of spheres based on comparative similarity of worlds.

The future and past systems are more like the deontic systems. They are neither centered nor weakly centered. They are not universal, and not absolute unless there is only one moment of time. They may or may not be normal. In the future system, the last moment of time is abnormal, if there is a last moment; all other times are normal. Therefore the future system is normal if and only if time has no end. Likewise in the past system, only the first moment, if there is a first, is abnormal; so the past system is normal if and only if time has no beginning.

The linearity of time does not guarantee that Stalnaker's Assumption holds, but it does make Stalnaker's Assumption equivalent to the Limit Assumption. Both hold, for all four systems, if the order of time is *discrete*: that is, if the moments of time can be placed in order-preserving correspondence with some or all of the integers. But if time is not discrete, for instance if the order of time is like the order of the rational or real numbers, or like the order of a transfinite ordinal, then somewhere in time there is either an infinite descending sequence of earlier and earlier times, with a time *i* before all the times in the sequence, or else an infinite ascending sequence of later and later times, with a time *i* after all the times in the sequence. If we have a sentence ϕ true at all and only the times in the sequence, then either there is no first ϕ-time after *i* (if the sequence is descending) or there is no last ϕ-time before *i* (if the sequence is ascending). If so, then either the future and semi-future systems or the past and semi-past systems violate Stalnaker's Assumption and the Limit Assumption.

The Limit Assumption taken both for $\$^F$ and $\$^P$ (whence it follows for $\$^f$ and $\$^p$ as well) amounts almost to the assumption that time is discrete. But not quite: $\$^F$ and $\$^P$ might satisfy the Limit Assumption by accident in non-discrete time of a certain sort, because the propositions that violate it happen not to be expressible. If all propositions were expressible, then the assumption that time is discrete, the Limit Assumption for $\$^F$ and $\$^P$, and Stalnaker's Assumption for $\$^F$ and $\$^P$ would all three be equivalent. What does follow from the Limit Assumption for $\$^F$ and $\$^P$ both is this: for every moment of time, there is a next moment after it (unless it is the end of time) and a last moment before it (unless it is the beginning of time). To see this, apply the Limit Assumption to any tautology. A time order of this sort has the structure of several copies of the integers one after the other, perhaps with the first or last (if there is a first or last) truncated. Time is discrete if there is only *one* copy, perhaps truncated at one or both ends.

The truth conditions for our variably strict conditionals, modal operators, and comparative possibility operators are to be given as usual according to the four systems of spheres. Let us mark each operator with the superscript *F*, *P*, *f*, or *p* to indicate whether its truth conditions are given according to $\$^F$, $\$^P$, $\$^f$, or $\$^p$. Now what do our operators mean?

All of our variably strict conditionals may be regarded as alternative versions of the temporal connectives 'When next' and 'When last', with differences in detail. All of

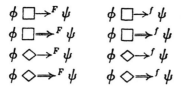

may be read as '*When it is next the case that ϕ, it will then be the case that ψ*', or more concisely as '*ψ the next time that ϕ*' or '*When next ϕ, ψ*'. The differences between them are these. (1) Those on the left pertain strictly to the future; those on the right pertain also to the present. The truth values at a time i of ϕ and ψ are irrelevant to the truth at i of the strictly future versions of 'when next'; whereas if ϕ is true already at i, then all the semi-future versions on the right are true at i if and only if ψ is true at i. (2) In the vacuous case, if ϕ is never true after i (or at i, for the semi-future versions) then $\phi \Box \rightarrow^F \psi$, $\phi \Diamond \Rightarrow^F \psi$, $\phi \Box \rightarrow^f \psi$, and $\phi \Diamond \Rightarrow^f \psi$ are vacuously true at i, whereas the other four are false. (3) Suppose that there are ϕ-times after i, but no first ϕ-time after i (or at i, for the semi-future versions). For instance, suppose ϕ holds at all times more than a year later than i, but no sooner. Suppose also that the initial ϕ-times after i are a *fuzz* of ϕ-times when ψ holds and ϕ-times when it does not: before every ϕ-time after i when ψ holds there is one when ψ does not hold, and before every ϕ-time after i when ψ does not hold there is one when it does. For instance, suppose that ψ holds a year and .1 seconds after i, a year and .01 seconds after i, a year and .001 seconds after i, and so on; and suppose ψ fails to hold a year and .2 seconds after i, a year and .02 seconds after i, a year and .002 seconds after i, and so on. Then the 'might'-like versions $\phi \Diamond \rightarrow^F \psi$, $\phi \Diamond \Rightarrow^F \psi$, $\phi \Diamond \rightarrow^f \psi$, and $\phi \Diamond \Rightarrow^f \psi$ are true at i, whereas the 'would'-like versions are false. But these differences arise only in special cases. The principal case is the case in which there is a first moment after i when ϕ holds (and ϕ does not hold already at i); and in that case, all eight alike are true at i if and only if ψ holds at that first ϕ-time after i.

Exactly the same goes, *mutatis mutandis*, for the eight mirror-image past and semi-past variably strict conditionals $\phi \Box \rightarrow^P \psi$ and so on. These may all be read as '*When it was last the case that ϕ, it was then the case that ψ*', or as '*ψ the last time that ϕ*' or as '*When last ϕ, ψ*'. The principal case is that in which there is a last moment before i when ϕ holds (and ϕ does not hold at i); then all eight versions of '*When last ϕ, ψ*' are true at i if and only if ψ holds at that last ϕ-time before i. The eight differ in respect to what happens when ϕ is true at present, what happens when ϕ has never been true, and what happens when there is a fuzz of ψ-times and $\sim\psi$-times among the last ϕ-times.

The future and past outer modalities are the usual basic operators of tense logic, sometimes written as *G, F, H*, and *P*.* $\Box^F\phi$ is true at *i* if and only if ϕ holds at all times after *i*, and may be read as '*Henceforth ϕ*'. $\Diamond^F\phi$ is true at *i* if and only if ϕ holds at some time after *i*, and may be read as '*It will be that ϕ*'. $\Box^P\phi$ is true at *i* if and only if ϕ holds at all times before *i*, and may be read as '*Hitherto ϕ*'. $\Diamond^P\phi$ is true at *i* if and only if ϕ holds at some time before *i*, and may be read as '*It has been that ϕ*'.

The semi-future and semi-past outer modalities are called the *Diodorean modalities*. (Sometimes the term 'Diodorean' is reserved for these modalities in discrete time.) $\Box^I\phi$ is true at *i* if and only if ϕ holds both at *i* and at all times after *i*, and so may be read as 'ϕ *now and henceforth*'. The others are likewise related to the corresponding future and past outer modalities. The Diodorean modalities are closer than the future and past outer modalities to sharing the properties of logical necessity and possibility, since $\Box^I\phi$ implies ϕ which in turn implies $\Diamond^I\phi$, and likewise for $\Box^P\phi$ and $\Diamond^P\phi$.

The future and past inner modalities pertain to the immediate future and the immediate past. $\boxdot^F\phi$ and $\diamondsuit^F\phi$ may both be read as '*It will be immediately that ϕ*'. If there is a next moment after *i*, then the two do not differ: both are true at *i* if and only if ϕ is true at that next moment after *i*. Both are true at *i* also if there is no next moment after *i*, but ϕ holds throughout some interval—however short—beginning at *i*. Both are false at *i* if ϕ is false throughout some such interval. But they may differ: (1) $\boxdot^F\phi$ is false and $\diamondsuit^F\phi$ is true, for any ϕ, at the end of time if such there be, and (2) if *i* is followed by a fuzz of ϕ-times and $\sim\phi$-times—if every ϕ-time after *i* is preceded by a $\sim\phi$-time after *i*, and vice versa—then at *i* $\diamondsuit^F\phi$ and $\diamondsuit^F\sim\phi$ are true but $\boxdot^F\phi$ and $\boxdot^F\sim\phi$ are false. As for the past, $\boxdot^P\phi$ and $\diamondsuit^P\phi$ may both be read as '*It has just been that ϕ*'; if there is a last moment before *i*, they are both true or false at *i* according as ϕ is true or false at that moment. Again, they may differ (1) at the beginning of time, or (2) at a time preceded by a fuzz of ϕ-times and $\sim\phi$-times.

In discrete time with no end and no beginning, however, there is no way for $\boxdot^F$ and $\diamondsuit^F$, or $\boxdot^P$ and $\diamondsuit^P$, to differ. Then the first pair can be consolidated into a single 'tomorrow' operator, and the second into a single 'yesterday' operator.‡

The conjunction $\boxdot^P\phi$ & ϕ & $\boxdot^F\phi$ is true at *i* (in any sort of time order) if and only if *i* is an interior point of an interval throughout which ϕ holds. Dana Scott has observed that a sentence with these truth conditions can be regarded as the present progressive tense of ϕ.§ A

---

* The principal account of tense logic is Arthur N. Prior, *Past, Present and Future* (Clarendon Press: Oxford, 1967).
‡ See *Past, Present and Future*: 66–70.   § 'Advice on Modal Logic'.

present progressive tense operator defined accordingly is of interest because it has the logic of an S4 necessity operator and yet cannot be interpreted, in general, as a universal quantifier over times restricted by an accessibility relation.

The semi-future and semi-past inner modalities are trivial, since $\$^f$ and $\$^p$ are centered. All of $\boxdot^f\phi$, $\diamondsuit^f\phi$, $\boxdot^p\phi$, and $\diamondsuit^p\phi$ are equivalent to ϕ.

Comparative possibility becomes comparative futurity or comparative pastness. $\phi \prec^F \psi$ may be read as '*It will next be that ϕ before it will be that ψ*', or more concisely as '*ϕ before ψ*', and it is true at i if and only if some ϕ-time after i precedes every ψ-time after i (including the case that there is a ϕ-time after i but no ψ-time after i). $\preccurlyeq^F$ and $\approx^F$ are defined as usual from $\prec^F$. Note that there are two ways for $\phi \approx^F \psi$ to be true at i; not only is it true when ϕ and ψ simultaneously begin to be true, but also when there is an initial fuzz of ϕ-times and ψ-times after i. Even $\phi \approx^F \sim\phi$ can be true by a fuzz; it is so in the same situation that makes both of $\diamondsuit^F\phi$ and $\diamondsuit^F\sim\phi$ true. As for the past, $\phi \prec^P \psi$ may be read as '*It was last that ϕ after it was that ψ*' or as '*ϕ after ψ*', and it is true at i if and only if some ϕ-time before i follows every ψ-time before i. We also have comparative semi-futurity and comparative semi-pastness. For instance $\phi \prec^f \psi$ may be read as '*It is or will be that ϕ before it is or will be that ψ*' and is true at i if and only if ψ is false at i and either ϕ is true at i or some ϕ-time after i precedes every ψ-time after i.

Given the future and past operators, the semi-future and semi-past operators are definable. All of them are definable from $\prec^f$ and $\prec^p$, for instance, and those are definable as follows.

$$\phi \prec^f \psi =^{\text{df}} \sim\psi \ \& \ (\phi \vee \phi \prec^F \psi),$$
$$\phi \prec^p \psi =^{\text{df}} \sim\psi \ \& \ (\phi \vee \phi \prec^P \psi).$$

But we cannot go the other direction. For instance, the future and past operators provide us with a sentence $\square^F\bot$ that is true precisely at the end of time, if such there be; whereas it is easy to show that no sentence built up from the semi-future and semi-past operators will distinguish between the end of time and the beginning of everlasting monotony (*monotony* being constancy of the truth values of at least all sentences that contain none of our tense operators).

We can write a sentence $\phi \prec^F \sim\psi$ (or, in terms of one of the 'when next' operators $(\phi \vee \sim\psi) \square\!\!\rightarrow^F (\phi \ \& \ \psi)$) which is true at i if and only if some ϕ-time after i precedes every $\sim\psi$-time after i; we could read this as '*Until ϕ, ψ*'. Likewise for the past: $\phi \prec^P \sim\psi$ (or the equivalent with $\square\!\!\rightarrow^P$) is true at i if and only if some ϕ-time before i follows every $\sim\psi$-time before i; we could read it as '*Since ϕ, ψ*' (with '*since*' understood as 'ever since', not as 'sometime since'). Hans Kamp has studied operators for 'since' and 'until' that give almost the same truth conditions, but not quite.* His version of '*Until ϕ, ψ*', written $U(\phi, \psi)$, is true at i if and only if some ϕ-time after i is not preceded by any $\sim\psi$-time after i; his '*Since ϕ, ψ*', written $S(\phi, \psi)$, is true at i if and only if some ϕ-time before i is not followed by any $\sim\psi$-time before i.

The small difference between my versions of 'until' and 'since' and Kamp's has a surprising consequence. Kamp proves that if the order of time is a complete linear order, then U and S suffice to define all possible tense operators; whereas my operators do not suffice because, in particular, they do not suffice to define U and S.‡ Suppose time has no end and no beginning; suppose the order of time is a complete linear order with a mixture of discrete stretches and dense stretches; and suppose monotony prevails throughout. With Kamp's operators we have sentences that vary in truth value: $U(\top, \bot)$ is true at i if and only if there is a next moment after i, hence true in the discrete stretches and false in the dense stretches. Likewise in mirror-image for $S(\top, \bot)$. But it is easily verified that any sentence built up by means of my operators has constant truth value.

In discrete time, however, my operators have the power of Kamp's; for mine can define U and S and they can define anything. For the special case of discrete time, the following definitions are correct.

$$U(\phi, \psi) =^{\mathrm{df}} \phi \leqslant^F \sim\psi \ \& \ \Diamond^F\phi,$$
$$S(\phi, \psi) =^{\mathrm{df}} \phi \leqslant^P \sim\psi \ \& \ \Diamond^P\phi.$$

Prior has noted that 'when next' and 'when last' can be used to define metric tense operators, if some periodic process is available.§ These would othewise need to be introduced into tense logic as new primitives. Suppose we can find some sentence χ that is alternately true and false, and we want to clock states of affairs by the truth and falsehood of χ. For instance χ might be '*The sun is setting*'. Now suppose I want to say that it was raining three sunsets ago. Let ϕ be '*It is raining*'. Then I say roughly this:

When last χ, (When last χ, (When last χ, ϕ)).

* '*On Tense Logic and the Theory of Order*' (Ph.D. dissertation, 1968, University of California at Los Angeles).

‡ The order is *complete* unless there are two nonempty, non-overlapping intervals such that the first has no last moment, the second has no first moment, and no moments fall between the two intervals. The order of the integers or of the real numbers is complete, but that of the rational numbers is not. A *tense operator*, in general, is any operator whose truth conditions can be formulated in terms of nothing but truth of sentences at times, the order of times, quantification over times, and truth-functional connectives.

§ *Past, Present and Future*: 106–112.

That will not quite work as it stands, however, since it takes time for the sun to set. We will not get different sunsets, but earlier and earlier times in the most recent one. What we need is a clock sentence true at one and only one time in each sunset—say, at the beginning. If a sunset has a first moment, χ & $\boxdot^P \sim \chi$ will do; if it is preceded by a last moment of non-sunset, $\sim\chi$ & $\diamondsuit^F\chi$ will do; if we think that there is either a first moment of sunset or a last moment of non-sunset but not both, and we do not know which, then we may take the disjunction. Given our corrected clock sentence, if we can find one, we proceed as before. It does not much matter whether we use $\Box\!\!\rightarrow^P$, $\diamondsuit\!\!\rightarrow^P$, $\Box\!\!\rightarrow^P$, or $\diamondsuit\!\!\rightarrow^P$ as our 'when last'; of course the semi-past ones will not work, since we will get stuck at the most recent time when the clock sentence was true. Suppose we choose $\Box\!\!\rightarrow^P$; then our metric sentence is

$$(\chi \;\Box\!\!\rightarrow^P (\chi \;\Box\!\!\rightarrow^P (\chi \;\Box\!\!\rightarrow^P \phi)))$$

where χ is our corrected clock sentence '*The sun is beginning to set*'.

We might also wish to clock things that do not occur exactly at the beginning of a sunset, and we can do that too. Suppose I want to say that it was raining some time during the day before yesterday. (Let each new day begin at the beginning of sunset on the previous night.) The sentence is

$$(\chi \;\Box\!\!\rightarrow^P (\chi \;\Box\!\!\rightarrow^P (\phi <^P \chi))).$$

Or suppose I want to say that it was raining all of the day before yesterday:

$$(\chi \;\Box\!\!\rightarrow^P (\chi \;\Box\!\!\rightarrow^P (\chi \leqslant^P \sim\phi))).$$

Prior defines a 'when last' operator for this use. It is none of mine; rather it is defined by means of Kamp's S:

When last ϕ, ψ $=^{\mathrm{df}} S(\phi$ & $\psi, \sim\phi)$.

This Prior-Kamp 'when last' can be approximated from my operators, just as Kamp's U and S can; and I think that mine serve equally well the purpose for which Prior introduced it. But I cannot define it. For *When last* T, T is equivalent to $S(\mathsf{T}, \bot)$, and we have already seen that $S(\mathsf{T}, \bot)$ cannot be defined from my tense operators.

5.3 Contextually Definite Descriptions

Still other coordinates may play the role of worlds or times. Let us think of sentences as being true or false at *things*, with the world and time and everything else tacitly held fixed. Propositions (though it is strange now to call them that) are sets of things, and systems of spheres are sets of sets of things.

What sort of sentence can be assessed for truth at a thing? A first person sentence, for instance. '*Cogito*' is true at me, and at any other thing that thinks. '*Sum*' is true at everything. '*I am a rock*' is true at any rock. '*I am even*' is true at 948, and '*I am prime*' at 2311. Roughly, ϕ is true at i if and only if ϕ is truly assertable by i; but that it is not quite right, because '*I cannot talk*' is true at anything that cannot talk. With the first person sentences in mind, we call sentences that can be assessed for truth at things *egocentric* sentences. The study of them is Prior's 'egocentric logic'.*

There is a problem, at least in English, with the first person reading of egocentric sentences. If we prefix to one of them an operator '*Everything is such that ____*', '*The Anighito meteorite is such that ____*', or the like, nothing happens. '*The Anighito meteorite is such that I am a rock*' is false at me because I am not a rock, even though the Anighito meteorite is a rock. '*I*' is like the present tense marked by '*now*', and unlike the unmarked present tense, in that we cannot shift its reference by putting it in the scope of a suitable operator.‡ Unless we pretend that '*I*' is shiftable, we have no non-trivial egocentric operators.

Prior reads egocentric sentences as gerunds. '*Thinking*' is an egocentric sentence true at me. '*Being such that being a rock is true of the Anighito meteorite*' is true at me, so '*Being such that ____ is true of the Anighito meteorite*' is a non-trivial shifting operator. But the gerunds are clumsy, so I would rather introduce into the language a shiftable variant of '*I*'. Write this as '*x*'. Now '*x is thinking*' is an egocentric sentence true at me, or anything else that is thinking. If '*x*' resembles a free variable, that is all to the good. It is a free variable, approached from a new direction. Egocentric logic is predicate logic with only one variable. Because there is only one variable, we can give truth conditions in a special way, confining our attention to the complete egocentric sentences and disregarding the meanings of the parts— '*x*' and the predicate, or whatever—that combine to form the smallest sentences. If we apply the customary way of disambiguating a mixture of free and bound occurrences of '*x*'—call it a variable or a shiftable version of '*I*' as you like—the egocentric sentence '*x is such that (the Anighito meteorite is an x such that x is a rock)*' is true at me, or anything else, because the Anighito meteorite is a rock; so we have a non-trivial shifting operator, as intended.

Now consider a system of spheres $ based on comparative salience of

* Arthur N. Prior, 'Egocentric Logic', *Noûs* **2** (1968): 191–207.
‡ See Hans Kamp, 'Formal Properties of "Now"'. For example, '*It will be the case in 2100 A.D. that there are men on Mars*' is probably true, whereas '*It will be the case in 2100 A.D. that there are men on Mars now*' contains an idle shifting operator, and is certainly false.

things. When i is a thing with a point of view—say, a person or an animal—then some things are more salient than others from the point of view of i. They loom larger in his mental life; they are more important to him; they come more readily to the center of his attention. Right now, as I sit writing this, my typewriter is more salient to me than my left shoe; that is more salient than the kitchen clock in the house where I grew up; that is more salient than the fourteenth brick from the right in the seventh row from the top in the garden wall outside my window; but all of these are salient to me to some extent, in contrast to the countless things that are outside my ken altogether. (I am speaking of how salient these things were *before* I started to think up examples of things that were not very salient; comparative salience is much shiftier even than comparative similarity.)

A sphere around i is to be any set of things in the ken of i such that all those in the set are more salient to i than any of those outside. Assuming that comparative salience orderings have the definitive properties of weak orderings, then these sets do indeed comprise a system of spheres $.

The system $ clearly does not satisfy any of the special conditions we have considered. It is not normal: there are no differences in comparative salience from the point of view of a rock, so there are no nonempty spheres around the rock. To be normal is to have some propensity to pay attention to something. Since $ is not normal, it is not centered or weakly centered. (It is not even *normally centered*, or *normally weakly centered*: that is, it is not the case that whenever i is normal, $_i$ is centered or weakly centered on i. We are not all such egotists; for at least some normal i, there is something even more salient to i than he is to himself.) The system $ is not universal (or normally universal) since for most things i there is something outside the ken of i. It is not absolute, since different ones of us pay attention to different things.

We may give the truth conditions of our operators as usual according to this system of spheres. The comparative possibility operators and inner modalities turn out to be nothing of interest. The outer modalities $\square$ and $\diamond$ are universal and existential quantifiers, restricted to the things one knows of. The variable of quantification is superfluous, of course, since we only have one variable. $\square\phi$ is true at i if and only if ϕ is true at everything in the ken of i; $\diamond\phi$ is true at i if and only if ϕ is true at something in the ken of i. We may read them as '*For everything known, ϕ*' and '*For something known, ϕ*', where 'known' makes the sentence subjective. Or if we prefer Prior's gerund readings, we may read them as '*Knowing only things of which ϕ holds*' and '*Knowing something of which ϕ holds*', where ϕ is itself a gerund.

The real object of the exercise, however, is to show that the variably strict egocentric conditional $\Box\!\!\rightarrow$ will serve as a connective of *contextually definite description*. Suppose we read $\phi \;\Box\!\!\rightarrow\; \psi$ as '*The x such that ϕ is such that ψ*', or some less clumsy paraphrase thereof. For instance, we may read

> *x is a pig* $\Box\!\!\rightarrow$ *x is grunting*

as '*The pig is grunting*'. I claim that this will give the correct truth conditions for such a sentence if we take 'the' not as the usual logicians' definite description operator (under any of the various treatments of improper descriptions) but in a different sense, no less familiar in ordinary language than the logicians' sense.

It is nothing special to parse 'the' as a connective rather than a term-maker. The same can advantageously be done for the logicians' definite description operator. Rather than writing

$$\psi(\imath x \phi_x)$$

as usual—this being the result of substituting $\imath x \phi_x$ for free occurrences of x throughout ψ_x—we can write something like

$$\imath x(\phi_x, \psi_x)$$

with the same meaning. (In our present one-variable language, there is no need for the explicit occurrences of 'x'.) This connective notation captures scope distinctions automatically, with no special scope marker. Further, it practices what Russell preached: that the seeming denoting term $\imath x \phi_x$ is not really a meaningful constituent of the sentence.*

Contextually definite descriptions, as I shall call them, are definite descriptions 'the so-and-so' suitable for use when it is perfectly well understood that there exist many different so-and-so's, not just one. It makes nonsense of them to take them as logicians' definite descriptions. Suppose I am walking past a piggery. I say to myself: '*The pig is grunting*', since my attention is centered on a certain conspicuously grunting pig. I do not mean that there is exactly one pig in existence, and that it is grunting. I know better than that. Nor do I mean that some pig somewhere, or every pig there is, is grunting. Still less do I mean that the null entity—something chosen arbitrarily to serve as an artificial denotation for all improper definite descriptions—is grunting. What I mean is more like this: among the things that have captured my attention just now there is exactly one pig, and it is grunting. But that is not quite right. If there are several pigs around, it seems that I might be able to assert all of these sentences together, and with them their negated opposites.

See Richard Sharvy, 'Things,' *Monist* 53 (1969): 489.

The pig is grunting.
The pig with floppy ears is not grunting.
The spotted pig with floppy ears is grunting.

Let S be a set of 'things that have captured my attention just now'. If S contains exactly one pig, and it is grunting, then it cannot also be that S contains exactly one pig with floppy ears, which is not grunting. If, on the other hand, S does contain exactly one pig with floppy ears, and it is not grunting, then it cannot be that S contains a grunting pig to make the first sentence true. Moreover, it cannot be that S contains exactly one spotted pig with floppy ears, which is grunting, to make the third sentence true.

Here we have another of our alternating sequences; and we know by now that such sequences are the mark of a variably strict conditional. We should not take a fixed set of the things that fall within a certain fixed degree of salience. Instead we should expand the set of things under consideration, starting with the most salient things and working outward until we have expanded enough to admit something that falls under the description in question. If the most salient pig does not have floppy ears, we must expand farther to reach a pig with floppy ears than to reach a pig; and if the most salient pig with floppy ears is not spotted, then we must expand farther still to admit a spotted pig with floppy ears.

That is what happens if we take the contextually definite description operator to be the variably strict egocentric conditional $\Box\!\!\rightarrow$. In general, $\phi \Box\!\!\rightarrow \psi$ is true at i if and only if there is some ϕ-permitting sphere based on comparative salience from the point of view of i, throughout which ψ is true at every ϕ-thing. If there is one ϕ-thing most salient to i, then $\phi \Box\!\!\rightarrow \psi$ is true at i if and only if ψ is true at that thing.

Suppose that only a few pigs are in my ken: the nine in the piggery I am walking past, and perhaps two or three others that I have met elsewhere. (I know *that* there are other pigs; but that is not to say that there are other particular pigs I know *of.*) It may be safe to assume that no two of these pigs are precisely equal in salience to me. Then the sentences

x is a pig $\Box\!\!\rightarrow$ *x is grunting*
x is a pig & x has floppy ears. $\Box\!\!\rightarrow$ *~x is grunting*
x is a pig & x has floppy ears & x is spotted. $\Box\!\!\rightarrow$ *x is grunting*

may all be true (at me) together. The first because the most salient of all the pigs in my ken is grunting; the second because the most salient pig with floppy ears is not; the third because the most salient spotted pig with floppy ears is. So $\Box\!\!\rightarrow$ works properly as the contextually definite description operator.

$\Box\!\!\rightarrow$, $\Diamond\!\!\rightarrow$, and $\Diamond\!\!\rightarrow$ would work as well in this case, but would go wrong in others. There are no aardvarks in my ken, so it is clear that '*The aardvark is grunting*' ought not to be true at me. That eliminates $\Box\!\!\rightarrow$ and $\Diamond\!\!\rightarrow$, since $\phi\,\Box\!\!\rightarrow\psi$ and $\phi\,\Diamond\!\!\Rightarrow\psi$ are true at i if there is no ϕ-thing in i's ken. '*The pig is grunting*' and '*The pig is not grunting*' sound inconsistent. They ought never to be true together at me, not even if there are two equally salient most salient pigs in my ken, one grunting and one not. That eliminates $\Diamond\!\!\rightarrow$ and (again) $\Diamond\!\!\Rightarrow$, since $\phi\,\Diamond\!\!\rightarrow\psi$ and $\phi\,\Diamond\!\!\Rightarrow\psi$ are true at i if ψ is true at even one most salient ϕ-thing in i's ken, and $\phi\,\Diamond\!\!\rightarrow\sim\psi$ and $\phi\,\Diamond\!\!\Rightarrow\sim\psi$ are true at i as well if $\sim\psi$ is true at another one.

Using $\Box\!\!\Rightarrow$, as I prefer, what happens when there are two equally salient most salient pigs? If neither is grunting, or one but not the other, then '*x is a pig* $\Box\!\!\Rightarrow$ *x is grunting*' is false, and that seems correct. It is true if both are grunting, and that seems more questionable. Hasn't a presupposition of uniqueness been violated? Granted; '*The pig is grunting*' is only appropriate under the presupposition (roughly speaking) that there is a unique most salient pig, just as '*The root of* $z^3 - 17z^2 - 1 = 0$ *is negative*' (a specimen of the logicians' 'the', presumably) is appropriate only under the presupposition that the equation has a unique solution. But I have rejected the view that presupposition failure must always produce untruth; and I do not think it does so in this case.

Consider that comparative salience is shifty in the extreme. Nothing is easier than to break the tie; and if it were broken *either way* the sentence would be true. Recognizing the inevitable vagueness of comparative salience, we see that we almost never will simply have a tie. What we will have is indeterminacy between many reasonable ways to resolve the vagueness. Some will break the tie in favor of one pig, some in favor of the other, and some will land exactly on the border and make a tie. Borders have zero thickness, so presumably most reasonable resolutions break the tie one way or the other and thereby make the sentence true. Then what would be the point of having untruth at the border? It would have negligible effect on what we really care about: truth under most, many, or few reasonable resolutions of vagueness.*

The presupposition carried by '*The pig is grunting*' is not exactly a uniqueness presupposition, if I am right that we can always expect uniqueness one way or another under most reasonable resolutions of vagueness. It is better called a presupposition of determinate uniqueness: that most reasonable resolutions will yield the *same* unique most salient pig. That is so if one pig is well ahead of the rest in salience; if he is

---

* A parallel proposal to make $\imath x(\phi_x, \psi_x)$ true when there are two or more ϕ-things, while granting that a presupposition has been violated, could not be defended in a parallel way by considerations about vagueness.

enough ahead on one resolution of vagueness, he probably will be ahead on the others too.

Finally, it is interesting to note a special case. Imagine that I am keenly interested in the natural numbers; so fanatically so that all of them are in my ken and nothing else is. Further, I pay most attention to the small ones: 1 is more salient than 2, 2 more than 3, and so on throughout. Then our contextually definite description operator $\Box\!\!\!\rightarrow$ is essentially the familiar μ-operator of recursion theory.

6. Logics

6.1 *Completeness Results*

Investigations in possible-world semantics traditionally culminate in completeness proofs. It is shown that the sentences of a specified language that must be true according to the proposed semantic analysis are exactly the theorems of a specified deductive system called a 'logic of' the concept under analysis. I am not sure how much completeness proofs really add to our understanding, but I here provide them for those readers who do find them helpful and for those—like myself—who find them interesting in their own right. Readers of other persuasions have no reason to read on, and are warned that this final chapter is more technical than the rest.

Our formal language has as its vocabulary (1) countably many sentence letters; (2) the sentential constants $\top$ and $\bot$; (3) the connectives $\sim$, &, $\vee$, $\supset$, and $\equiv$; (4) our special operators $\leqslant$, $<$, $\approx$, $\diamondsuit$, $\square$, $\lozenge$, $\boxdot$, $\square\!\!\rightarrow$, $\diamondsuit\!\!\rightarrow$, $\square\!\!\rightarrow$, and $\diamondsuit\!\!\rightarrow$; and (5) punctuation. The sentences comprise the smallest superset of the sentence letters and sentential constants that is closed under compounding by means of the connectives and operators (with the aid of suitable punctuation, which we can leave to take care of itself).

An *interpretation* of this language, *over* a nonempty set I and *based on* a system of spheres \$ over I, is a function $[\![\ ]\!]$ mapping all sentences of the language onto the subsets of I in such a way that the following conditions hold for all sentences ϕ and ψ.

(Let $A \bullet B =^{\mathrm{df}} A \cap B \neq \Lambda$; that is, A overlaps B.)

(1) $[\![\top]\!] = I$
(2) $[\![\bot]\!] = \Lambda$
(3) $[\![\sim\!\phi]\!] = I - [\![\phi]\!]$
(4) $[\![\phi\ \&\ \psi]\!] = [\![\phi]\!] \cap [\![\psi]\!]$
(5) $[\![\phi \vee \psi]\!] = [\![\phi]\!] \cup [\![\psi]\!]$
(6) $[\![\phi \supset \psi]\!] = (I - [\![\phi]\!]) \cup [\![\psi]\!]$

$(7) \quad [\![\phi \equiv \psi]\!] = ([\![\phi]\!] \cap [\![\psi]\!]) \cup ((I - [\![\phi]\!]) \cap (I - [\![\psi]\!]))$

$(8) \quad [\![\phi \leqslant \psi]\!] = \{i \in I: \forall S \in \$_i([\![\psi]\!] \cdot S \supset [\![\phi]\!] \cdot S)\}$

$(9) \quad [\![\phi < \psi]\!] = \{i \in I: \exists S \in \$_i([\![\phi]\!] \cdot S \ \& \ \sim[\![\psi]\!] \cdot S)\}$

$(10) \quad [\![\phi \approx \psi]\!] = \{i \in I: \forall S \in \$_i([\![\phi]\!] \cdot S \equiv [\![\psi]\!] \cdot S)\}$

$(11) \quad [\![\Diamond\phi]\!] = \{i \in I: [\![\phi]\!] \cdot \bigcup\$_i\}$

$(12) \quad [\![\Box\phi]\!] = \{i \in I: \bigcup\$_i \subseteq [\![\phi]\!]\}$

$(13) \quad [\![\boxdot\phi]\!] = \{i \in I: \forall S \in \$_i(S \neq \Lambda \supset [\![\phi]\!] \cdot S)\}$

$(14) \quad [\![\boxdot\phi]\!] = \{i \in I: \exists S \in \$_i(S \neq \Lambda \ \& \ S \subseteq [\![\phi]\!])\}$

$(15) \quad [\![\phi\Box\!\!\rightarrow \psi]\!] = \{i \in I: \exists S \in \$_i(\Lambda \neq [\![\phi]\!] \cap S \subseteq [\![\psi]\!])\}$

$(16) \quad [\![\phi\Diamond\!\!\rightarrow \psi]\!] = \{i \in I: \forall S \in \$_i([\![\phi]\!] \cdot S \supset [\![\phi]\!] \cap [\![\psi]\!] \cdot S)\}$

$(17) \quad [\![\phi\Box\!\!\rightarrow \psi]\!] = \{i \in I: [\![\phi]\!] \cdot \bigcup\$_i \supset \exists S \in \$_i(\Lambda \neq [\![\phi]\!] \cap S \subseteq [\![\psi]\!])\}$

$(18) \quad [\![\phi\Diamond\!\!\rightarrow \psi]\!] = \{i \in I: [\![\phi]\!] \cdot \bigcup\$_i \ \& \ \forall S \in \$_i([\![\phi]\!] \cdot S \supset [\![\phi]\!] \cap [\![\psi]\!] \cdot S)\}$

Call I the *index set* of the interpretation, and call its members *indices*.
Call $[\![\phi]\!]$ the *proposition* expressed by ϕ *(under* the interpretation). ϕ is
true at index i *(under* the interpretation) if and only if i is in $[\![\phi]\!]$. Thus
the equations above give truth conditions for compound sentences by
means of an algebra of propositions, as discussed in Section 2.2. ϕ is
valid (under the interpretation) if and only if $[\![\phi]\!] = I$, so that ϕ is true
at every index. A set of sentences or sentence schema is *valid (under* the
interpretation) if and only if all its members or instances are.

We are concerned now only with the formal aspects of my analyses of
comparative possibility, inner and outer modalities, and variably strict
conditionals. Therefore we leave it open what the index set I is; it can be
the set of worlds, the set of times, the set of things, or any other nonempty set whatever. We leave it open likewise whether the system of
spheres $\$$ is based on comparative similarity, on comparative goodness,
on the order of time, on comparative salience, on something else, or on
nothing in particular. We require only that it have the formal properties
of a system of spheres; that is, it must assign to each index i in I a set $\$_i$ of
subsets of I such that (1) $\$_i$ is nested, (2) $\$_i$ is closed under unions, and
(3) $\$_i$ is closed under (nonempty) intersections.*

A sentence, set of sentences, or sentence schema is *valid unconditionally* if and only if it is valid under every interpretation (of the kind
specified above). It is *valid under* a given combination of conditions if

---

* Closure under unions and intersections is inessential. It is easily seen that all
my soundness results would hold even if these closure requirements were dropped;
as of course would the completeness results, since we never could get more valid
sentences by relaxing constraints on interpretations. In my 'Completeness and
Decidability of Three Logics of Counterfactual Conditionals' these closure requirements on systems of spheres were not imposed.

and only if it is valid under every interpretation based on a system of spheres that satisfies the conditions. We shall consider conditions of two sorts: conditions on the system of spheres by itself, and conditions on the system of spheres in relation to an interpretation based on it.

We shall be concerned in particular with the conditions listed below. We have met most of them before.

(N) \$ is *normal* if and only if, for each i in I, $\bigcup \$_i$ is nonempty.

(T) \$ is *totally reflexive* if and only if, for each i in I, i belongs to $\bigcup \$_i$.

(W) \$ is *weakly centered* if and only if, for each i in I, i belongs to every nonempty member of $\$_i$, and there is at least one nonempty member of $\$_i$.

(C) \$ is *centered* if and only if, for each i in I, $\{i\}$ belongs to $\$_i$.

(These four conditions are increasingly strong. (C) implies (W), (W) implies (T), (T) implies (N); but the converse implications do not hold.)

(L) \$ satisfies the *Limit Assumption* in relation to $[\![\ ]\!]$ if and only if, for any ϕ, if $[\![\phi]\!]$ overlaps $\bigcup \$_i$ there is some smallest member of $\$_i$ that overlaps $[\![\phi]\!]$.

(S) \$ satisfies *Stalnaker's Assumption* in relation to $[\![\ ]\!]$ if and only if, for any ϕ, if $[\![\phi]\!]$ overlaps $\bigcup \$_i$ there is some member of $\$_i$ whose intersection with $[\![\phi]\!]$ contains exactly one index.

((S) implies (L), but not conversely. (S) and (W) together imply (C).)

(U-) \$ is *locally uniform* if and only if, for each i in I and j in $\bigcup \$_i$, $\bigcup \$_i$ and $\bigcup \$_j$ are the same.

(U) \$ is *uniform* if and only if, for each i and j in I, $\bigcup \$_i$ and $\bigcup \$_j$ are the same.

(A-) \$ is *locally absolute* if and only if, for each i in I and j in $\bigcup \$_i$, $\$_i$ and $\$_j$ are the same.

(A) \$ is *absolute* if and only if, for each i and j in I, $\$_i$ and $\$_j$ are the same.

((U) implies (U-) but not conversely; (A) implies (A-) but not conversely; (A) implies (U) but not conversely.)

(UT) \$ is *universal* if and only if, for each i in I, $\bigcup \$_i$ is I.

((UT) is equivalent to the combination of (T) and (U). It is for the sake of this combination that the hitherto unmentioned conditions (T) and (U) have been listed.)

(WA) \$ is *weakly trivial* if and only if, for each i in I, I is the only nonempty member of $\$_i$.

(CA) \$ is *trivial* if and only if I contains exactly one member i, and $\$_i$ contains both Λ and $\{i\}$.

((WA) is equivalent to the combination of (W) and (A); (CA) is equivalent to the combination of (C) and (A). (CA) implies (WA), but not conversely. (CA) implies (S), and (WA) implies (L), in relation to any interpretation based on $. Note that (CA) implies *all* the listed conditions.)

We can associate *characteristic axioms* (or axiom schemata, or pairs of axiom schemata) with the listed conditions, as follows. In all cases, the axioms are valid under the corresponding conditions. It follows that combinations of the axioms also are valid under the corresponding combinations of conditions.

Conditions		*Axioms*
(N)	Normality	N: $\top \prec \bot$
(T)	Total reflexivity	T: $\Box \phi \supset \phi$
(W)	Weak centering	W: $\Box \phi \lor \boxdot \phi . \supset \phi$
(C)	Centering	C: $\Diamond \phi \supset \phi$
(L)	Limit Assumption	(none)
(S)	Stalnaker's Assumption . . .	S: $(\phi \ \& \ \psi) \approx (\phi \ \& \ {\sim}\psi) \supset {\sim}\Diamond \phi$
(U-)	Local uniformity	U: $\begin{cases} \Diamond \phi \supset \Box \Diamond \phi \\ \Box \phi \supset \Box \Box \phi \end{cases}$
(U)	Uniformity	
(A-)	Local absoluteness	A: $\begin{cases} \phi \preccurlyeq \psi \supset \Box (\phi \preccurlyeq \psi) \\ \phi \prec \psi \supset \Box (\phi \prec \psi) \end{cases}$
(A)	Absoluteness	
(UT)	Universality	U and T
(WA)	Weak triviality	W and A; or $\phi \preccurlyeq \psi \equiv . \Diamond \psi \supset \Diamond \phi$
(CA)	Triviality	C and A; or $\phi \preccurlyeq \psi \equiv . \psi \supset \phi$

There is no special characteristic axiom corresponding to the Limit Assumption. We can therefore say that if any combination of axioms corresponds to a combination of conditions without the Limit Assumption, then the same combination of axioms corresponds also to that combination of conditions with the Limit Assumption added.

The characteristic axiom corresponding to weak triviality provides a definition of $\preccurlyeq$, and thence of all our other operators, by means of outer modalities and truth functions. Under an interpretation based on a weakly trivial system of spheres, moreover, the outer modalities are simply the logical modalities. Our language, so interpreted, therefore collapses into the simplest sort of modal logic. The case of triviality is still worse: the characteristic axiom defines $\preccurlyeq$ from truth functions alone, so that our language collapses into ordinary truth-functional logic.

Local uniformity and uniformity have the same pair of characteristic axioms; as do local absoluteness and absoluteness. Indeed, so far as validity is concerned, there is no difference between local uniformity and uniformity, or between local absoluteness and absoluteness. Suppose two combinations of our conditions are alike except that uniformity or absoluteness in the first is replaced by local uniformity or local absoluteness in the second. Then exactly the same sentences are valid under both. Proof: The first is a special case of the second, so whatever is valid under the second is valid under the first. Conversely, suppose ϕ is valid under the first; and let $[\![\ ]\!]$ be any interpretation, with index set I, based on a system of spheres $\$$ satisfying the second. For any i in I, let I^i be $\{i\} \cup \bigcup \$_i$, let $[\![\psi]\!]^i$ be $[\![\psi]\!] \cap I^i$ for any ψ, and let $\$^i$ be $\$$ restricted to I^i. It is easily verified, given that $\$$ is at least locally uniform, that each $[\![\ ]\!]^i$ is an interpretation over I^i based on $\$^i$; that if $\$$ is normal, totally reflexive, weakly centered, or centered then so is each $\$^i$; that if $\$$ satisfies the Limit Assumption or Stalnaker's Assumption in relation to $[\![\ ]\!]$ then so does each $\$^i$ in relation to $[\![\ ]\!]^i$; and that if $\$$ is locally uniform or locally absolute then each $\$^i$ is uniform or absolute. We have eliminated the local quality of the uniformity or absoluteness by cutting away part of the index set. By hypothesis, ϕ is valid under each $[\![\ ]\!]^i$. But each of them gives the same truth values within its index set as the original interpretation, and the index sets cover I; so ϕ is valid also under $[\![\ ]\!]$. Q.E.D.

Thanks to this replacement result, we can prove theorems about validity under the local versions of uniformity or absoluteness, and they will carry over to uniformity or absoluteness proper. That is the only point of introducing local uniformity and absoluteness; they are of no interest in themselves.

Our task now is to specify, by means of axiomatized deductive systems, the sets of sentences valid under various combinations of our listed conditions. I call these systems *V-logics*—'*V*' stands for 'variable strictness'. We may identify the system with the set of its theorems (so we can have different axiomatizations for one *V*-logic, not different *V*-logics with the same theorems). That gives us an implication relation as well: ϕ *implies* ψ *in* a given system if and only if $\phi \supset \psi$ is a theorem. For sets of premises: Φ *implies* ψ if and only if some finite conjunction of members of the premise-set Φ implies ψ in the previous sense. A *V*-logic is *sound for* a combination of conditions if and only if its theorems are valid under those conditions; *complete for* a combination of conditions if and only if every sentence valid under those conditions is a theorem. We want systems that are both sound and complete for various combinations of conditions, so that the theorems are exactly the sentences valid under the combination of conditions.

The *V*-logics will be specified by means of axioms (given often by schemata) and rules of inference. The system *generated* by such an axiomatization has as theorems the sentences obtainable from the axioms by repeated application of the rules. More precisely: it is the smallest superset of the axioms that is closed under the rules. Note that since the rules are used only to go from theorems to theorems—not to draw conclusions from premises that are not theorems—we need not require them to preserve truth, but only validity.

Let us specify the V-logics by axiomatizations as follows.

Rules: (1) *Modus Ponens,*
 (2) *Rule for Comparative Possibility: for any* $n \geqslant 1$,

$$\frac{\vdash \phi \supset (\psi_1 \vee \ldots \vee \psi_n)}{\vdash (\psi_1 \leqslant \phi) \vee \ldots \vee (\psi_n \leqslant \phi)};$$

Axioms: (1) *Truth-functional tautologies,*
 (2) *Definitions of operators,*
 (3) **Trans:** $((\phi \leqslant \psi) \,\&\, (\psi \leqslant \chi)) \supset (\phi \leqslant \chi),$
 (4) **Connex:** $(\phi \leqslant \psi) \vee (\psi \leqslant \phi),$
 (5) *Characteristic axioms for conditions: some combination (zero or more) of* **N, T, W, C, S, U, A.**

Given any combination of our conditions, we have an axiomatization of this form, with the combination of characteristic axioms that corresponds to the given combination of conditions. The V-logic generated thereby also will be said to *correspond* to the combination of conditions, and conversely. We name this logic by writing 'V' followed by the list of characteristic axioms. Example: corresponding to the combination of centering and uniformity, we have the V-logic **VCU** generated by the rules, the basic axioms (1)–(4), and the characteristic axioms **C** and **U** corresponding, respectively, to centering and uniformity. A special case: the basic V-logic, **V**, is generated by the rules and basic axioms alone; there are no characteristic axioms, and the logic corresponds to the empty combination of conditions.

By taking *Modus Ponens* as a rule and all tautologies as axioms, we provide for all of ordinary truth-functional logic: not only the truth-functional theorems, but also the truth-functional consequences of other theorems. Inclusion of the tautologies makes there be infinitely many axioms, as does the fact that most of the listed axioms are really axiom schemata, but no harm is done since the set of axioms remains decidable. Having chosen $\leqslant$ as primitive for purposes of axiomatization—it gives more perspicuous axioms than $\Box\!\!\rightarrow$, and easier proofs—we need to reintroduce our other ten operators by a sequence of definitions starting from $\leqslant$; the needed definitions are found in Section 2.5. (Replace ' $=^{\mathrm{df}}$ ' by ' $\equiv$ ' throughout, so that the definitions become object-language schemata.) The Rule for Comparative Possibility combines two intuitive principles. One is that a premise cannot be more possible than a conclusion it implies; the other is that a (finite) disjunction cannot be more possible than all of its disjuncts.* **Trans** and **Connex** express the fact that comparative possibility is a weak ordering.

The *V*-logics are sound for their corresponding combinations of conditions. Proof: Each characteristic axiom is valid under its corresponding condition, and hence under any combination that includes that condition. The tautologies, the definitions, **Trans**, and **Connex** are valid unconditionally, and hence under any combination of conditions. *Modus Ponens* preserves truth, and therefore preserves validity under any combination of conditions. The Rule for Comparative Possibility, although it does not preserve truth in general, also preserves validity under any combination of conditions. So, for any combination of conditions, the axioms for the corresponding *V*-logic are valid, and the rules preserve validity, under that combination of conditions. Therefore the theorems also are valid under it.

There are interpretations based on systems of spheres that satisfy any combination of our conditions; most simply, there are interpretations based on trivial systems of spheres, and these satisfy all the conditions at once. Hence our soundness results are not vacuous. Therefore the *V*-logics are *consistent*: none of them has ⊥ as a theorem. For if one did, then by its non-vacuous soundness, ⊥ would be valid under some interpretation; which is impossible.

It remains to show that the *V*-logics are complete, as well as sound, for their corresponding combinations of conditions. To prove this, I adapt a standard method for proving completeness results in modal logic.‡

A set Σ of sentences is *consistent* in a given deductive system if and only if it does not imply ⊥; it is *consistent with* a sentence φ if and only if the union Σ ∪ {φ} is consistent. A *maximal consistent* set of sentences

---

* If we prefer, we can embody the first principle in a simpler rule, and the second in another axiom, as follows:

$$\frac{\vdash \phi \supset \psi}{\vdash \psi \leqslant \phi} \quad \text{and} \quad (\phi \leqslant (\phi \lor \psi)) \lor (\psi \leqslant (\phi \lor \psi)).$$

Together, these can replace the Rule for Comparative Possibility.

‡ I rely principally on work of John Lemmon and Dana Scott; see E. J. Lemmon, *An Introduction to Modal Logic* (Blackwell: Oxford, 1977), Sections 2 and 4. Similar methods were developed independently in David Makinson, 'On Some Completeness Theorems in Modal Logic', *Zeitschrift für mathematische Logik und Grundlagen der Mathematik* **12** (1966): 379–384. A third source is David Kaplan, review of Saul Kripke, 'Semantical Analysis of Modal Logic I', *Journal of Symbolic Logic* **31** (1966): 120–122.

is one that is consistent, but not consistent with any sentence that is not already in it. All our V-logics satisfy *Lindenbaum's Lemma*: any consistent set of sentences can be extended to a maximal consistent set. Proof: the countably many sentences in our language can all be arranged in a sequence $\phi_1, \phi_2, \ldots$. Given any consistent set of sentences Σ_0, we define a parallel sequence of sets of sentences: for each $n > 0$, if Σ_{n-1} is consistent with ϕ_n, let $\Sigma_n = \Sigma_{n-1} \cup \{\phi_n\}$; if not, let $\Sigma_n = \Sigma_{n-1}$. Σ_0 is consistent by hypothesis, and an inconsistent Σ_n never can follow a consistent Σ_{n-1}, so every set in the sequence is consistent. Let Σ_∞ be the union of all the sets in the sequence. Σ_∞ is consistent; if not, a finite subset of Σ_∞ implies $\bot$, but that finite subset must already be included in some Σ_n, contradicting the consistency of each Σ_n. Σ_∞ is maximal consistent; if not, it is consistent with some sentence that does not belong to it, say ϕ_n. Either Σ_{n-1} is consistent with ϕ_n, contradicting the absence of ϕ_n from Σ_∞, or Σ_{n-1} is inconsistent with ϕ_n, contradicting the consistency of Σ_∞ with ϕ_n. Finally, Σ_∞ includes Σ_0. Q.E.D.

If a logic is valid under a certain interpretation, then whenever Σ is the set of all sentences true together at some index under the interpretation, Σ is a maximal consistent set. The converse is not ordinarily true; but we shall now consider special interpretations such that *every* maximal consistent set is the set of all sentences true together at some index.

We define the *canonical interpretation* for any V-logic to be the function $[\![\ ]\!]$ that assigns to any sentence ϕ the set $[\![\phi]\!]$ of all maximal consistent sets having ϕ as a member. That is, letting I be the set of all sets of sentences that are maximal consistent in the given V-logic, $[\![\phi]\!] =^{\mathrm{df}} \{i \in I: \phi \in i\}$. Under the canonical interpretation, truth at an index is membership therein. Since all maximal consistent sets are indices, every maximal consistent set of sentences comprises the sentences true together at some index—namely, at itself.*

We shall shortly see that the so-called canonical interpretation really is an interpretation, based on a system of spheres satisfying one of the combinations of conditions corresponding to the V-logic: the one with local uniformity rather than uniformity if the axiomatization includes U, with local absoluteness rather than absoluteness if it includes A, and with the Limit Assumption no matter what.

All and only theorems of the V-logic are valid under its canonical interpretation. Proof: Any theorem is valid; an index that did not

---

* Have I reverted to the idea, denounced in Section 4.1, of identifying possible worlds with respectable linguistic entities? No; sets of sentences are indices in canonical interpretations, just as worlds or times or things are indices in our intended interpretations, but that does not mean that they *are* the worlds or times or things. Canonical interpretations are *un*intended interpretations. Their purpose is mathematical, not metaphysical.

contain it would be inconsistent with it and hence inconsistent, so it must be in—true at—every index. Any non-theorem ϕ is invalid: $\{\sim\phi\}$ is consistent and can be extended to a maximal consistent set i; ϕ is false at i, otherwise both ϕ and $\sim\phi$ would be in i, making i inconsistent. Q.E.D.

Given this coincidence of theoremhood and validity, and given also—what we have yet to prove—that the canonical interpretation is based on a system of spheres satisfying the appropriate conditions, our completeness results are forthcoming at once. First case: suppose ϕ is valid under a combination of conditions without uniformity or absoluteness, and with the Limit Assumption. Then the canonical interpretation for the corresponding V-logic is based on a system of spheres satisfying those conditions, so ϕ is valid in particular under that interpretation, so ϕ is a theorem of the V-logic. Second case: suppose ϕ is valid under *any* combination of conditions. Revise the combination, if necessary, as follows. Replace uniformity by local uniformity, replace absoluteness by local absoluteness, and add the Limit Assumption. ϕ is still valid under the new combination: we saw that the difference between uniformity and local uniformity, or absoluteness and local absoluteness, makes no difference to validity, and adding a condition cannot diminish the valid sentences. Then by the first case, ϕ is a theorem of the V-logic corresponding to the revised combination. But that is the same V-logic that corresponds to the original combination: local uniformity and uniformity have the same characteristic axiom, so do local absoluteness and absoluteness, and the Limit Assumption has no characteristic axiom at all.

It has yet to be shown that the so-called canonical interpretation really is an interpretation, and that it is based on a system of spheres that satisfies the appropriate conditions.

First: the index set I is nonempty. Proof: the V-logic itself is a consistent set of sentences, and can be expanded to a maximal consistent set belonging to I. Q.E.D.

Next: the canonical interpretation gives the correct truth conditions for the sentential constants and truth-functional connectives. Proof: T is a tautology, hence a theorem, hence in every maximal consistent set, so $[\![T]\!] = I$. $\perp$ belongs to no consistent set, maximal or otherwise, so $[\![\perp]\!] = \Lambda$. $[\![\sim\phi]\!] = I - [\![\phi]\!]$, since a maximal consistent set contains just one of ϕ and $\sim\phi$; if it contained both it would be inconsistent, and if it contained neither it would be consistent with neither, so it would be inconsistent with the theorem $\phi \vee \sim\phi$, so it would be inconsistent. A maximal consistent set contains every sentence that it implies; otherwise it would be inconsistent with some such sentence and hence inconsistent. Therefore $[\![\phi \,\&\, \psi]\!] = [\![\phi]\!] \cap [\![\psi]\!]$ for any ϕ and ψ, and likewise for the remaining truth-functional connectives. Q.E.D.

Now I define a system of spheres $, called the *canonical basis* for the logic in question. Call any set Ψ of sentences a *cut around* any index i if and only if (1) $\psi \leqslant \phi$ is false at i whenever ψ does and ϕ does not belong to Ψ, and (2) ⊥ belongs to Ψ. Associate with every cut Ψ a subset of I called the *co-sphere* of Ψ: the set of all and only those indices where no sentence in Ψ is true. Let $ assign to each index i the set $_i$ of all unions of sets of co-spheres of cuts around i.

Note that $_i$ contains all co-spheres of cuts around i. Each $_i$ is nested. Proof: the cuts around i are nested; otherwise we would have two cuts Φ and Ψ around i, a sentence ϕ in Φ but not in Ψ, and a sentence ψ in Ψ but not in Φ. Then both $\phi \leqslant \psi$ and $\psi \leqslant \phi$ would be false at i, contradicting the truth at i of instances of **Connex**. It follows that the co-spheres also are nested, since if one cut around i includes another, then the co-sphere of the former cut is included in the co-sphere of the latter. It then follows that unions of sets of co-spheres also are nested. Q.E.D.

Each $_i$ is closed under unions. Proof: a union of unions of sets of co-spheres is itself the union of a set of co-spheres. Q.E.D.

Similarly, each $_i$ is closed under nonempty intersections. Proof: the union of any given nonempty set of cuts around i is itself a cut around i since (1) whenever ψ does and ϕ does not belong to it, then also ψ does and ϕ does not belong to one of the given cuts, so that $\psi \leqslant \phi$ is false at i, and (2) ⊥ belongs to it. The intersection of the co-spheres of any given nonempty set of cuts around i is the co-sphere of the union of the cuts. So we have closure of the co-spheres under nonempty intersections. Now our general result follows by distribution of intersection over union. Q.E.D. This completes the proof that $ is a system of spheres.

Before I can proceed to show that $ gives the correct truth conditions for comparative possibility, I shall need this lemma. *Co-sphere Lemma:* if S is the co-sphere of a cut Ψ around some i (under the canonical interpretation of some consistent V-logic) then a sentence ϕ belongs to Ψ if and only if $[\![\phi]\!]$ does not overlap S. Proof: Suppose ϕ belongs to Ψ. Then by definition of a co-sphere, ϕ is true nowhere in S, so $[\![\phi]\!]$ does not overlap S. Conversely, suppose ϕ does not belong to Ψ. If the set $\{\sim\psi: \psi \in \Psi\}$ of negations of sentences in Ψ is consistent with ϕ, then the union of this set and $\{\phi\}$ can be extended to a maximal consistent set j. Since the interpretation is canonical, this j is a member of I. No sentence in Ψ is true at j, and ϕ is true at j; so $[\![\phi]\!]$ overlaps S, since j belongs to both. But suppose on the other hand that the set $\{\sim\psi: \psi \in \Psi\}$ is not consistent with ϕ. Then for some sentences $\psi_1, \ldots, \psi_n$ in Ψ we have in the logic a theorem

$$(\sim\psi_1 \,\&\ldots\&\, \sim\psi_n \,\&\, \phi) \supset \perp$$

By truth-functional logic we have also a theorem

$$\phi \supset (\psi_1 \vee \ldots \vee \psi_n),$$

and by the Rule for Comparative Possibility we have also a theorem

$$(\psi_1 \leqslant \phi) \vee \ldots \vee (\psi_n \leqslant \phi).$$

The theoremhood, and hence truth at i, of this disjunction contradicts the falsehood at i, by definition of a cut, of each of its disjuncts. Q.E.D.

$\$$ gives the correct truth conditions for comparative possibility: $\phi \leqslant \psi$ is true at i if and only if every S in $\$_i$ that overlaps $[\![\psi]\!]$ also overlaps $[\![\phi]\!]$. Proof: Suppose some member of $\$_i$ overlaps $[\![\psi]\!]$ but not also $[\![\phi]\!]$. Then so does the co-sphere S of some cut Φ around i. By the Co-sphere Lemma, ϕ does and ψ does not belong to Φ. By definition of a cut, $\phi \leqslant \psi$ is false at i. Conversely, suppose every S in $\$_i$ that overlaps $[\![\psi]\!]$ also overlaps $[\![\phi]\!]$. Let Φ be the set of all sentences χ such that $\phi \leqslant \chi$ is true at i. By the validity of **Connex**, $\phi \leqslant \phi$ is true at i and hence ϕ belongs to Φ. Φ is a cut around i since (1) whenever η does and ζ does not belong to it, then $\phi \leqslant \eta$ is true and $\phi \leqslant \zeta$ is false at i, so by validity of **Trans** $\eta \leqslant \zeta$ is false at i, and (2) $\perp$ belongs to Φ because $\phi \leqslant \perp$ is a theorem (proved easily from the Rule for Comparative Possibility). Let S be the co-sphere of Φ. By the Co-sphere Lemma, S does not overlap $[\![\phi]\!]$; so by hypothesis S does not overlap $[\![\psi]\!]$; so by the Co-sphere Lemma ψ belongs to Φ; so $\phi \leqslant \psi$ is true at i. Q.E.D.

$\$$ gives the correct truth conditions also for the other ten operators defined from $\leqslant$: given that the truth conditions for $\leqslant$ are correct, the validity of the definitions ensures the correct derived truth conditions for the others.

Now we have verified that the canonical interpretation $[\![\ ]\!]$ is an interpretation based on the canonical basis $\$$. It remains to show that $\$$ satisfies the proper conditions—those whose characteristic axioms were included in the axiomatization of the given V-logic.

If the axiomatization includes N, then $\$$ is normal. Proof: If any $\bigcup \$_i$ were empty, N would be false at i. Q.E.D.

If the axiomatization includes T, then $\$$ is totally reflexive. Proof: For any i, let Φ be the set of all sentences ϕ such that $\square \sim \phi$ is true at i. It is easily verified that Φ is a cut around i; let S be its co-sphere. Every sentence in Φ is false at i, by T, so i belongs to S. Hence i belongs to $\bigcup \$_i$. Q.E.D.

If the axiomatization includes W, then $\$$ is weakly centered. Proof: First, W implies N; hence $\$$ is normal; hence each $\$_i$ contains at least one nonempty sphere. Now suppose S' is a nonempty member of some $\$_i$. Then S' includes a nonempty S which is the co-sphere of a cut Φ around i. Since S is nonempty, $[\![\top]\!]$ overlaps S, so by the Co-sphere

Lemma T is not in Φ, and for any sentence ϕ in Φ, $\phi \leqslant T$ is false at i. Then $\diamondsuit\phi$ is false at i, and so is ϕ itself by **W**. Since every sentence in Φ is false at i, i belongs to S and hence to S'. Q.E.D.

If the axiomatization includes **C**, then \$ is centered. Proof: for any i, let Ψ be the set of all sentences ψ such that $\diamondsuit\psi$ is false at i. It is easily verified that Ψ is a cut around i; let S be its co-sphere. $\diamondsuit T$ is a theorem, hence true at i, so T is not in Ψ; then by the Co-sphere Lemma, $[\![T]\!]$ overlaps S. Hence S is nonempty. Consider any j in S. If j is not the same as i, there is a sentence ϕ in j but not in i, hence true at j but not at i. Since ϕ does not belong to Ψ, by definition of co-sphere, $\diamondsuit\phi$ is true at i. But then ϕ also is true at i, by **C**, contrary to the choice of ϕ. Hence any j in S is the same as i; so since S is nonempty, S is $\{i\}$. Therefore $\{i\}$ belongs to $\$_i$. Q.E.D.

No matter what characteristic axioms are included in the axiomatization, \$ satisfies the Limit Assumption in relation to $[\![\ ]\!]$. Proof: Suppose $[\![\phi]\!]$ overlaps $\bigcup\$_i$. Let Φ be the union of all cuts around i that do not contain ϕ; there are such, by the Co-sphere Lemma and the fact that $[\![\phi]\!]$ overlaps some co-sphere. Then Φ itself is a cut around i that does not contain ϕ. Let S be its co-sphere; by the Co-sphere Lemma S overlaps $[\![\phi]\!]$. No smaller member of $\$_i$ does so; else $[\![\phi]\!]$ would overlap the co-sphere of some cut which was larger than Φ yet did not contain ϕ, which is impossible. Q.E.D.

If the axiomatization includes **S**, then \$ satisfies Stalnaker's Assumption in relation to $[\![\ ]\!]$. Proof: Suppose $[\![\phi]\!]$ overlaps $\bigcup\$_i$; then $\diamondsuit\phi$ is true at i. Let Φ be the set of all sentences χ such that $\chi \leqslant \phi$ is false at i. Φ is a cut around i; let S be its co-sphere. By the Co-sphere Lemma, the intersection $[\![\phi]\!] \cap S$ is nonempty. Suppose it contains two indices; then some sentence ψ belongs to one but not the other, so $[\![\phi\ \&\ \psi]\!]$ and $[\![\phi\ \&\ \sim\psi]\!]$ both overlap S, so by the Co-sphere Lemma neither $\phi\ \&\ \psi$ nor $\phi\ \&\ \sim\psi$ belongs to Φ, so both $(\phi\ \&\ \psi) \leqslant \phi$ and $(\phi\ \&\ \sim\psi) \leqslant \phi$ are true at i. By **Trans**, and the theorems $\phi \leqslant (\phi\ \&\ \psi)$ and $\phi \leqslant (\phi\ \&\ \sim\psi)$ (consequences of the Rule for Comparative Possibility) we have $(\phi\ \&\ \psi) \approx (\phi\ \&\ \sim\psi)$ true at i; whence we have $\sim\diamondsuit\phi$ true at i by **S**, which is impossible. Therefore $[\![\phi]\!] \cap S$ contains exactly one index. Q.E.D.

If the axiomatization includes **U**, then \$ is locally uniform. Proof: Take any i and j such that j is in $\bigcup\$_i$. By **U**, any sentence of the form $\diamondsuit\phi$ is true at both or neither of i and j. The set of all sentences ϕ such that $\diamondsuit\phi$ is false at i is the smallest cut around i, so its co-sphere is the largest sphere around i, $\bigcup\$_i$. Likewise $\bigcup\$_j$ is the co-sphere of the set of all sentences ϕ such that $\diamondsuit\phi$ is false at j; since this is the same set of sentences, $\bigcup\$_i$ and $\bigcup\$_j$ are the same. Q.E.D.

If the axiomatization includes **A**, then \$ is locally absolute. Proof:

Take any i and j such that j is in $\bigcup \$_i$. By A, any sentence of the form $\phi \leqslant \psi$ is true at both or neither of i and j. Hence a set of sentences is a cut around both or neither of i and j, and a subset of I is a co-sphere of a cut around both or neither of i and j. Thus $\$_i$ and $\$_j$ are the same. Q.E.D.

This completes the proof that the canonical basis $\$$ satisfies those of our conditions (except non-local uniformity and absoluteness) whose characteristic axioms are included in the axiomatization by which we specify the V-logic in question. Therefore we have proved the desired general soundness and completeness result for the V-logics: *the V-logic corresponding to any combination of our conditions is sound and complete for that combination of conditions.*

Figure 5 is a chart of the V-logics. There are 26 in all—one for each of the 26 non-equivalent combinations of our principal conditions. Whenever one system is connected to another by a path of upward lines, the higher one is an extension of the lower—that is, the higher system has all the theorems of the lower and more besides. The upward paths diverge from the basic system V at the bottom and reconverge to the trivial system VCA—truth-functional logic in disguise—at the top. A little below the top is the weakly trivial system VWA, which is nothing but the modal logic $S5$.

In my analysis of counterfactuals, I officially imposed centering and none of the other conditions. VC is therefore my official logic for the counterfactual interpretation.* I left open the question whether to assume universality as well, in order to forget the bothersome accessibility restrictions and identify the outer modalities with the logical modalities. If universality were assumed, the resulting system would be VCU. (Universality is uniformity plus total reflexivity, but since the latter is already implied by centering, only the axiom U for uniformity needs to be added.) Anyone who would like to weaken centering for the reasons considered in Section 1.7 will prefer VW, or perhaps VWU if he opts for universality. The only real difference between Stalnaker's theory and mine is the addition of Stalnaker's Assumption. His 'conditional logic' $C2$ is therefore a system equivalent to VCS.‡ Universality has its appeal on Stalnaker's theory as on mine, so $VCSU$ is another contender. None of the other V-logics would do at all for counter-

---

* VC is definitionally equivalent to the system $C1$ of my paper 'Completeness and Decidability of Three Logics of Counterfactual Conditionals'; I there endorsed $C1$ as the correct logic of counterfactuals. V is definitionally equivalent to the system there called CO; VCS to the system there called $C2$.

‡ Thomason calls the same system CS, or FCS in the Fitch-style formulation. Its quantificational extension is called CQ. See the papers of Stalnaker and Thomason cited in Section 3.4.

factuals, since we surely need at least weak centering and we surely must reject absoluteness.

Turning next to deontic interpretations: we must reject centering and weak centering, and I have argued that in this case also we do not want

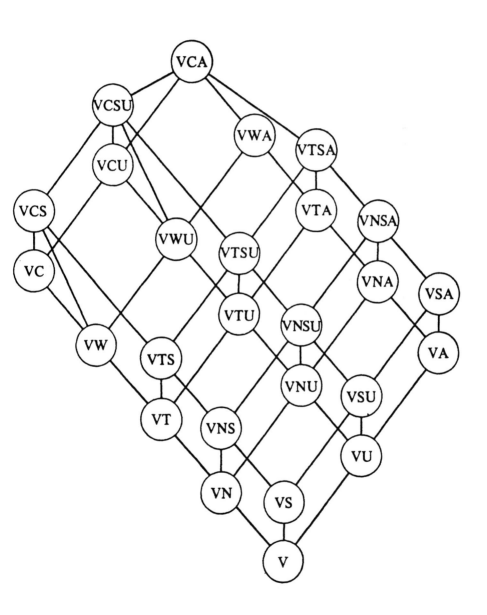

FIGURE 5

Stalnaker's Assumption. For some deontic interpretations we definitely want absoluteness; for others we definitely do not. I argued inconclusively for normality; universality again simplifies things, but I know of no strong arguments pro or con. Uniformity might come as a consequence either of absoluteness or of universality; I know of no reason to want it by itself. Likewise I know of no reason to want total reflexivity except as part of universality. It seems, therefore, that the proper V-logics for deontic interpretations are **V, VN, VTU, VA, VNA, VTA**.*

Temporal interpretations divide into two cases. For the semi-future and semi-past interpretations we have centering; for the future and past interpretations we must reject centering, weak centering, and total reflexivity, and we want normality only if we want to build in the assumption that time has no end (or no beginning). Stalnaker's Assumption amounts roughly to the implausible assumption that time is discrete. Uniformity and absoluteness must be rejected. However, none of the V-logics really fit the temporal interpretations: there are further conditions to be imposed, arising from the linear order of time, and for these I have been unable to find characteristic axioms.

Finally the egocentric interpretation, based on comparative salience: here, I argued, all of our conditions must be rejected. The proper V-logic is the basic system **V**.

Since our principal interest has been the analysis of counterfactuals, it is incumbent on me to provide an alternative axiomatization for **VC**, my official logic of counterfactuals, with the 'would' counterfactual itself as primitive. The simplest one I know is as follows.

Rules: (1) *Modus Ponens,*

(2) *Deduction within Conditionals: for any $n \geqslant 1$,*

$$\frac{\vdash (\chi_1 \,\&\, \ldots \,\&\, \chi_n) \supset \psi}{\vdash ((\phi \,\square\!\!\rightarrow\, \chi_1) \,\&\, \ldots \,\&\, (\phi \,\square\!\!\rightarrow\, \chi_n)) \supset (\phi \,\square\!\!\rightarrow\, \psi)},$$

(3) *Interchange of Logical Equivalents;*

Axioms: (1) *Truth-functional tautologies,*

(2) *Definitions of non-primitive operators,‡*

(3) $\phi \,\square\!\!\rightarrow\, \phi$,

(4) $(\sim\!\phi \,\square\!\!\rightarrow\, \phi) \supset (\psi \,\square\!\!\rightarrow\, \phi)$,

(5) $(\phi \,\square\!\!\rightarrow\, \sim\!\psi) \vee (((\phi \,\&\, \psi) \,\square\!\!\rightarrow\, \chi) \equiv (\phi \,\square\!\!\rightarrow\, (\psi \supset \chi)))$,

(6) $(\phi \,\square\!\!\rightarrow\, \psi) \supset (\phi \supset \psi)$,

(7) $(\phi \,\&\, \psi) \supset (\phi \,\square\!\!\rightarrow\, \psi)$.

* **VN** is equivalent to the system **CD** in van Fraassen, 'The Logic of Conditional Obligation'.

‡ Definitions of our other operators from $\square\!\!\rightarrow$ may be assembled from Sections 1.5, 1.6, 1.7, and 2.5. Replace ' $=^{df}$ ' by ' $\equiv$ ' to make them into object-language schemata.

(For **VW**, delete (7). For **VCS** add Conditional Excluded Middle:

(8) $(\phi \;\square\!\!\rightarrow \psi) \vee (\phi \;\square\!\!\rightarrow \sim\!\psi)$.

For **VCU**, or **VWU** or **VCSU**, it is best to add the previous schemata **U**, with the outer modalities defined now from the counterfactual.)

I apologize for (5). It is because there seems to be no way to take the counterfactual as primitive without at least one such long and obscure axiom that I prefer axiomatizations in terms of comparative possibility.*

It would be tedious to make sure that this really is an axiomatization of **VC** by showing that the axioms and rules of this axiomatization are theorems and derived rules of the former axiomatization, and vice versa. It is easier and more illuminating to show that the system generated by the new axiomatization must be **VC** because it, like **VC**, has all and only the sentences valid under centering as theorems.

Its soundness under centering is routine: we can verify that the rules preserve validity, and axioms (1)–(5) are valid, under any interpretation; that (6) is valid under weak centering and *a fortiori* under centering; and that (7) is valid under centering. It follows that the theorems are valid under centering; that is, that the system is at least included in **VC**.

To show its completeness for centering, we define the canonical interpretation for the system as before, show that the canonical interpretation is based on a centered system of spheres, and argue that any sentence valid under centering—any theorem of **VC**, that is—is valid under the canonical interpretation and therefore a theorem.

This time, however, we go by two steps to the system of spheres. First we show that the canonical interpretation is based on a certain (centered) selection function, in the way described in Section 2.7. Then it follows that the canonical interpretation also is based on a centered system of spheres; for in Section 2.7 it was shown that any (centered) selection function is derived from a centered system of spheres, and agrees on the truth conditions for counterfactuals with the system of spheres whence it is derived.

Let $[\![\;]\!]$ be the canonical interpretation for the system generated by the new axiomatization: the index set I is the set of maximal consistent sets of sentences and $[\![\phi]\!] = \{i \in I: \phi \in i\}$. For any ϕ and i, let $\Theta(\phi, i)$—the *counterfactual theory* for ϕ at i—be the set $\{\psi: i \in [\![\phi \;\square\!\!\rightarrow \psi]\!]\}$ of sentences ψ such that $\phi \;\square\!\!\rightarrow \psi$ holds at i; and let the *canonical selection function* be the function f that assigns to each ϕ and i the set $f(\phi, i)$ of all maximal consistent extensions of the counterfactual theory $\Theta(\phi, i)$. It is easily verified that f is indeed a (centered) selection function according

* The present axiomatization, however, is a great improvement on the axiomatization for VC—there called **C1**—in 'Completeness and. Decidability of Three Logics of Counterfactual Conditionals'.

to the four defining conditions given in Section 2.7 (reading 'index' now in place of 'world'). Also f gives the correct truth conditions:

$$[\![\phi \;\Box\!\!\rightarrow\psi]\!] = \{i \in I : f(\phi, i) \subseteq [\![\psi]\!]\}.$$

Proof: Suppose i is in $[\![\phi \;\Box\!\!\rightarrow\psi]\!]$; then ψ is in $\Theta(\phi, i)$, and hence in every maximal consistent extension thereof, so $f(\phi, i) \subseteq [\![\psi]\!]$. Conversely, suppose $f(\phi, i) \subseteq [\![\psi]\!]$. Then $\Theta(\phi, i)$ implies ψ; otherwise $\Theta(\phi, i) \cup \{\sim\psi\}$ would be consistent and could be extended to a maximal consistent set in $f(\phi, i)$, contrary to the supposition that ψ belongs to all such sets. By the rule of Deduction within Conditionals $\Theta(\phi, i)$ is closed under implication—that is why it is called a theory—and hence contains ψ; therefore i is in $[\![\phi \;\Box\!\!\rightarrow\psi]\!]$. Q.E.D. In this way the canonical interpretation is based on the canonical selection function; and therefore based also on the system of spheres whence the canonical selection function is derived.

6.2 Decidability Results

Theoremhood in the V-logics is effectively decidable. There is a mechanical procedure which, if asked whether a given sentence is a theorem of a given V-logic, always answers correctly after a finite time. (A long finite time in most cases; I do not know any practical decision procedure.) We know by our soundness and completeness results that questions of theoremhood reduce to questions of validity. Now we shall see that those questions reduce in turn to questions of validity under a finite bound on the size of the index set; and these last are decidable.

Suppose we wish to decide whether a certain sentence ϕ is a theorem of a certain V-logic. We may safely assume that $\leqslant$ is the only one of our special operators to appear in ϕ, since if we could decide theoremhood for any such sentence then we could decide theoremhood for other sentences by first eliminating the other operators by means of their definitions in terms of $\leqslant$. Take the combination of conditions corresponding to the given V-logic; use uniformity rather than local uniformity, use absoluteness rather than local absoluteness, and omit the Limit Assumption. A triple $\langle I, \$, [\![\;]\!]\rangle$ is a *counterexample* to the validity of ϕ under these conditions if and only if (1) $[\![\;]\!]$ is an interpretation over I based on $\$$, (2) $\$$ satisfies the conditions, and (3) ϕ is invalid under $[\![\;]\!]$. The triple is a *small counterexample* if and only if, in addition, there are at most 2^n members of the index set I, n being the number of subsentences of ϕ. (Count ϕ as one of its own subsentences.) If ϕ is a theorem of the given V-logic, then by soundness there is no counterexample, small or otherwise, to its validity under the conditions. But if

ϕ is not a theorem, then by completeness there is a counterexample; and we shall prove that if there is any counterexample, then there is a small one. We can therefore decide whether ϕ is a theorem of the given V-logic by deciding whether there exists any small counterexample to the validity of ϕ under the corresponding combination of conditions. And that is obviously a decidable question. Of course, we cannot search through all the infinitely many $\langle I, \$, [\![\ ]\!] \rangle$ triples with small enough I; however, most of the differences between the triples can be ignored, so it suffices to search through finitely many finitely specifiable structural types, checking in each case whether triples of that type are small counterexamples to the validity of ϕ under the conditions.

It only remains to prove that if there is any counterexample $\langle I, \$, [\![\ ]\!] \rangle$ to the validity of ϕ under the conditions, then there also is a small counterexample. We can obtain a small counterexample $\langle I^*, \$^*, [\![\ ]\!]^* \rangle$, called a *filtration* through ϕ of the original counterexample, as follows.‡

Call i and j in I *indistinguishable* if and only if any subsentence of ϕ is true, under $[\![\ ]\!]$, at both or neither of them. There exist subsets of I that contain, for any i in I, one and only one index indistinguishable from i. Let I^* be any such subset. I^* is small enough: there are at most 2^n ways to assign truth values to the n subsentences of ϕ (fewer ways, in general, under the constraints imposed by the truth conditions for connectives in ϕ), no two members of I^* are indistinguishable, and hence I^* has at most 2^n members.

Define a function $*$ as follows. For any i in I, $*i$ is the unique index in I^* that is indistinguishable from i. For any subset S of I, $*S$ is the set of all indices in I^* that are indistinguishable from members of S—that is, $*S = \{*i : i \in S\}$.

Now we define $\$^*$ as follows. For any i in I^*, $\$_i^*$ is the set of all sets $*S$ such that S belongs to $\$_i$. $\$^*$ is a system of spheres. Proof: whenever $S \subseteq T$, then $*S \subseteq *T$, so that each $\$_i^*$ inherits the nesting of $\$_i$. Because each $\$_i^*$ is nested and finite, it is closed under unions and nonempty intersections. Q.E.D.

It is easy to verify that if $\$$ is normal, totally reflexive, weakly centered, centered, uniform, or absolute, then so is $\$^*$. Also, if $\$$ satisfies Stalnaker's Assumption in relation to $[\![\ ]\!]$, then $\$^*$ satisfies Stalnaker's Assumption in relation to any interpretation based on $\$^*$. Proof: It is enough to show that whenever two indices j and k belong to some $\bigcup \$_i^*$, then there is some sphere in $\$_i^*$ that contains one of them but not the other. Let χ_j be a sentence true under $[\![\ ]\!]$ at all and only indices indistinguishable from j, and let χ_k likewise be true at all and only indices

‡ I am adapting the method of filtrations used in modal logic; see Lemmon, *An Introduction to Modal Logic*, Sections 3 and 6.

indistinguishable from k; such sentences always can be formed as conjunctions of subsentences of ϕ and negated subsentences of ϕ. Since j and k are in $\bigcup \$_i^*$, $[\![\chi_j \lor \chi_k]\!]$ overlaps $\bigcup \$_i$. Then by Stalnaker's Assumption for $\$$ there is some S in $\$_i$ whose intersection with $[\![\chi_j \lor \chi_k]\!]$ contains exactly one index h. This h is indistinguishable from one of j and k; but not from both since they are both in I^* and so not indistinguishable from one another. Then $*S$ is a member of $\$_i^*$ that contains whichever one of j and k is indistinguishable from h, but not the other. Q.E.D.

Now we are ready to define the interpretation $[\![\ ]\!]^*$. If σ is any sentence letter, let $[\![\sigma]\!]^*$ be $[\![\sigma]\!] \cap I^*$; and stipulate that $[\![\ ]\!]^*$ is to be an interpretation over I^* based on $\$^*$. That is enough to determine $[\![\psi]\!]^*$ for any sentence ψ, since the truth conditions for the connectives and operators by which ψ is built up from its sentence letters are written into the definition of an interpretation.

Call a sentence ψ *invariant* if and only if $[\![\psi]\!]^*$ is $[\![\psi]\!] \cap I^*$, so that ψ has the same truth value under both $[\![\ ]\!]$ and $[\![\ ]\!]^*$ at any index in I^*. Suppose both that ψ is invariant and that ψ is a subsentence of ϕ. Then for any subset S of I, $[\![\psi]\!]$ overlaps S if and only if $[\![\psi]\!]^*$ overlaps $*S$. Proof: Suppose $[\![\psi]\!]$ overlaps S; let i belong to both. Then $*i$ belongs to $*S$. Also, since $*i$ and i are indistinguishable and ψ is a subsentence of ϕ, $*i$ belongs to $[\![\psi]\!]$; so since ψ is invariant and $*i$ belongs to I^*, $*i$ belongs to $[\![\psi]\!]^*$. Conversely, suppose $[\![\psi]\!]^*$ overlaps $*S$; let j belong to both. By invariance, j belongs to $[\![\psi]\!]$; also j is $*i$ for some i in S. Since i and j are indistinguishable and ψ is a subsentence of ϕ, i belongs to $[\![\psi]\!]$. Q.E.D.

Now suppose ψ and χ both are invariant subsentences of ϕ; then $\psi \leqslant \chi$ is invariant. Proof: For any i in I^*, i is in $[\![\psi \leqslant \chi]\!]$ if and only if, for every S in $\$_i$, if $[\![\chi]\!]$ overlaps S then so does $[\![\psi]\!]$; that is, by our last result, if and only if, for every S in $\$_i$, if $[\![\chi]\!]^*$ overlaps $*S$ then so does $[\![\psi]\!]^*$; that is, if and only if, for every S in $\$_i^*$, if $[\![\chi]\!]^*$ overlaps S then so does $[\![\psi]\!]^*$; that is, if and only if i is in $[\![\psi \leqslant \chi]\!]^*$. Q.E.D.

It follows that all subsentences of ϕ are invariant. For sentence letters are invariant by definition of $[\![\ ]\!]^*$; truth-functional compounds of invariant sentences are obviously invariant; and we have just seen that compounds with $\leqslant$ are invariant so long as the combined sentences are subsentences of ϕ. In particular, ϕ itself is invariant.

By hypothesis, ϕ is invalid under $[\![\ ]\!]$. Let i be an index where ϕ is false under $[\![\ ]\!]$; then since i and $*i$ are indistinguishable, ϕ is false under $[\![\ ]\!]$ at $*i$ also; then since ϕ is invariant and $*i$ belongs to I^*, ϕ is false at $*i$ under $[\![\ ]\!]^*$. Therefore ϕ is invalid under $[\![\ ]\!]^*$. This completes the proof that the filtration $\langle I^*, \$^*, [\![\ ]\!]^* \rangle$ is a small counterexample to the validity of the given sentence ϕ under the combination of conditions corresponding to the given V-logic.

6.3 Derived Modal Logics

An *outer modal sentence* of our language is one that contains none of our special operators except perhaps the outer modal operators. It is built up from sentence letters, T, and ⊥ by means of nothing but □ and ◇ and truth-functional connectives. Likewise an *inner modal sentence* is one that contains none of the operators except perhaps the inner modal operators ⊡ and ◈.

For each of the *V*-logics, there is a *derived outer modal logic* comprising those theorems of the *V*-logic that are outer modal sentences; also a *derived inner modal logic* comprising the inner modal theorems of the *V*-logic. All of the outer modal logics, and most of the inner modal logics, can be axiomatized in the following familiar form. (For inner modal logics, replace □ and ◇ throughout by ⊡ and ◈.)

Rules: (1) *Modus Ponens,*
(2) *Necessitation:* $\vdash\phi/\vdash \Box\,\phi$;

Axioms: (1) *Truth-functional tautologies,*
(2) *Definition:* $\Diamond\,\phi \equiv\, \sim \Box \sim\phi$,
(3) $\Box(\phi \supset \psi) \supset (\Box\phi \supset \Box\psi)$,
(4) *Some combination (zero or more) of:*

$$\textbf{D:}\quad \Box\phi \supset \Diamond\phi$$
$$\textbf{T:}\quad \Box\phi \supset \phi$$
$$\textbf{P:}\quad \Diamond\phi \supset \Box\phi$$
$$\textbf{E:}\quad \Diamond\phi \supset \Box\Diamond\phi$$
$$\textbf{4:}\quad \Box\phi \supset \Box\Box\phi.$$

Nomenclature (after Lemmon, except for my addition of **P**): the name of the logic is its axiom list, preceded by '**K**' unless the list begins with '**D**' or '**T**'. **TE** is **S5**, the best-known modal logic. **K** (with no special axioms), **D**, and **T** are well known under those names. **TP** is the trivial modal logic—truth-functional logic in disguise—since it has theorems to the effect that $\Box\phi$ and $\Diamond\phi$ are equivalent simply to ϕ.*

The derived outer modal logics, and the derived inner modal logics for *V*-logics at least as strong as **VN**, are as follows.

V-Logic	*Outer Modal Logic*
V, VS	K
VN, VNS	D
VT, VW, VC, VTS, VCS	T

* DP is the system W of Krister Segerberg, 'On the Logic of "To-morrow"', *Theoria* 33 (1967): 45–52. I prefer to think of it as Prussian deontic logic, whence the name.

VU, VA, VSU, VSA	**KE4**
VNU, VNA, VNSU, VNSA	**DE4**
VTU, VWU, VCU, VTA, VWA, VTSU, VCSU, VTSA	**S5 (TE)**
VCA	Trivial **(TP)**

V-Logic	*Inner Modal Logic*
VN, VT, VNU, VTU	**D**
VW, VWU	**T**
VNA, VTA	**DE4**
VWA	**S5 (TE)**
VNS, VTS, VNSU, VTSU	**DP**
VNSA, VTSA	**DPE**
VC, VCU, VCA, VCS, VCSU	Trivial **(TP)**

In each case listed, the rules of inference for the modal logic preserve theoremhood in the V-logic, and the axioms for the modal logic are theorems—indeed, often axioms—of the V-logic. Therefore all theorems of the modal logic are theorems of the V-logic as well. In particular, for the outer modalities: **VN** and its extensions give axiom **D**; **VT** and its extensions give axiom **T** (which we took as an axiom for those V-logics); **VU** and its extensions give axioms **E** and **4** (the upper and lower halves of **U**); and **VCA**, the trivial V-logic, gives axiom **P**. For the inner modalities: all V-logics give axiom **D**; **VW** and its extensions give axiom **T**; **VNA** and its extensions give axioms **E** and **4**; and **VC** and **VNS** and their extensions give axiom **P**.

In each case listed, conversely, the modal logic yields all the modal theorems—outer or inner, as the case may be—of the V-logic. Proof: In each case, we have a completeness theorem for the modal logic, saying that any modal sentence valid under a certain condition on accessibility is a theorem of the logic. (These theorems are mostly well-known; they can be proved in much the same way as my completeness results in Section 6.1, but more easily. I state them here in terms of an assignment of spheres of accessibility, as in Section 1.2, rather than an accessibility relation.) Contrapositively: let ϕ be any modal sentence—outer or inner, as the case may be—that is not a theorem of the modal logic; then ϕ is invalid under some interpretation $[\![\ ]\!]$ of the modal sentences of our language, over a set I, based on an accessibility assignment S that satisfies the condition given in the completeness theorem. That is, S assigns to each i in I a sphere of accessibility S_i (a subset of I) and the interpretation is based on these spheres as follows:

$$[\![\Box\psi]\!] = \{i \in I : S_i \subseteq [\![\psi]\!]\},$$

$$[\![\Diamond\psi]\!] = \{i \in I : S_i \bullet [\![\psi]\!]\} \quad (\text{where } A \bullet B =^{\text{df}} A \cap B \neq \Lambda),$$

in the case of outer modality, and likewise but with □ and ◇ replaced by ⊡ and ◈ in the case of inner modality. Say that a system of spheres $ over *I matches* this accessibility assignment *S*, in the case of outer modality, if and only if each S_i is the outermost sphere in $_i (that is, ∪$_i); or, in the case of inner modality, if and only if each S_i is the innermost nonempty sphere in $_i (which is possible only if $ is such that each $_i *has* an innermost nonempty sphere). Given a system of spheres $ that matches *S* in the appropriate way, we can expand the interpretation ⟦ ⟧ into an interpretation, based on $, of our full language; that is possible because the matching ensures that $ gives the same truth conditions as *S* for the modal sentences. ϕ remains invalid under the expanded interpretation. Suppose further that $ satisfies conditions corresponding to a certain *V*-logic; then ϕ is invalid under those conditions, and hence not a theorem of the *V*-logic. The modal logic did not omit any modal theorems of that *V*-logic. Nor did it omit any modal theorems of any weaker *V*-logic, since the theorems of the weaker system are among those of the stronger.

Now we turn to particular cases. First we consider the outer modal cases; take the modal logics discussed to be outer.

For **K** we are given no condition on the accessibility assignment *S*. We can nevertheless match *S* with a system of spheres $ that satisfies Stalnaker's Assumption (in relation to any interpretation based on it), as follows. For each *i* in *I*, take an arbitrary well-ordering of S_i; let the spheres in $_i be all and only those subsets of S_i such that whenever *j* belongs to the subset and *k* belongs to S_i but not to the subset, then *j* precedes *k* in the well-ordering. Hence **K** captures all the outer modal theorems of **VS**, including those of **V**.

For **D**, we have the condition that each S_i is nonempty. We can match *S* with a normal system of spheres that satisfies Stalnaker's Assumption: use an arbitrary well-ordering of each S_i as before. Hence **D** captures all the outer modal theorems of **VNS**, including those of **VN**.

For **T**, we have the condition that each S_i contains *i*. We can match *S* with a centered system of spheres that satisfies Stalnaker's Assumption: this time, use a well-ordering of each S_i that is arbitrary except that *i* comes first. Hence **T** captures all the outer modal theorems of **VCS**, including those of **VTS**, **VC**, **VW**, and **VT**.

For **KE4**, we have the condition that S_i is the same for every *i* in *I*. We can match *S* with an absolute system of spheres that satisfies Stalnaker's Assumption: use the same arbitrary well-ordering of S_i for every *i*. Hence **KE4** captures all the outer modal theorems of **VSA**, including those of **VSU**, **VA**, and **VU**.

For **DE4**, we have the condition that S_i is the same for every *i* in *I*, and further that it is nonempty. We can match *S* with a normal, absolute system of spheres that satisfies Stalnaker's Assumption: again, use the same well-ordering for every i. Hence **DE4** captures all the outer modal theorems of **VNSA**, including those of **VNSU**, **VNA**, and **VNU**.

For **S5 (TE)**, we have the condition that each S_i is the whole index set I. We can match S with a totally reflexive, absolute system of spheres that satisfies Stalnaker's Assumption: use the same well-ordering of I for every i. Hence **S5** captures all the outer modal theorems of **VTSA**, including those of **VTSU**, **VTA**, and **VTU**. Alternatively, we can match S with a centered, uniform system of spheres that satisfies Stalnaker's Assumption: for each i, use a well-ordering of I that is arbitrary except that i comes first. Hence **S5** captures all the outer modal theorems of **VCSU**, including those of **VCU** and **VWU**. Alternatively, we can match S with a weakly trivial system of spheres: for each i, let I be the only nonempty sphere around i. Hence **S5** captures all the outer modal theorems of **VWA**—no surprise, since we already noted that **VWA** is nothing but (a definitional extension of) **S5**.

For the trivial system **TP**, we have the condition that there is only one index i, and S_i is $\{i\}$. We can match S with a trivial system of spheres: let $\{i\}$ be the only nonempty sphere around i. Hence **TP** captures all the outer modal theorems of **VCA**—as expected, since both of them are nothing but truth-functional logic.

Now for the inner modal cases; henceforth take the modal logics discussed to be inner.

For **D**, we have again the condition that each S_i is nonempty. We can match S with a totally reflexive, uniform system of spheres: for each i, let the nonempty spheres around i be S_i and I. Hence **D** captures all the inner modal theorems of **VTU**, including those of **VNU**, **VT**, and **VN**.

For **T**, we have again the condition that each S_i contains i. We can match S with a weakly centered, uniform system of spheres: as before, let the nonempty spheres around any i be S_i and I. Hence **T** captures all the inner modal theorems of **VWU**, including those of **VW**.

For **DE4**, we have again the condition that S_i is the same for every i in I, and further that it is nonempty. We can match S with a totally reflexive, absolute system of spheres: let the nonempty spheres around any i be S_i—now constant—and I. Hence **DE4** captures all the inner modal theorems of **VTA**, including those of **VNA**.

For **S5**, we have again the condition that each S_i is I. We can match S with a weakly trivial system of spheres: let I be the only nonempty sphere around any i. Hence **S5** captures all the inner modal theorems of **VWA**.

For **DP**, we have the condition that each S_i contains exactly one index j_i. We can match S with a totally reflexive, uniform system of spheres that satisfies Stalnaker's Assumption: for each i, use a well-ordering of I, arbitrary except that j_i comes first. Hence **DP** captures all the inner modal theorems of **VTSU**, including those of **VNSU**, **VTS**, and **VNS**.

For **DPE**, we have the condition that each S_i contains exactly one index j, the same for every i. We can match S with a totally reflexive, absolute system of spheres that satisfies Stalnaker's Assumption: use a fixed well-ordering of I, arbitrary except that j comes first. Hence **DPE** captures all the inner modal theorems of **VTSA**, including those of **VNSA**.

For the trivial system **TP**, we have again the condition that there is only one index i, and S_i is $\{i\}$. We can match S with a trivial system of spheres: let $\{i\}$ be the only nonempty sphere around i. Hence **TP** captures all the inner modal theorems of **VCA**, including those of **VCSU**, **VCS**, **VCU**, and **VC**—all the systems in which the inner modalities are trivialized. Q.E.D.

I have so far ignored the inner modal logics derived from **V**, **VU**, **VA**, **VS**, **VSU**, and **VSA**. It turns out that these derived logics do not belong to the well-known family of modal logics we have been considering hitherto. Rather, they are among the so-called *non-normal modal logics* —systems in which the rule of necessitation fails to preserve theoremhood.[*] In fact, the rule of necessitation never yields theorems; these derived logics have no theorems whatever of the form $\boxdot \phi$. Recall this consequence of our truth conditions for inner modality: if there are no nonempty spheres around an index i—if i is an *abnormal* index—then no sentences of the form $\boxdot \phi$ are true at i. (Contrariwise, if there are nonempty spheres around i—if i is a *normal* index—then some such sentences are true at i. In particular $\boxdot T$, an inner modal sentence definitionally equivalent to our axiom **N**, is true at all and only normal indices.) A sentence of the form $\boxdot \phi$ therefore cannot be valid under a combination of conditions unless the conditions somehow prohibit abnormal indices. Our normality condition does exactly that. Total reflexivity, weak centering, · or centering also prohibits abnormal indices. But Stalnaker's Assumption, uniformity, and absoluteness, singly or in combination, do nothing to prohibit abnormal indices. Hence the V-logics we are considering, which correspond to the combinations of these three conditions, have no theorems of the form $\boxdot \phi$. That is why their derived inner modal logics have no such theorems;

---

[*] See John Lemmon, 'Algebraic Semantics for Modal Logic', *Journal of Symbolic Logic* 31 (1966): 46–65 and 191–218; and Saul Kripke, 'Semantical Analysis of Modal Logic II: Non-normal Modal Propositional Calculi', in J. W. Addison, L. Henkin, and A. Tarski, *The Theory of Models* (North-Holland: Amsterdam, 1965): 206–220.

and (since they do have *some* theorems, as we shall see) it follows that they are systems in which the rule of necessitation does not preserve theoremhood.

I shall not attempt a catalog of the non-normal derived inner modal logics, but shall be content to discuss one case: the inner modal logic derived from our basic system **V**. This is the non-normal modal logic called **D2** by Lemmon, and it may be axiomatized as follows.

Rules: (1) *Modus Ponens,*
           (2) *Weakened Necessitation:* $\vdash \phi \supset \psi / \vdash \Box \phi \supset \Box \psi$;

Axioms: (1) *Truth-functional tautologies,*
           (2) *Definition:* $\Diamond \phi \equiv \sim \Box \sim \phi$,
           (3) $\Box(\phi \supset \psi) \supset (\Box \phi \supset \Box \psi)$,
           (4) **D**: $\Box \phi \supset \Diamond \phi$.

The rules preserve theoremhood in **V**, and the axioms are theorems of **V**; so all theorems of **D2** are theorems of **V** (and therefore of all *V*-logics). Conversely, **D2** captures all the inner modal theorems of **V**. Proof: There is a completeness theorem for **D2**, according to which any inner modal sentence ϕ that is not a theorem of **D2** is invalid under some interpretation $[\![\ ]\!]$ of the inner modal sentences, over a set *I*, based on a *partial accessibility assignment S*—one that may be undefined at some indices in *I*—satisfying the condition that whenever *S* is defined at *i*, then S_i is nonempty.* The interpretation is based on *S* as follows.

$$[\![\Box \psi]\!] = \{i \in I : S \text{ is defined at } i \text{ and } S_i \subseteq [\![\psi]\!]\},$$
$$[\![\Diamond \psi]\!] = \{i \in I : S \text{ is undefined at } i \text{ or } S_i \bullet [\![\psi]\!]\}.$$

Now let $ be a system of spheres over *I* such that if *S* is defined at *i*, then S_i is the only nonempty sphere around *I*, and if *S* is undefined at *i*, then there is no nonempty sphere around *i*; and expand the interpretation $[\![\ ]\!]$ into an interpretation, based on $, of our full language. ϕ remains invalid, and hence is not a theorem of **V**. Therefore **D2** captures all inner modal theorems of **V**. Q.E.D.

* If we were using accessibility relations instead of assignments of spheres of accessibility, we would need a second item to specify the indices here specified as those where *S* is undefined; and we would raise idle questions about accessibility from such indices.

Appendix:
Related Writings by David Lewis

'Completeness and Decidability of Three Logics of Counterfactual Conditionals', *Theoria* **37** (1971): 74–85.

I consider the three logics here called **V**, **VC**, and **VCS**, formulated with the counterfactual connective as primitive. They are shown to be complete, first for a semantic analysis in terms of selection functions, and derivatively for analyses in terms of systems of spheres and in terms of comparative similarity relations. They are shown to be decidable, using the method of filtrations.

'Causation', *Journal of Philosophy* **70** (1973): 556–567; reprinted in Ernest Sosa, *Causation and Conditionals* (Oxford University Press: Oxford, 1975). German translation by Günter Posch (with additions) published as 'Kausalität', in Günter Posch, *Kausalität—Neue Texte* (Philip Reclam: Stuttgart, 1981); reprinted with added postscripts in David Lewis, *Philosophical Papers*, Volume II (Oxford University Press: Oxford, 1986).

I propose a counterfactual analysis of causal dependence and causation between particular events. First, an event *e depends causally* on a (wholly distinct) event *c* iff *c* and *e* both occur, but if *c* had not occurred then *e* would not have occurred. Second, *c* is a *cause* of *e* iff either *e* depends on *c*, or *e* depends on *d* which depends in turn on *c*, or . . . . The counterfactuals must be of the proper, non-backtracking sort.

In the added postscripts, I extend the treatment to cover probabilistic causation under indeterminism; piecemeal causation, in which *c* is said to cause *e* because some part of *c* causes *e* according to the original analysis; and certain forms of redundant causation which are not covered by the original treatment.

'Counterfactuals and Comparative Possibility', *Journal of Philosophical Logic* **2** (1973): 418–446; reprinted in Donald Hockney *et al.*, *Contemporary Research in Philosophical Logic and Linguistic Semantics* (D. Reidel: Dordrecht, 1975); Italian translation by Claudio Pizzi published as 'Controfattuali e possibilità comparativa', in Claudio

Pizzi, *Leggi di natura, modalità, ipotesti* (Feltrinelli: Milano, 1978); reprinted in W. L. Harper *et al.*, *Ifs* (D. Reidel: Dordrecht, 1981); reprinted in David Lewis, *Philosophical Papers*, Volume II.

For the most part, the article is a summary presentation of material from this book. But also I mention two extensions: (1) a selection-function treatment in which the Limit Assumption is ensured by supplementing the genuine worlds with artificially constructed impossible limit worlds; and (2) a kind of quantitative counterfactual, intermediate between 'would' and 'might' counterfactuals, which holds iff, roughly, the consequent holds throughout a certain fraction of the closest antecedent-worlds.

'Semantic Analyses for Dyadic Deontic Logic', in Sören Stenlund, *Logical Theory and Semantic Analysis: Essays Dedicated to Stig Kanger on His Fiftieth Birthday* (D. Reidel: Dordrecht, 1974).

I compare several treatments of conditional obligation and permissibility similar to the one given in this book, attempting to separate substantive differences from differences between equivalent formulations.

'Intensional Logics Without Iterative Axioms', *Journal of Philosophical Logic* 3 (1974): 457–466.

I present an easy method for proving the completeness and decidability of any sentential intensional logic which can be axomatized without the iteration of intensional operators. The method applies *inter alia* to all the *V*-logics considered here except for those with axioms U or A.

'The Paradoxes of Time Travel', *American Philosophical Quarterly* 13 (1976): 145–152; reprinted in Fred D. Miller, Jr., and Nicholas D. Smith, *Thought Probes* (Prentice-Hall: Englewood Cliffs, N.J., 1981); reprinted in David Lewis, *Philosophical Papers*, Volume II.

In the course of a general defense of the possibility of time travel, I consider the question what would have happened if a time traveler visiting the past had succeeded in killing his grandfather. I reply that if so, the killer would not after all have been the time-traveling grandson of his victim.

'Probabilities of Conditionals and Conditional Probabilities', *Philosophical Review* 85 (1976): 297–315; reprinted in W. L. Harper *et al.*, *Ifs* (D. Reidel: Dordrecht, 1981); reprinted with an added postscript in David Lewis, *Philosophical Papers*, Volume II.

I ask whether we can interpret $\rightarrow$ so as to guarantee an equality between the probability $P(\phi \rightarrow \psi)$ of a conditional and the revised probability $P_\phi(\psi)$ of the consequent, where P_ϕ is the result of revising probability function P so as to make the antecedent certain. If the revision of probability works by conditionalizing whenever possible, then it cannot be done (except in certain trivial cases). However it can be done if $\rightarrow$ is the Stalnaker conditional and P_ϕ comes from P by a process of 'imaging' in which each world's original share of probability is shifted to the closest ϕ-world.

'Possible-World Semantics for Counterfactual Logics: A Rejoinder', *Journal of Philosophical Logic* **6** (1977): 359–363.

I discuss an article by Brian Ellis, Frank Jackson, and Robert Pargetter,* in which they had suggested that no sort of possible-world semantics for counterfactuals could validate the inference from 'If χ or ψ, it would be that ϕ' to 'If ψ, it would be that ϕ'. I reply that the problem can be solved in various ways within possible-world semantics. But any solution will involve treating counterfactuals with disjunctive antecedents as a special case, not covered directly by my treatment in this book.

'Truth in Fiction', *American Philosophical Quarterly* **15** (1978): 37–46; reprinted with added postscripts in David Lewis, *Philosophical Papers*, Volume I (Oxford University Press, 1983).

I treat operators of truth in fiction as if they were counterfactual suppositions, so that 'In fiction f, ϕ' means roughly that ϕ holds at the closest f-worlds. The f-worlds are those worlds where the fiction f really is what here it only purports to be—truthful history, perhaps. 'Closeness' of these f-worlds may be closeness to actuality; or alternatively it may be closeness to the collective belief-worlds of the community wherein fiction f originated. Inconsistent fictions pose extra problems, which may be addressed by considering what is true in the various consistent corrections or fragments of the original fiction.

'Reply to McMichael', *Analysis* **38** (1978): 85–86.

I discuss an article by Alan McMichael,† in which he had shown that the treatment of conditional obligation in Section 5.1, combined with a utilitarian measure of the goodness of worlds, would yield the unwelcome conclusion that ordinary statements of conditional obligation are seldom true. I reply that this is due to the peculiarity of the utilitarian measure, not the treatment of conditional obligation.

* 'An Objection to Possible-World Semantics for Counterfactual Logics', *Journal of Philosophical Logic* **6** (1977): 355–357.
† 'Too Much of a Good Thing: A Problem in Deontic Logic', *Analysis* **38** (1978): 83–84.

'Counterfactual Dependence and Time's Arrow', *Noûs* **13** (1979): 455–476; reprinted with added postscripts in David Lewis, *Philosophical Papers*, Volume II.

I seek to explain an asymmetry of counterfactual dependence: subject to several qualifications, it seems that if the present were different, then the future but not the past would also be different. I argue that we should not build the asymmetry into the analysis of counterfactuals, or into the weighting of respects of comparison that we bring to an analysis in terms of similarity of worlds, since that would give us the asymmetry in too unqualified a form. I show how a symmetric analysis, and symmetric standards of similarity, can join with *de facto* temporal asymmetries in the world to explain the asymmetry of counterfactual dependence.

In discussing the asymmetry for the indeterministic case (in a postscript) I change what I say about 'might' counterfactuals. Besides the 'not-would-not' sense that I admit in this book, I find reason to admit also a 'would-be-possible' sense, which holds iff each of the closest antecedent worlds is one where the objective chance of the consequent is positive. I argue that 'If it were that ϕ, it would be that not ψ' is compatible with 'If it were that ϕ, there would have been some chance that ψ' and hence with 'If it were that ϕ, it might have been that ψ' taken in the 'would-be-possible' sense; for instance, if the antecedent is 'The coin was fair and fell heads' and the consequent is 'The coin fell tails'.

'Veridical Hallucination and Prosthetic Vision', *Australasian Journal of Philosophy* **58** (1980): 239–249; reprinted with an added postscript in David Lewis, *Philosophical Papers*, Volume II.

I propose that what distinguishes vision from other cases in which the scene before the eyes causes matching visual experience is the existence of a suitable pattern of counterfactual dependence whereby any one of a wide range of alternative scenes would have caused matching visual experience.

'Causal Decision Theory', *Australasian Journal of Philosophy* **59** (1981): 5–30; reprinted with an added postscript in David Lewis, *Philosophical Papers*, Volume II.

I take it that Newcomb's problem (in its down-to-earth forms) teaches us that we must formulate decision theory in terms of the causal dependence of outcomes upon the agent's actions. I define expected utility in terms of *dependency hypotheses*: conjunctions of counterfactuals about the objective chance distributions that would follow if the agent were to take one or another of his alternative narrowest options. I argue that, despite superficial differences, my proposal is in essential agreement with proposals of Gibbard and Harper, Skyrms, and Sobel.*

'Ordering Semantics and Premise Semantics for Counterfactuals', *Journal of Philosophical Logic* **10** (1981): 217–234.

I compare ordering semantics—like my treatment in Section 2.3 of this book, but generalized to permit similarity orderings of worlds to be merely partial—with Kratzer's treatment of counterfactuals.† According to Kratzer, we have for each world a certain set of premises true at that world; and (in the simple finite case) a counterfactual holds at a world iff, whenever S is a subset of the given premise set, and S is consistent with the antecedent, and S is a maximal such set, then S and the antecedent imply the consequent. Ordering semantics and premise semantics turn out to be equivalent: to any system of orderings there corresponds a system of premise sets, and to any system of premise sets there corresponds a system of orderings, such that the two systems make the same counterfactuals true.

The two approaches face parallel choices about how to respond to the threat that the Limit Assumption might fail; and here a complication in Kratzer's premise semantics corresponds to a complication in my ordering semantics, and to a worse complication when provision for failure of the Limit Assumption is combined with provision for merely partial orderings.

I note also that there is little difference between supposing we have one determinate partial ordering and supposing instead that we have indeterminacy between several disagreeing total orderings.

'Are We Free to Break the Laws?', *Theoria* **47** (1981): 113–121; reprinted in David Lewis, *Philosophical Papers*, Volume II.

On behalf of compatibilism, I deny that a free agent in a deterministic world is able to break the laws of nature. For we should distinguish between 'If I had raised my hand, some law of nature would have been broken', which is true if the world is deterministic and I didn't raise my hand, and 'If I had raised my hand, some act of mine would have been, or would have caused, a law-breaking event', which is false.

---

* Allan Gibbard and William Harper, 'Counterfactuals and Two Kinds of Expected Utility', in C. A. Hooker *et al.*, *Foundations and Applications of Decision Theory*, volume I (D. Reidel: Dordrecht, 1978); Brian Skyrms, 'The Role of Causal Factors in Rational Decision', in Skyrms, *Causal Necessity* (Yale University Press: New Haven, 1980); and Jordan Howard Sobel, *Probability, Chance and Choice: A Theory of Rational Agency* (unpublished).

† Angelika Kratzer, 'Partition and Revision: The Semantics of Counterfactuals', *Journal of Philosophical Logic* **10** (1981): 201–216.

On the Plurality of Worlds (Blackwell: Oxford, 1986).

I defend realism about possible worlds, and make various objections against the plan of using abstract representations in place of genuine worlds. However, I retract some of the arguments given in Section 4.1 of this book, as follows.

(1) I had argued (page 85) that mathematical consistency could not be characterized without quantifying over worlds, since a deductive characterization would be inadequate; but I accept the reply that we can somehow make reference to 'intended' models and therefore a model-theoretic characterization is adequate.

(2) I had argued (page 86) that if I took maximal consistent sets of sentences as ersatz possible worlds, I would have to believe that I and all my surroundings are a set of sentences; but surely part of the ersatzer's plan will be to distinguish the world itself from the actualized ersatz world that correctly represents it.

(3) I had argued (page 90n.) that there are not enough maximal consistent sets of sentences to cover all possibilities without omitting or conflating some, since there are more possibilities than there are finite strings over a finite alphabet; but there is no reason why the ersatzer's worldmaking language should be finite either in its alphabet or in the length of its sentences.

Index

CPSIA information can be obtained at www.ICGtesting.com
Printed in the USA
LVOW082141250911

247825LV00005B/183/P